INTRODUCTION TO
SOCIAL POLICY ANALYSIS
Illuminating welfare

Stephen Sinclair

P P

First published in Great Britain in 2016 by

Policy Press   North American office:
University of Bristol   Policy Press
1-9 Old Park Hill   c/o The University of Chicago Press
Bristol BS2 8BB   1427 East 60th Street
UK   Chicago, IL 60637, USA
t: +44 (0)117 954 5940   t: +1 773 702 7700
e: pp-info@bristol.ac.uk   f: +1 773-702-9756
www.policypress.co.uk   e:sales@press.uchicago.edu
                                      www.press.uchicago.edu

British Library Cataloguing in Publication Data
A catalogue record for this book is available from the British Library.

Library of Congress Cataloging-in-Publication Data
A catalog record for this book has been requested.

ISBN 978-1-4473-1392-2 paperback
ISBN 978-1-4473-1391-5 hardcover
ISBN 978-1-4473-1393-9 ePub
ISBN 978-1-4473-1394-6 Mobi

Cover design by Tony Sinclair
Front cover: image kindly supplied by Stephen Sinclair
Printed and bound in Great Britain by CMP, Poole
Policy Press uses environmentally responsible print partners

Woodland
CARBON
www.woodlandcarbon.co.uk
CMP (UK) LTD
Printed on Carbon Captured paper

Dedicated to my brothers and sisters
and to the memory of our parents.

Contents

Acknowledgements

I would like to express my gratitude to the late Chelly Halsey for enabling me to continue my postgraduate studies in Social Policy, to Peter Taylor-Gooby for years of support and to Stephen Moore for giving me my first job teaching Social Policy and being such a generous colleague. I would particularly like to thank Adrian Sinfield for the encouragement he has provided over a long time and his many helpful comments and advice on this book. I am grateful to Tony Sinclair for designing the cover, and Policy Press editors Laura Vickers and Emily Watt for their patience. I hope they all find something here that made it worth the wait.

ONE

Analysing social policies

Analysing social policies: key points
- Social Policy analyses social challenges and collective measures to enhance well-being.
- Social Policy considers both scientific and moral questions.
- Social Policy analysis extends beyond what is usually thought of as the 'welfare state'.
- There are four dimensions to Social Policy analysis: empirical, distributional, ethical and critical.
- Theories and concepts are indispensable to Social Policy analysis. The qualities of a useful theory are consistency, comprehensiveness, parsimony, fruitfulness and elegance.
- The most illuminating theories and concepts in Social Policy clarify the causes of and inform response to the most damaging conditions confronting societies.

Understanding Social Policy

My aim in this book is to introduce readers to Social Policy[1] analysis and to help them think coherently about social problems and how societies collectively respond to them. It is not intended to be a systematic introduction to social policies or to the 'welfare state' in general. There are already many such books and readers can turn to them to learn more about the details of policies. Instead, the purpose is to introduce the distinctive nature of Social Policy analysis and some of the insights provided by this way of looking at social issues. I hope to show readers how to think like a Social Policy analyst by illustrating how a selection of ideas provides insights into some of the basic questions raised by social welfare. Thinking about such issues requires analysis, that is, unravelling the relationships between the different components of complex issues, examining how social systems function, unpicking arguments and interrogating the evidence used to justify social policies. Studying Social Policy also requires synthesis: recognising connections between different concepts and factors, such as how poverty relates to inequality, or the relationship between social exclusion and citizenship.

Each chapter considers an important question about social well-being and introduces what, in my experience, have been some of the most illuminating ideas applied to understand and answer them. My aim is to describe and demonstrate the value of these concepts: how they contribute to understanding the social world, help summarise the key features of important developments or make sense of large amounts of information, and how they cast new light on social issues and challenge ill-considered assumptions. These concepts, theories and ways of thinking provide powerful insights into some of the perennial and pressing issues facing society.

Social Policy is concerned with addressing serious social problems and it can be earnest and even upsetting at times. Most Social Policy analysts are motivated by concern for those experiencing problems and a desire to improve the world, so we do not often express how stimulating it is to analyse these issues as this might appear frivolous, or even exploitative. However, studying Social Policy is not just about struggling with unappealing technical issues and troubling social problems. The intellectual excitement when a theory or insight makes sense of what appears to be a mass of complex detail and reveals the social forces and factors that explain it is a deeply rewarding experience.

The questions and concepts outlined in this book are not intended to be exhaustive or definitive; they are a starting point to illustrate what is involved in Social Policy analysis and to show the insights that it can provide. While I hope to show readers how to think about Social Policy issues, it is not my aim to tell anyone *what* to think, although, for reasons outlined later, I do not believe that social problems and policies can be analysed with complete neutrality. The insights that I think are provided by the ideas selected and applied here do not amount to an overall perspective. There are also many other books that offer those, and I hope that the ideas and analyses provided in this book will help readers to assess them.

Social Policy involves continuous debate rather than settling on a dogma of fixed ideas. This characteristic will not appeal to everyone, but for those willing to accept the challenge of questioning received opinion, including their own, then Social Policy analysis provides an invigorating freshness. The evidence, arguments and insights produced by the best Social Policy analyses can transform our understanding of the world and change ourselves and society in the process. This is why Social Policy is worth studying.

What is Social Policy?

Much of what governments do could be described as social policy. For example, providing social security benefits, funding or delivering health and education services, regulating industry and employment, and providing cultural and leisure services are all examples of actions that governments take to promote social welfare. Many private companies are also heavily involved in delivering social policies – education, health, transport and even prisons in some countries are provided as commercial services, sometimes through complex partnerships with government or voluntary and community organisations. Even more welfare is provided by families and within households, although these might not usually be thought of as matters of 'policy' at all. This last point is itself an important issue. What should count as a social or welfare policy is discussed in Chapters Two and Three.

The scale of welfare

As there is so much at stake, debates over the size of the 'welfare state' are controversial and technically challenging.[2] For example, in the autumn of 2014, the UK government sent a letter to every household outlining how tax revenues were used.[3] This estimated that approximately 25% of all UK public expenditure was spent on welfare. However, this could be regarded as an overestimate as it included pension payments to National Health Service (NHS) staff and police and fire officers, which would be counted separately under other definitions and accounting rules. In a different report, the UK Office for Budget Responsibility argued that spending on health services, long-term care, education, social housing and security, and tax credits were all part of the welfare state, and that including these in the calculations meant that the UK spends £410 billion a year on the welfare state, which is about 57% of all public spending.[4] One thing is clear, irrespective of how it is defined and expenditure is calculated, welfare is certainly a major factor in the budgets of developed countries and a significant feature of their economies.

Given its significance and ubiquity, it is perhaps surprising that Social Policy – the discipline that is devoted to studying social problems and welfare policies – is not familiar to many people. This is not because it is a new subject. In the UK, it first developed as an academic discipline in the early 20th century, initially at the University of Liverpool and the London School of Economics.[5] At that time, it was known as Social Administration, and focused on the education of social workers. Nor is it the case that government welfare policies are a recent development. The date of the earliest social policies or first welfare states is debatable. The English Poor Laws can be traced back to at least the 1600s, and the first national unemployment insurance scheme was introduced in Germany in 1883, so welfare systems have a long history.

What defines the academic subject of Social Policy is its field of inquiry – the issues that it is concerned with and the questions that it addresses. However, there is even debate over that. There are many alternative definitions of what Social Policy is and what it studies, for example:

- 'The term "social policy" refers to forms of state intervention which affect the social opportunities and conditions under which people live.'[6]
- 'Social Policy studies the ways in which societies provide for the social and economic needs of their members.'[7]
- 'Social Policy is the study of human wellbeing.'[8]

It might be discouraging for those studying a subject for the first time to learn that experts cannot agree on how to define it. However, this lack of consensus is not a sign of failure, but reflects the complexity of what is involved in analysing social problems and the varied responses to them. First of all, considering all the possible factors that affect well-being or the interventions that have an impact on social and economic conditions, it is clear that Social Policy is a wide-ranging subject. One implication of this is that 'welfare', however it might be regarded, certainly extends beyond what is often thought of as the 'welfare state'.

A second distinctive factor that complicates Social Policy analysis is that the issues with which it deals are not merely technical and scientific, but also moral. For example, it is often suggested that – compared to the past or conditions in the developing world – there is no real **poverty** in a developed society such as the UK or the US.[9] This view depends upon beliefs about what 'poverty' is and how it should be defined and measured (see Chapter Four). Defining poverty involves judgements about what we think people ought to have and not go without. Should poverty mean only not having whatever is necessary to survive, or are there forms of deprivation short of destitution that should be regarded as poverty? Are members of contemporary societies entitled only to the standard of living of 20, 50 or 100 years ago? If this applies to living standards and incomes, should it apply also to housing conditions, education or health care? These questions lead to larger and deeper questions that have both moral and analytical aspects:

- What do people need to 'fare well' – what do they require for their well-being?
- Are social problems caused by the behaviour of those who experience them or are they produced by conditions beyond individual control?
- What makes an issue a *social* problem as opposed to a purely personal one?
- If a particular issue *is* a social problem, does that make it a government responsibility, or should some other social institution deal with it?
- Do people have the right to receive welfare support from others, and, if so, what is the basis of that right?

It is clear that answering these questions involves more than merely gathering facts. These are also **normative** issues, that is, they concern beliefs about right and wrong. Thinking about Social Policy questions involves considering ideas of **justice, fairness, rights** and **obligations**, and several other important principles. It is unlikely that agreement will be reached over such matters any time soon, and this might lead some to give up on studying Social Policy. However, neglecting such issues as poverty, caring for those in need, unemployment or inadequate housing is an even worse option, so addressing them requires Social Policy analysis. As Chapter Six shows, just because ideas about social issues are held passionately does not mean that they are always informed and well founded, and studying social issues and policies rigorously and methodically can bring some light to these heated controversies. While it is important from the outset to be aware that the answers to these questions are not easy, and the solutions to social problems are unlikely to be simple, Social Policy analysis is indispensable to properly understand, let alone begin to try to fix, these kinds of problems.

Social science: no easy answers

The distinctive nature of the issues with which Social Policy deals means that it is necessary to appreciate what is possible in any 'answer' to the questions and problems it considers. The cognitive psychologist and linguist Steven Pinker once summarised what he regarded as the difference between the natural sciences and the humanities:

> I once went to an interdisciplinary conference with scientists and humanities professors. At the end of a talk exploring a painting, the speaker said: 'Well, I hope to have complicated the subject matter in several ways.' I thought, that's the difference between a scientist and a critic – the scientist would say: 'I hope to have simplified the matter in several ways'.[10]

Pinker specifically refers here to the humanities rather than social sciences, but the contrasting approaches he claims to find expresses what some feel about disciplines such as Social Policy. Social scientists have a reputation for overcomplicating and obscuring issues rather than providing 'proper' answers. Some critics argue that the difference between genuine natural science and pseudo-social science is that the former provides precise answers to the questions it asks, often expressed in equations or scientific laws. These findings are verified by experiments and can be practically implemented in technology. In contrast, social sciences are dismissed as producing obscure jargon, endless debate and failed interventions.

It is true that the nature of the issues with which it deals – complex, multidimensional and involving both moral and technical considerations – means that Social Policy rarely provides simple answers. This might seem frustrating, but it is unavoidable rather than a result of incompetence or deliberate obscurity. Those who believe that there ought to be simple common-sense answers to complex moral, social and political disputes have not properly understood the issue. In some cases, an important contribution of Social Policy analysis might be to show that the most familiar and comforting opinions on social problems are unfounded and perhaps even prejudiced (see Chapter Six). Intellectual maturity and progress in thinking sometimes means recognising that an issue might be more complicated than it initially appears. This does not mean that Social Policy analysis is always difficult and only frustrating: it can be a stimulating and enlightening subject that can transform understanding and open up new perspectives on complex and important social challenges.

Personal life and Social Policy

Peter Townsend – one of the most important thinkers in Social Policy – once remarked that 'The sciences of economics and sociology sometimes seem to be imprisoned within narrow specialisms which discount the flesh and blood, and the problems, of ordinary life.'[11] This is not a criticism that can be made of Social Policy. Some of the issues with which Social Policy deals might appear remote and impersonal – unfortunate conditions perhaps, but if you are lucky, ones that mostly affect other people. Few problems impact equally upon everyone at all times, but many of those who do not suffer directly from particular issues are still influenced by them indirectly as users, providers or funders of welfare services. Personal life is also shaped by social policies in numerous subtle ways. One example of this is fertility – the capacity to bear children. Fertility is clearly a biological matter but the opportunity to have children is influenced by wider social and economic conditions. Obvious examples of this are such factors as the availability of contraception, medical technology or laws on abortion. More basic even than this, the child-bearing age of women is bounded by the onset of puberty and the menopause, both of which are influenced by diet and physical well-being, themselves shaped by economic development and social conditions. Fertility rates also decline with economic development, when general conditions and standards of living improve (as shown by the experience of South Korea since the 1960s), and also during periods of economic crisis and upheaval, as in several European countries after 2008.[12]

A final example of how fertility is influenced by socio-economic conditions and public policies is the 'baby gap': the difference between the number of children women say they would like to have had and the number that they were actually able to have. This gap, in part, reflects the economic circumstances of women (and couples) due to the nature of employment and career opportunities (including flexible working and parental leave), the availability of childcare, the housing market, the costs of education and accumulated debts, and several other factors that are, or could be, the subject of social policies. It has been estimated that the cumulative cost of raising a child to the age of 21 in the UK is £227,266.[13] It is perhaps not surprising therefore that the UK baby gap was estimated to be 90,000 births per year.[14]

Fertility is just one example of how the social environment and policy context influences personal life. The personal is certainly political, and also social and economic – in some subtle and surprising ways.

Dimensions of Social Policy analysis

To understand and inform responses to complex social issues, Social Policy draws upon a range of social sciences and applies elements from them in a distinctive way. Social Policy analysis is characterised by four dimensions:

- empirical;
- distributional;
- ethical; and
- critical.

Empirical analysis

Social Policy is a **science**. Social Policy analyses and arguments must be assessed using the criteria that apply to all social sciences. They must be logical and coherent, consistent with the known evidence, and tested by valid and reliable research methods. Social Policy arguments and theories must constantly be examined against new data, and only the fittest survive. This is what makes Social Policy a rigorous intellectual discipline rather than mere opinion or polemic.

Carefully gathering facts has been a traditional strength of Social Policy. Although the term was not used at the time, some of what could be regarded as the earliest Social Policy studies were concerned with documenting social conditions, such as Charles Booth's (1889) *Labour and Life of the People in London* and Seebohm Rowntree's (1901) *Poverty: A Study of Town Life* (discussed in Chapter Four). This empirical orientation remains vital: it is impossible to have an informed commentary on the nature and scale of social problems or the impact of policies without valid and reliable data.

In the 1990s, the empirical dimension of Social Policy was given added impetus by the idea of **evidence-based policy**, and the argument that what is important for a policy is not its underlying ideology, but that 'what matters is what works'.[15] A vital contribution of Social Policy analysis is to test policy against evidence, and this often produces illuminating findings. One example of this is the evaluation of measures to deter young offenders from committing further crimes. 'Scared Straight' and similar programmes involve taking young people judged to be at risk of persistent offending to visit prisons. The theory behind this policy is that witnessing the conditions of imprisonment and learning from the experiences of older convicts will deter young people from committing further offences. In fact, a systematic review of the randomised experimental tests of these kinds of programme concluded that they actually did more harm than good, that is, the young people who experienced them were *more* likely to reoffend.[16] Despite this evidence, this policy remains popular among many politicians and criminal justice officials, and it has now been tried in at least six different countries. Why would a policy persist when not only is there no evidence to support it, but research shows that it is actively harmful? This question is one that Social Policy analysts have considered at length (see Chapter Two). What it demonstrates is that social policies are not always decided by considering what works.

Distributional analysis

Lord Robbins once defined the subject of Economics as dealing with the problem of allocating scarce resources between alternative uses.[17] Economics is therefore ultimately concerned with choices – the decisions required when resources are limited but demands and alternative uses are potentially infinite. Economic questions are central to Social Policy analysis, such as: 'What is the most efficient and effective use of resources to maximise welfare?' or 'What is the best way to pay for services?' However, when considering whether or not a particular welfare service is affordable, it is necessary to acknowledge the cost of *not* providing it. As the geneticist Steve Jones once observed: 'If you think education is expensive try ignorance'.[18] A particular example of this is the cost of child poverty, which was estimated in 2013 to be £25 billion a year in the UK.[19] These costs arise from the additional expenditure on education, social work services, social security benefits and the police and criminal justice system required to deal with the legacy of childhood poverty. Added to these costs are the lower taxes paid and the reduced expenditure on goods and services of those unemployed or with lower incomes as a result of the effects of childhood poverty. For these reasons, the European Union uses the level of child poverty as an indicator in forecasting future social and economic problems in different countries.[20]

The 'do nothing' option in response to a social problem is not a neutral position as the issue does not simply disappear, and the costs of addressing it always fall somewhere. For example, if society as a whole does not provide care and support for its vulnerable members, then – unless they are left to whatever fate befalls them – someone must, and this responsibility often falls upon families, and disproportionately upon women. For this reason, it has been argued that reducing public spending on social care services involves redistributing resources from female carers (who provide unpaid labour and lose earnings from employment) to male taxpayers, who pay less tax than they would otherwise.[21]

In such cases, the moral and economic aspects of Social Policy analysis are intertwined. Who benefits and pays for a policy are often as much political as economic questions. Identifying the contributors to and beneficiaries of social policies is a complicated but fascinating issue (see Chapter Three). For example, who benefits from state-funded education: children, their parents, employers or future pensioners who rely upon working-age people to generate profits and dividends and pay taxes? Perhaps it is all of them and others not mentioned here. Can we identify which group benefits most, and would it be fair for whoever that is to fund education? Or, would it be fairer to require whichever groups can best afford to pay more towards the costs of education to do so, even if they might not benefit so much directly?

Even identifying who uses a service is less straightforward than it initially appears. It might seem simple enough to count the number of service users, but what if particular groups make less use not because they do not need a service, but for other reasons? For example, it has long been known that there is an **inverse care law** in publicly funded health services: that some of the groups who most need health care are among those least likely to receive it.[22] This might be due to access barriers such as discrimination or social exclusion (see Chapter Four), or to less obvious factors. Complicating the issue yet further is the fact that older people on average make greater use of health services than other age groups but not every section of society has an equal prospect of living to an age when most care is needed. In particular, lower-income groups have a lower life expectancy than wealthier ones so that, overall, the more affluent sections of society are likely to receive most health-care provision (as are women relative to men).[23] Rather than criticising Social Policy for complicating such matters, the insights gained from asking better questions should be appreciated. Demonstrating that an issue is less straightforward than is supposed by simplistic and mistaken ideas is a valuable contribution. Informed doubt might be preferable to dogmatic ignorance, although it may be less comfortable.

Social Policy is also concerned with the costs and benefits of social issues and welfare arrangements in a wider sense than the calculations of conventional economics. This means that a **multidimensional** approach to analysing social problems and policy responses is required. The limitations of the one-dimensional approach to social policies taken by some economists are evident from the bestseller *Freakonomics* and its offshoots.[24] The authors once challenged the apparent attachment of British Prime Minister David Cameron to an NHS that provides care free at the point of use. They argued that such a policy was as unwise as offering free universal transport – such a service is inevitably unaffordable as if there are no costs in using it, demand will be insatiable.[25] In fact, a US research institution reported in 2014 that the British NHS was the best in the world in terms of quality, access and efficiency, while health-care provision in the US was the worst of the 11 countries examined.[26] This highlights the limitations of an ill-considered one-dimensional approach to social issues. First, as mentioned earlier, it fails to consider the implications of alternative forms of provision or not providing a service at all. There are pros and cons to every system of healthcare provision that have to be compared, and some of the costs of limited public provision should be evident to authors from the US. In particular, markets respond to the ability to pay rather than the intensity of need, and a market-based health-care system creates incentives for medical professionals to provide more treatment than might be required to those patients who can afford to pay the fees. Neither a public health-care system free at the point of use nor a private health market is a perfect response to health-care needs. It is likely that such a complex social issue requires a range of forms of funding and provision and insights from different perspectives. It is also unlikely that there will be a definitive solution to this issue: the health-care requirements of the post-Second World War period are not the same as those of the early 21st century, with its distinctive issues of ageing and 'lifestyle' illnesses, such as cardiovascular conditions and obesity. Similarly, the nature and the challenges of providing health care in the developing world are different from those of the developed world, and may require distinctive models of provision.

Beyond this, the authors of *Freakonomics* illustrate the old saying that if all you have is a hammer then every problem looks like a nail. Economic costs and benefits are not the only, or even the determining, calculation in health-care policy, or many other areas of social policy. Elected politicians answerable to voters must consider whether a policy is practical and deliverable. In the current British political climate, the outright privatisation of the NHS would be an act of political suicide, although this is not necessarily a fixed and inevitable situation (see Chapter Two).

Social Policy analysis therefore involves asking a wider set of questions than conventional economics: not only who financially benefits from and pays for different interventions and non-interventions, but which social and political factors shape a particular policy and the outcomes it produces.[27] Social Policy is about **value** as much as cost; as well as who gets what and why, it is concerned with whether this outcome *ought* to be the case. This is not an economic, but an ethical, question.

Ethical analysis

A distinguishing feature of academic Social Policy is its practical orientation. The name of the discipline itself makes this clear, and, as mentioned earlier, the subject has its origins in training practitioners and studying social conditions with the aim of social reform. Social Policy aims not only to analyse and understand social conditions, but also to reshape society in various ways. This is a feature that attracts many to study Social Policy.

Not every Social Policy analyst can point directly to the impact of their research on policy and practice, and there are many reasons for this that have nothing to do with the quality of research (see Chapter Six). However, if studying social problems and those who suffer from them is not to be a voyeuristic intrusion, then there must be some justification beyond intellectual curiosity.[28] As the football manager Bill Nicholson once said in another context: 'If you're not interfering with play, what are you doing on the pitch?' Respecting those who experience social problems or use welfare services and treating them as equals underpins arguments for **participatory research** and analysis in Social Policy.[29] This approach actively involves service users and undertakes research 'with' them as **human subjects** rather than 'on' them as though they were mere objects.

Social Policy deals with issues not only of what *is*, but also of what *ought to be* the case. It involves ideas about how we should live, about the **good society**. Obviously, this leads to controversy as there is disagreement about how society ought to be, and the heat and intensity of social policy disputes reflects this inescapable ethical aspect. Social Policy does not face the tortuous problem of trying to be **value-neutral** with which other social sciences have (unsuccessfully) wrestled.[30] As Social Policy is about informing change, it need not try to disguise its partisanship. Instead of a futile aspiration to neutrality, Peter Townsend argued that Social Policy analysts should be honestly morally and politically engaged:

> As policy analyst, the sociologist cannot just be a servant of society.... He cannot but also be its judge. However hard he strives for detachment, particular values and selected standards of comparison are inevitably built into his work. This is best acknowledged and openly discussed.[31]

As it informs interventions, some critics accuse Social Policy of political bias. Certainly, those who favour 'political minimalism' or who are suspicious of government accuse Social Policy of providing an ideological case for intervention and reform.[32] However, there is a difference between partisanship and bias.

Possessing values and informing interventions does not mean that Social Policy is ideological. The science of Medicine is not neutral between illness and health but clearly 'interventionist', so it seems unusual to suggest that studying social problems and proposing remedies to them is a form of bias. Furthermore, as Chapter Three explains, interventions to address social problems do not necessarily have to come from the public sector.

As with Medicine, Social Policy students must be aware of the ethical issues involved in their work. The 'Guidelines on Research Ethics' issued by the Social Policy Association state that:

> While it is inevitable that the choice of research topics and methods will be influenced by individuals' values and beliefs, researchers should reflect critically on the ways in which their values and beliefs influence their research approach and the conduct, analysis and reporting of research.[33]

This echoes the argument of Titmuss, who urged Social Policy analysts to be aware of the influence of their personal values, do what they can to hold them in check and, above all, be open with others about them so that they can judge what influence these values might have had on research and analysis:

> We all have our values and prejudices … we have a responsibility for making our values clear, and we have a special duty to do so when we are discussing such a subject as social policy which, quite clearly has no meaning at all if it is considered to be neutral in terms of values.[34]

Self-criticism and public scrutiny are essential to the integrity of Social Policy analysis, and further reasons why it should be regarded as a science. Objectivity in science is not achieved by believing that researchers can be detached and neutral, but comes from their following the proper rules of inquiry. These include refusing to knowingly distort data, submitting findings and the methods used to reach them to collective scrutiny, and holding others to these standards. One ethical duty of Social Policy analysts is to expose weak arguments even if they would like to support their principles or consequences. Social Policy scholars are members not of a party, but of a community of independent critical analysts, and their self-criticism and peer review guard against 'the terrible certainties peddled by the ideologically possessed'.[35]

Critical analysis

Social Policy is critical not only of itself, but also of social conditions and of policy. It has been noted that 'There is a sense in which social science is inherently disturbing or critical'.[36] The word 'critic' comes from the Greek word for 'judge' – κριτης (*crit-es*) – and a critical approach to an issue involves assessing and weighing up its worth. To be critical in this sense does not mean being hostile or opposed to something – a literary critic does not only write negative book reviews. A good critic provides a reasoned and evidence-based evaluation of the quality of whatever is being examined, whether that be a book, a theory or a hypothesis. A critic may also clarify and explain what is being studied, for example, by putting it into context or comparing it with examples of similar things. A critical perspective therefore involves analysing how things – such as social conditions or social policies – have come about and take the form that they do, and evaluating the evidence for and against particular positions. Critical analysis of social issues and social policies involves asking whether the current situation is the only way things could be, whether conditions have been different in the past or elsewhere, and, if so, what accounts for such differences? The literary critic Edward Said describes this as adopting an 'exile standpoint', which requires critics to:

> see things not simply as they are, but as they have come to be that way. [To] Look at situations as contingent, not as inevitable, look at them as the result of a series of historical choices made by men and women, as facts of society made by human beings, and not as natural or god-given, therefore unchangeable, permanent, irreversible.[37]

Questioning social conditions and common-sense opinions in this way may appear disrespectful or even subversive, and is one reason why social sciences are often thought to be politically radical.[38] Critical Social Policy analysis involves considering the foundation of ideas about welfare and the rationale for social policies. This means uncovering the assumptions on which policies are based, including the often unarticulated ideas about what motivates people to behave in particular ways, implicit theories of how society works and beliefs about what rights people have. Social Policy analysis brings such beliefs to the surface for examination and may require challenging what Richard Dawkins calls the 'argument from personal incredulity', where people find it difficult to accept some counter-intuitive scientific facts or theory and seek more comforting explanations.[39] Scientific training and method involves 'taming the authority of one's intuition' by applying rigorous logical and empirical analysis.[40] A consequence of this approach is that science may challenge received opinion or cherished beliefs. Some of the most illuminating and exciting scientific ideas challenge common sense in this way but, in doing so, allow us to see the world in a new light. Over time, some of the insights of these theories become so compelling and irresistible that they are incorporated into common sense so that, in retrospect, it is difficult to understand why they initially caused fuss or even to identify what contribution critical analysis ever made to our understanding. It is the fate of some of the greatest findings and insights of social science to be absorbed in this way so that their originality and impact are overlooked. In some cases, the contribution of Social Policy analysis might be that it has changed how an issue is thought of or the terms of the debate (see Chapter Two). This subtle but transformational impact is a quality of some of the most valuable concepts in the discipline.

Concepts and theory in Social Policy analysis

Theoretical discussions and conceptual analyses are sometimes dismissed as impractical or self-indulgent – a dry and abstract distraction from what really matters, which is *doing* something about social problems or producing real research findings. This criticism is mistaken – it is impossible to separate theory from valuable research or from effective practice. The psychologist Kurt Lewin once suggested that 'There is nothing so practical as a good theory'.[41] This is because useful theories inspire new ways of thinking about issues and are an indispensable guide to research. Theories tells us what to look for and what to test; they offer accounts of how the different aspects of an issue relate to each other, for example, how one thing impacts upon or causes another. Without a theory to provide some context and understanding, research becomes merely **mindless empiricism** – a collection of unconnected and meaningless data.[42]

One example of this is the current interest in 'Big Data' as a source of insight into social issues. The principle behind this approach is that there is now so much data produced by contemporary systems of telecommunications and online information exchange that this can be mined by ever-more powerful computer analysis programs to reveal significant patterns. With enough data and the right algorithms, previously hidden processes and relationships can be identified from a mass of facts without the need to propose theories and design research projects. This approach has proven useful in some branches of genomics and physics. The idea that data alone is sufficient to understand social processes and inform policy was boosted by Google's Flu Trends analysis, which used Internet search queries about influenza symptoms and related issues to predict the spread of influenza epidemics.[43] The initial results were impressive and Google Flu Trends was able to provide a more accurate and timely estimate of the spread of influenza than the US government's Centre for Disease Control and Prevention.[44] However, Google Flu Trends' estimates of influenza cases in subsequent years were very inaccurate – over 50% higher than actual recorded cases in 2011/12.[45] There are several reasons for this, but an important factor was that Big Data analysis operates without an adequate theory of what causes the correlations on which it draws. Without an explanatory model of what causes flu to spread, Google's analysis could mistake mere associations for significant relationships and fail to distinguish between important and insignificant patterns. Although the analysis of massive data sets is a promising area for future social research, this example illustrates that this cannot progress if theory is neglected. Theories are necessary to organise data and make it coherent by explaining *why* particular factors correlate.[46]

Theories and concepts are ideas that offer accounts that explain what is observed from experience and research. Without evidence to test or verify them, these ideas are only empty speculations. Useful scientific concepts not only provide insights and alternative ways of thinking about issues, but can also be applied practically in research or policy, and the best of them can change our understanding of the world.

Rethinking the nature of welfare regimes

There are many alternative ways of categorising national welfare systems. One of the most influential approaches was proposed by Esping-Andersen in *The Three Worlds of Welfare Capitalism*.[47] This classified welfare regimes using three criteria:

1. decommodification – the extent to which access to a welfare service is independent from market purchasing power (ie income and employment);
2. effect on stratification – whether the welfare service reduces or reinforces social divisions, particularly class differences; and
3. form of state intervention – how directly involved the government is in providing the service.

Using these criteria, Esping-Andersen identified three types of welfare regime:

1. Liberal welfare states (such as the UK and the USA) – which have a low level of decommodification, are highly stratified and provide many welfare services through markets;
2. social-democratic regimes (such as those in Scandinavia) – where services are highly decommodified, are intended to reduce class divisions and there is significant direct state provision; and
3. conservative-corporatist systems (eg Germany and France) – where welfare services are decommodified but not designed to reduce stratification, and state intervention is through the regulation of markets or finance.

Lewis proposed an alternative approach to categorising welfare regimes. She suggested that welfare states could be classified in terms of their assumptions about gender roles and a 'male breadwinner' within households.[48] Lewis also identified three forms of welfare regime:

1. strong male-breadwinner model (eg UK and Ireland) – draws a firm line between the 'public' sphere of state-provided welfare and the 'private' or domestic sphere, where there is no state responsibility (eg childcare);
2. modified male-breadwinner model (eg France) – enables female employment by supporting 'horizontal' redistribution between different types of household, for example, towards families with children; and
3. weak male-breadwinner model (eg Denmark and Sweden) – supports working parents through childcare provision and taxation policies and therefore enables a dual- rather than male-breadwinner household.

The male-breadwinner model makes explicit the sometimes unspoken and unquestioned assumptions about families and the respective roles of men and women within them upon which some social policies are based, and which these policies then reinforce. It implies that Social Policy should pay particular attention to the situation of women, as: most informal care within households is provided by women; women are often the majority of those employed in delivering welfare services; and women have particular roles as welfare service users, for example, as parents (particularly lone parents), and as they are more likely to be pensioners. Lewis's classification of welfare regimes showed welfare policies in a new light and raised important questions about why services are provided as they are. In these ways, it exemplifies many of the qualities of an illuminating concept.

What a good idea

The criteria to assess the quality of Social Policy theories and ideas are the same as in other sciences: consistency, reach, parsimony, fruitfulness and elegance.[49] Consistency (ie logical coherence) is a basic feature of a useful idea but the other elements require some explanation. The 'reach' of a theory is how much information it accounts for: 'The mark of any good theory is that it makes coordinated sense of a string of observations otherwise independent and inexplicable'.[50] A good idea is one that summarises and makes sense of a lot of data. As part of this, useful theories and concepts are comprehensive in terms of the groups, times and contexts to which they refer and are not restricted to specific circumstances.

Parsimony means making few assumptions:

> A powerful idea assumes little to explain much. It does lots of explanatory 'heavy lifting', while expending little in way of assumptions or postulations. It gives you plenty of bangs for your explanatory buck. Its Explanatory Ratio – what it explains, divided by what it needs to assume in order to do the explaining – is large.[51]

One of the most parsimonious and powerful ideas in science is Darwin's theory of evolution by natural selection, which relies upon a few plausible propositions to explain the enormous diversity of forms of life. Darwin's theory proposes that all living things produce more offspring than can possibly survive; while very similar, there are minor differences between these offspring, and those variations that provide an advantage in the struggle to survive enable some to live to reproduce the next generation so that, over time, new species evolve in relation to their environment.[52] The parsimony of Darwin's theory is an example of a principle of reasoning known as **Occam's razor**. This is named after William of Ockham, a 14th-century English philosopher, who argued that the best option between competing theories was whichever assumed the least. A theory that depends upon many conditions is weaker than one that assumes little. This is why many conspiracy theories are implausible: they beg more questions than more mundane alternatives. Evidence alone will never be enough to rebut fanatics, but comparing the plausibility of alternative theories can separate reasonable explanations from fantasy.

The fruitfulness of an idea means that it provides new understanding and explains what was previously obscure. One test of a useful concept or theory is that it can account for evidence uncovered after it was first proposed. The richest theories and concepts are also suggestive, dynamic and capable of further development and application. A valuable concept prompts thinking in ways that would otherwise have been overlooked, for example, by revealing contrasts, similarities or connections not noticed before. It is easy to become trapped by habit and conventional ways of thinking, and the most illuminating insights challenge the blinkers of received opinion. This is not unique to science; one of the effects of art is to enable us to see what is a taken for granted in new ways. The literary critic Viktor Shklovsky described this as **defamiliarisation** or estrangement, and argued that the purpose of art was 'to overcome the deadening effects of habit by representing familiar things in unfamiliar ways'.[53] This is the heart of originality in creative art, and the very best scientific ideas also have this quality. Original scientific insights have a **Copernican effect**,[54] that is, they revolutionise how we look at things. Another way of expressing this is that novel and inspiring scientific insights puts things in a new light. Illumination is a common metaphor in discussing the best of both science and art: it is common to talk of seeing something 'in light of something' else, of becoming enlightened or of the **Enlightenment** as a new dawn of understanding or an awakening.

The final characteristic of the best scientific concepts and theories also overlaps with art: some ideas are more beautiful than others, that is, more elegant and aesthetic. This is part of the attraction of powerful equations and scientific laws, not only are they right (ie they stand up to tests against evidence and enable understanding of future events), but they are also satisfyingly neat and correct.[55] Something of this sentiment was expressed when James Watson, who, along with Francis Crick, discovered the double helix structure of DNA, said that it was so beautiful that it had to be true.[56] It might surprise those who regard science as a detached and technical pursuit that there is an aesthetic aspect to it, and it is certainly the case that ideas and theories cannot be accepted merely *because* they are beautiful. However, much of scientific understanding has progressed through searching for simplicity and an underlying order that explains a mass of detail. This is what Steven Pinker meant when he described science as simplifying rather than complicating matters. The Periodic Table of the chemical elements is a beautiful example of this – systematising and providing a foundation to explain what was previously complex and incomprehensible.[57]

The concepts and ideas discussed in this book demonstrate some of these qualities. They offer insights and new understanding that shed light on important social problems and the varied responses that different societies have taken to address them. They provide vantage points from which large areas of social welfare can be understood, and they are particularly illuminating when used in conjunction with one another. The following chapters aim to demonstrate the power of their insight by turning them to illuminate particular questions. These illustrations are not exhaustive. My hope is that by introducing exemplary Social Policy thinking (mostly that of other scholars), readers will be encouraged to adopt, adapt and apply these ideas to analyse some of the major challenges that contemporary societies face.

Any selection of particular concepts and theories raises the 'What about?' question. It is reasonable to ask what the justification is for the selection provided in this book and why other insightful ideas are not included. The aim of this book is to introduce Social Policy analysis rather than pretend to be exhaustive. It is not suggested that these are indisputably the 'best' concepts, ideas and analyses in Social Policy, only that I can testify from experience – and I hope to show by illustration – that they are excellent examples of the discipline *at* its best. The chemist and author Primo Levi once remarked that a chemist's career can be shaped and mapped out by their relationship with particular chemical elements. Something similar can be said about theories and concepts in the careers of social scientists. I have learned a lot about social issues and policies by applying the concepts outlined in the following chapters. Inevitably, the selection is partial, in the sense of being incomplete – not partisan. I hope that the concepts outlined in this book will provide similar inspiration in others, encourage readers to study the important questions that Social Policy considers and contribute to the promotion of human welfare.

Notes

[1] Throughout the book, I shall follow the convention of distinguishing the academic discipline of Social Policy from actual social policies and interventions by using capital letters for the former.

[2] HM Treasury (2014) *Public Expenditure Statistical Analyses, 2014.* Cm 8902. London: HM Treasury.

[3] Milligan, B. (2014) 'The Truth About Welfare Spending: Facts or Propaganda?', BBC News, 4 November. Available at: http://www.bbc.co.uk/news/business-29898083

[4] Office for Budget Responsibility (2014) 'Welfare Trends Report'. Available at: http://budgetresponsibility.org.uk/wordpress/docs/Welfare_trends_report_2014_dn2B.pdf

[5] Pinker, R. (1971) *Social Theory and Social Policy*. London: Heinemann.

[6] Burden, T. (1998) *Social Policy and Welfare: A Clear Guide*. London: Pluto Press, p xi.

[7] Social Policy Association (2009) 'Guidelines on Research Ethics'. Available at: http://www.social-policy.org.uk/downloads/SPA_code_ethics_jan09.pdf

[8] Dean, H. (2006) *Social Policy*. Cambridge: Policy Press, p 1.

[9] See, for example, Lanchester, J. (2014) 'There's Poverty in the UK, But We Are Better off Calling it Inequality', *The Guardian*, 5 September.

[10] Quoted in Tucker, I. (2012) 'Science Writing: How Do You Make Complex Issues Accessible and Readable?', *The Observer*, 2 December.

[11] Townsend, P. (2010) 'The Meaning of Poverty', *British Journal of Sociology*, 61, p 94.

[12] Lanzieri, G. (2013) *Towards a 'Baby Recession' in Europe? Differential Fertility Trends During the Economic Crisis*. Luxembourg: Eurostat.

[13] Osborne, H. (2014) 'Cost of Raising a Child Surges Past £225,000', *The Guardian*, 23 January.

[14] See: Dixon, M. and Margo, J. (2006) *Population Politics*. London: Institute for Public Policy Research, p 80.

[15] The recent use of this phrase is attributed to a speech delivered by Tony Blair at the Corn Exchange in the City of London on 7 April 1997 (see: http://blogs.independent.co.uk/2013/03/09/reinventing-blairism/). However, the wide appeal of this view is apparent in the creation of such organisations as 'What Works: Evidence Centres for Social Policy' (see: https://www.gov.uk/government/publications/what-works-evidence-centres-for-social-policy) and the Alliance for Useful Evidence (see: http://www.alliance4usefulevidence.org/).

[16] Petrosino, A. and Turpin-Petrosino, C. (2003) 'Scared Straight and Other Juvenile Awareness Programs for Preventing Juvenile Delinquency: A Systematic Review of the Randomized Experimental Evidence', *Annals of the American Academy of Political and Social Science*, 589(1). See also Haynes, L., Service, O., Goldacre, B. and Torgerson, D. (2012) *Test, Learn, Adapt: Developing Public Policy with Randomised Controlled Trials*. London: Cabinet Office Behavioural Insights Team.

[17] Robbins, L. (1935) *An Essay on the Nature and Significance of Economic Science*. London: MacMillan.

[18] BBC Radio 4 (2011) 'In Our Time', 9 June. Available at: http://www.bbc.co.uk/programmes/b011pldm

[19] Hirsch, D. (2013) *An Estimate of the Costs of Child Poverty in 2013*. Loughborough: Centre for Research in Social Policy. Available at: http://www.cpag.org.uk/sites/default/files/Cost%20of%20child%20poverty%20research%20update%20(2013).pdf (accessed 13 August 2015).

[20] Vandenbroucke, F. (2014) 'We Must Act Now to Defuse Europe's Timebomb', *Europe's World*, 15 June. Available at: http://europesworld.org/2014/06/15/we-must-act-now-to-defuse-europes-child-poverty-timebomb/#.U63FEU1OV94

[21] Himmelweit, S. and Land, H. (2008) *Reducing Gender Differences to Create a Sustainable Care System*. York: Joseph Rowntree Foundation.

[22] Tudor Hart, J. (1971) 'The Inverse Care Law', *The Lancet*, 297.

[23] See Sefton, T. (2002) *Recent Changes in the Distribution of the Social Wage*. York: Joseph Rowntree Foundation. Hills, J. (2014) *Good Times, Bad Times: The Welfare Myth of Them and Us*. Bristol: The Policy Press.

[24] Levitt, S.D. and Dubner, S.J. (2007) *Freakonomics: A Rogue Economist Explores the Hidden Side of Everything*. London: Penguin. This book has become the basis for a franchise, see: http://freakonomics.com/

[25] Levitt, S.D. and Dubner, S.J. (2014) 'Think Like a Freak Extract: Joining the Dots Between Hot Dogs, Van Halen and David Cameron', *The Observer*, 11 May.

[26] Davis, K., Stremikis, K., Squires, D. and Schoen, C. (2014) *Mirror, Mirror on the Wall, 2014 Update: How the U.S. Health Care System Compares Internationally*. Washington, DC: The Commonwealth Fund.

[27] Walker, A. (1984) *Social Planning: A Strategy for Socialist Welfare*. Oxford: Basil Blackwell, p 40.

[28] Piachaud, D. (1987) 'Problems in the Definition and Measurement of Poverty', *Journal of Social Policy*, 16(2), p 161: 'the study of poverty is only ultimately justifiable if it influences individual and social attitudes and actions. This must be borne in mind constantly if discussion on the definition of poverty is to avoid becoming an academic debate worthy of Nero – a semantic and statistical squabble that is parasitic, voyeuristic and utterly unconstructive and which treats "the poor" as passive objects for attention, whether benign or malevolent – a discussion that is part of the problem rather than part of the solution.'

[29] Beresford, P. (2002) 'User Involvement in Research and Evaluation: Liberation or Regulation?', *Social Policy and Society*, 1(2).

[30] Gouldner, A.V. (1973) 'Anti-Minotaur: The Myth of a Value-Free Sociology', in *For Sociology: Renewal and Critique in Sociology Today*. London: Allen Lane.

[31] Townsend, P. (1975) *Sociology and Social Policy*. Harmondsworth: Penguin, p 9.

[32] Heffer, S. (2008) 'Do Nothing', BBC Radio 4, 9 and 16 January. Available at: http://www.bbc.co.uk/programmes/b008s4ds/broadcasts/2008/01

[33] Social Policy Association (2009) 'Guidelines on Research Ethics'. Available at: http://www.social-policy.org.uk/downloads/SPA_code_ethics_jan09.pdf

[34] Titmuss, R.M. (1974) *Social Policy: An Introduction*. London: George Allen & Unwin, p 27.

[35] Hennessey, P. (1996) 'The Glories and Blemishes of the British Governing Class', *Fabian Review*, 108(1), p 9.

[36] Platt, J. (1992) 'The Contribution of Social Science', in Loney, M. (ed) *The State or the Market: Politics and Welfare in Contemporary Britain* (2nd edn). London: Sage, p 242.

[37] Said, E.W. (1994) *Representations of the Intellectual: The 1993 Reith Lectures*. London: Vintage, p 45.

[38] Giddens, A. (1986) *Sociology: A Brief but Critical Introduction*. London: Palgrave Macmillan.

[39] Dawkins, R. (1986) *The Blind Watchmaker: Why the Evidence of Evolution Reveals a Universe without Design*. London: Penguin.

[40] Orr, H.A. (2013) 'Awaiting a New Darwin', *The New York Review of Books*, 7 February, p 27.

[41] Lewin, K. (1951) *Field Theory in Social Science; Selected Theoretical Papers*. (ed Cartwright, D.). New York, NY: Harper & Row, p 169.

[42] Mills, C.W. (1970) *The Sociological Imagination*. Harmondsworth: Penguin.

[43] Ginsberg, J., Mohebbi M.H., Patel, R.S., Brammer, L., Smolinski, M.S. and Brilliant, L. (2009) 'Detecting Influenza Epidemics Using Search Engine Query Data', *Nature*, 457(19 February).

[44] Naughton, J. (2014) 'Google and the Flu: How Big Data Will Help Us Make Gigantic Mistakes', *The Observer*, 6 April.

[45] Lazer, D., Kennedy, R., King, G. and Vespignani, A. (2014) 'The Parable of Google Flu: Traps in Big Data Analysis', *Science*, 343(14).

[46] The physicist Steven Weinberg explains that theories played a crucial role in the development of elementary particle physics, where there was a deluge of data that was difficult to understand: 'Progress when it came was generally initiated by theoretical advances, with experimentation serving as a referee between competing theories'. See Weinberg, S. (2013) 'Physics: What We Do and Don't Know', *New York Review of Books*, 7 November.

[47] Esping-Andersen, G. (1990) *The Three Worlds of Welfare Capitalism*. Cambridge: Polity.

[48] Lewis, J. (1992) 'Gender and the Development of Welfare Regimes', *Journal of European Social Policy*, 2(3).

[49] Boote, D.N. and Beile, P. (2005) 'Scholars Before Researchers: On the Centrality of the Dissertation Literature Review in Research Preparation', *Educational Researcher*, 34(6).

[50] Gould, S.J. (2007) *The Richness of Life* (ed McGarr, P. and Rose, S.). London: Vintage, p 201.

[51] Dawkins, R. (2007) 'Why Darwin Matters', *The Guardian*, 9 February.

[52] Rose, S. (2013) 'Swamp-Man Strikes Again', *The Guardian*, 18 May.

[53] Lodge, D. (1992) *The Art of Fiction*. London: Penguin, p 53.

[54] Nicolaus Copernicus was a Polish astronomer who proposed in 1543 that the Sun rather than the Earth was the centre of our solar system.

55   Farmelo, G. (ed) (2003) *It Must Be Beautiful: Great Equations of Modern Science*. London: Granta.

56   Maddox, B. (2013) 'DNA's Double Helix: 60 Years Since Life's Deep Molecular Secret was Discovered', *The Guardian*, 22 February.

57   Strathearn, P. (2001) *Mendeleyev's Dream: The Quest for the Elements*. London: Thomas Dunne Books.

TWO

What is a 'social problem'?
The social construction of welfare

Social construction: key points

- Social construction refers to the difference between the representation and reality of social issues.
- There are three broad uses of the term 'social construction' in Social Policy analysis: (1) issues have social causes; (2) issues are represented in selective ways; and (3) social issues should be regarded as processes.
- Social constructionism implies that it is important to consider carefully the language and discourses used to discuss issues.
- Social constructionism suggests that ideas about social problems vary over time and between different perspectives.
- Perceptions of social issues and policy responses to them are determined by political processes rather than an objective consideration of the facts.

Introduction

The meaning of the word '**welfare**' has changed over time. It was originally used to wish someone well on a journey, which is still apparent in the word 'farewell'. By the 14th century, it meant happiness or prosperity.[1] The term '**welfare state**' was first used in 1941 by the then Archbishop of Canterbury, where he contrasted it with the 'warfare state' of fascism and Nazism.[2] However, the term was not generally known until the former US President Herbert Hoover used it in 1949 to describe it as 'a disguise for the totalitarian state'.[3] Very quickly, therefore, the concept of a welfare state had a negative meaning for some, and by the early 1960s, Richard Titmuss observed that 'to many people, "welfare state" is now a term of abuse'.[4] It is significant that Titmuss made this comment at the height of what has sometimes been regarded as a 'Golden Age' of political consensus and support for the welfare state[5]; it shows that state welfare provision has always been controversial and disputed. In the US, the word 'welfare' is now 'a term of opprobrium', although 'social security' (meaning social insurance for old age and disability) remains relatively popular.[6] In contrast, in much of Europe, public welfare and **social protection** are still favourably regarded. Public attitudes towards welfare in the UK are somewhere between the US and European positions.[7] There is support for some of the principles behind a welfare state and attachment to particular policies and institutions in the UK, but there is also ambivalence about some aspects of state welfare. With careful phrasing and a selective use of evidence, it is possible to claim that public support exists for radically opposing welfare reforms.

This history and the varied interpretations of the terms 'welfare' and 'welfare state' show that the meaning of some of the concepts central to Social Policy analysis are neither fixed nor agreed upon. It is important to understand this in order to begin to answer the question of what a social problem actually is. As some of the terms used in social policy debates are disputed, it is essential to examine how social problems and welfare issues are presented and discussed, and to appreciate that some social policy controversies might arise because people see the 'same' issue in different ways. This phenomenon is expressed by the idea of **social construction** – a phrase that has been used in various ways in social science but that, in essence, expresses the insight that how an issue is perceived or represented is not necessarily how it *really* is. Social construction (sometimes called discursive construction) highlights the importance of considering how issues are portrayed, and how ideas about social problems and policies might be shaped in particular ways.

As the term 'social construction' has been used in a variety of ways in the Social Policy literature, it is not easy to summarise its rich history and development. However, broadly speaking, three main uses of the term are evident: first, there is the idea that issues and social problems are caused by social conditions and practices; second, that problems are defined or presented in particular ways; and, third, that social problems are not things, but the outcomes of social and political processes. In their different ways, each of these uses suggests that there is a difference between the appearance and reality of social conditions. In extreme cases, the idea of social construction challenges the very existence of any 'objective' social reality at all. However, it is not necessary to agree with that viewpoint to believe that social construction is a concept that provides valuable insights. This includes answers to the question of what a social problem *is*, although this answer is less straightforward than it might initially appear.

The social construction of 'youth crime'

Ideas about and debates over 'youth crime', or 'juvenile delinquency' as it has sometimes been called, illustrate several issues captured by the concept of social construction. The fact that different terms have been used to describe this issue itself suggests that ideas about it vary, and there are several other ways in which youth crime could be described as socially constructed.

A social constructionist analysis would first of all ask whether there is such a thing as 'youth' crime at all? Is there anything distinctive about the criminal behaviour of younger age groups that requires a distinctive term? Second, crime itself is obviously not a natural phenomenon, but one that is socially defined. What counts as a criminal act at one time or in one society may not be a crime elsewhere. Lord Atkin observed in 1931 that the only thing that all 'crimes' have in common is that 'they are prohibited by the State'.[8] The *institutionalist* perspective in Criminology theory argues that the criminal justice system effectively 'makes' crime by designating certain acts as criminal.[9] From this perspective, the key question is not 'What causes crime?', but 'What leads certain acts to be defined as criminal and who makes these decisions?'

A third issue raised by social constructionist analysis is that the 'facts' about the extent of youth or any other kind of crime (such as whether the level of crime is rising or falling, who commits or is a victim of particular crimes, etc) depend on how incidents are defined and recorded. Criminal statistics reflect how the police and criminal justice systems operate and record incidents, as well as social conventions and attitudes. It is known that certain types of crime are far more likely to be reported and prosecuted than others, for example, theft from vehicles compared to sexual offences.[10] Crime figures therefore require careful interpretation. A change in the number of recorded offences might not reflect any real change in their actual incidence, but, instead, reflect the fact that more incidents are being reported, recorded or acted upon as crimes.[11] Therefore, the evidence about crime in a society at a particular time is not an objective body of facts, but the product of social processes.

A fourth point about 'youth crime' that social constructionism highlights is that public understanding of and debates about it are influenced by the activities of interest and campaigning groups, how the media covers the issue, and the ideologies and agendas of politicians and other opinion leaders. How social issues are conceptualised, thought about, defined and perceived is shaped by the language and arguments of these competing voices.

Finally, policy responses to youth crime and other social issues are the output of complex policymaking systems. In the course of producing policies, issues are processed by institutions and reshaped by the requirements of resource limitations and the pressure of deadlines. Social issues are also framed by the opinions and understanding of those responsible for making policy, and compromised by the demands of political reality.

In summary, a social constructionist perspective would suggest that ideas about and policy responses to an issue such as 'youth crime' are the end result of a series of complex social processes of conceptualisation, representation, interpretation and negotiation. From this perspective, whether there is a 'real' social problem at all is itself problematic, let alone how effective any policies might be.

A short history of 'social construction'

It is clear that 'the abstract thought that some things are created by societies and the thought that some beliefs owe more to social values than they do to the evidence in their favor, are as old as reason itself'.[12] There are two forms of the argument that the perception of issues reflects social conditions in some way, both of which can be traced to classical Greek philosophy. The first is the idea of **moral relativism**: that there are no universal principles of right and wrong. Aristotle summarised this view in his *Nicomachean Ethics*, written about 350 BC, where he observes that 'Fire burns both in Hellas and Persia, but men's ideas of right and wrong vary from place to place'. The separate idea of **epistemological relativism** is the argument that there are no objective facts independent from the perspective of the observer. This argument can be traced back to at least the Sceptics around 80 BC. For example, Aenesidemus argued that we can only know what appears to us, and since the perception of appearances depends on the viewpoint of the observer, it is not possible to reach absolute knowledge of the true nature of anything.

The full philosophical history of relativism and how it relates to ideas of social construction cannot be discussed here, but another significant stage in the development of the concept has been the field of study known as the **sociology of knowledge**. This examines how beliefs vary across different societies and between groups, and the relationship between ideas and social circumstances. The term 'knowledge', here, is potentially misleading as the sociology of knowledge is not only interested in the philosophical question of what counts as genuine knowledge (ie the branch of philosophy known as epistemology), but also interested in the social context of any idea, belief or perception. There are overlaps between the sociology of knowledge and other branches of sociology and anthropology that study belief systems and different forms of understanding, such as the sociology of art and culture, of religion, and of science.

Karl Marx was one of the pioneers of the sociology of knowledge, proposing what he called a **materialist** view of history in opposition to the **idealist** position of the philosopher **Hegel** (1770–1831). Marx argued that social circumstances shape – and perhaps even determine – social conventions and institutions, including ideas and beliefs: 'It is not the consciousness of men that determines their being, but, on the contrary, their social being that determines their consciousness'.[13] Marx also believed that it was not just *any* set of beliefs that people came to hold and that have a hold on them. He argued that groups with the greatest power were able to ensure that their ideas and values were dominant: that 'The ideas of the ruling class are in every epoch the ruling ideas'.[14] Later generations of Marxists have offered various theories explaining how the ruling class are able to exercise this ideological domination.[15]

The Marxist position can lead to the view that there are no ideas, arguments or policy proposals that are uncontaminated by class bias. This can lead to a damaging relativism, where political arguments become reduced to unmasking opponents' ideological limitations, and any shared basis for debate about social issues becomes impossible. However, it is possible to argue that beliefs and opinions have a social dimension – perhaps even a social origin – without this leading to a cynical relativism. **Karl Mannheim**, another key thinker in the development of the sociology of knowledge, argued that demonstrating that an outlook or argument was associated with a particular social system or place in society did not mean that these ideas were refuted. Furthermore, although all viewpoints might be limited by the perspective of the viewer, developing a critical self-awareness of this enables one to partially detach oneself from the social context so that this does not entirely determine one's outlook. Mannheim argued that training in the scientific method provided this **reflexivity**, and that social scientists could serve as mediators between different viewpoints, ensuring that constructive political debate and an interchange of ideas remained possible.[16]

A second major contribution to the idea of social construction comes from two different stands of sociology, both of which were particularly prominent in the US in the 20th century. Although drawn from different philosophical backgrounds, both investigated how people interpret the world and shape social reality through the meanings that inform their behaviour. The first is a strand of sociology influenced by the philosophy of **Phenomenology** pioneered by Edmund Husserl (1859–1938) in Germany in the early 20th century and subsequently developed and applied to social issues by Alfred Schütz (1899–1959). Phenomenology proposed that people do not respond unthinkingly to external events, but filter and process their experiences through frameworks of beliefs. The term 'social construction' was popularised by Berger and Luckmann in their influential book *The Social Construction of Reality*,[17] which applied Phenomenology to study the processes that create what come to be accepted as **common-sense knowledge**. They were interested in understanding 'what people "know" as "reality" in their everyday … lives … [and the] "knowledge" that constitutes the fabric of meanings without which no society could exist'.[18] Berger and Luckmann suggested that there may be different taken-for-granted beliefs about what is common sense: 'What is "real" to a Tibetan monk may not be "real" to an American businessman'.[19] They discussed how these different 'realities' came about and the social processes that maintained them.

The second strand of sociology that contributed significantly to the idea of social construction was the Symbolic Interactionist perspective, which built upon the theories of the social psychologist G.H. Mead (1863–1931). The term **Symbolic Interactionism** was coined by one of Mead's pupils, Herbert Blumer, to express the view that social behaviour involves a regulated exchange of meanings. Symbolic Interactionism proposes that interaction can only be understood if we grasp the meaning and significance of the symbols people use to communicate with each other. The meaning of a word, gesture or interaction is not inherent in it, but attributed by those using and interpreting it. There is an obvious difference between a flag and a piece of coloured cloth, and many actions could not be understood unless we appreciated the significance invested in such symbols. Symbolic Interactionists propose that social order is constructed by the rule-governed behaviour of actors. From this perspective, what is most important about social issues are people's ideas about them. Therefore, social problems are not objective external conditions, but constituted by people's perceptions and reactions to circumstances and events. This is expressed by a principle of Symbolic Interactionism that has come to be known as the **Thomas theorem**, which proposes that 'a situation defined as real is real in its consequences'.[20] This means that if someone truly *believes* that something is the case, they will act on the basis of that belief, even if they are mistaken. Therefore, to understand an actor's behaviour, it is necessary to see the world from their perspective, as far as this is possible. Consequently, Symbolic Interactionism is interested in the 'eye of the beholder' and how people's interpretations of social conditions and relations influence their actions. Douglas Hofstadter used the term **default assumption** to describe how unquestioned beliefs can shape how and what actors think about certain issues.[21] Default assumptions are comparable to what psychologists call **heuristics**, that is, intuitive and standardised rules of thumb that people rely upon to make quick assessments of situations and form the basis of their reaction to them.[22] Some of these assumptions may be embedded in the language that people learn and the categories that they use to think about and describe social reality.[23] The word 'mother', for example, has powerful associations that reflect and shape expectations about behaviour and beliefs about what is 'normal'. At the same time, ideas about what a 'mother' is or is expected to be vary across different groups, between societies and over time. Therefore, ideas about this role – and other potent concepts and symbols – can be contested and changed, albeit with difficulty and perhaps only through conflict in the case of particularly powerful ideas and sentiments.

Researchers influenced by Symbolic Interactionism have been particularly interested in investigating ideas of normality and **deviance**. Howard Becker argued that what makes an act 'deviant' is the social reaction to it, in particular, the perception of those with the power to define what is deviant or criminal, such as the medical and legal professions.[24] Becker questioned the authority of such groups to determine what counted as 'normal' and 'deviant', and advocated an 'underdog' perspective in which the conventional **hierarchy of credibility** was challenged and inverted.[25]

Social construction is an important concept for the critical dimension of Social Policy analysis discussed in Chapter One. This concept makes us aware that how issues are portrayed and commonly perceived might not be how they really are, and that social circumstances and how they are thought of can be changed. Social constructionism also suggests that interest groups may portray social issues in particular ways that reflect their own beliefs and priorities. The various uses of the term 'social construction' therefore highlight several questions that Social Policy analysts should always ask:

- Why is a particular issue or condition regarded as a 'social problem' at all? Who says that something is a problem?
- Who defines what the problem is, for example, what causes it?
- Is the definition of the problem or beliefs about its causes agreed or disputed?
- How is the policy response to the problem decided, that is, who is involved in shaping the policy and how open is decision-making in determining this?

The concept of social construction equips Social Policy analysis with an alternative way of seeing issues and therefore the capacity to exam them critically. The potential usefulness and insights that this provides can be illustrated by discussing in more detail the three main ways in which the term has been applied to the study of social issues and policies.

The social generation of problems

The first use of the term 'social construction' suggests that social problems are the outcome of particular social conditions and arrangements. For all the increase in resources and opportunities that they provide, contemporary societies generate many social problems. In fact, large-scale social welfare systems are, in part, a response to the problems created by the transition from an agricultural to an industrial economy and society. **Industrialisation** transforms societies and creates new challenges while making the systems that previously dealt with them outmoded. For example, the development of an industrial economy and society involves millions of people relocating to urban areas in search of employment: the population of Glasgow increased from 77,000 in 1801 to 275,000 in 1841 and 760,000 by the turn of the 20th century. This migration uprooted settled rural communities and separated smaller nuclear families from the larger extended families and community support networks that they previously relied upon. It takes time for new support networks to develop in these dynamic and rapidly expanding cities, and social problems often accumulate in the meantime. Often, the supply of housing and other essential infrastructure does not match rapid urbanisation, leading to problems of overcrowding, inadequate public sanitation and the spread of contagious diseases. The resulting social conditions were documented by Friedrich Engels, who described in detail the squalor of early industrialisation and urbanisation in Manchester, where thousands were crammed together in inadequate accommodation and 'thickly populated districts are without any sewers whatsoever'.[26] Similar conditions have developed in dozens of cities across the world during the early stages of industrialisation.[27]

An industrial economy generates other problems, such as industrial injuries and illnesses, and periodic (and sometimes locally concentrated) unemployment. To minimise the social disruption and political conflict that such issues cause, governments often respond with new forms of regulation and other social policies. For example, in the UK, which experienced the first Industrial Revolution in the 19th century, the role of the state expanded through a series of Factory Acts, which regulated working conditions, and reform of the Poor Law to deal with some of the casualties of the new economy (see Chapter Six).[28]

Dependence and the division of labour

Adam Smith's *An Inquiry into the Nature and Causes of the Wealth of Nations*,[29] published in 1776, is generally regarded as one of the foundations of economic analysis, and many of its ideas and arguments remain influential. In Chapter One, Smith discussed the productivity and efficiency gains created by increased specialisation. He used the example of pin making to show how output is greatly increased if the production process is organised into stages and workers repeatedly perform the same task rather than a range of functions. Smith argued that increasing the **division of labour** was a crucial factor in economic progress: 'The greatest improvement in the productive powers of labour, and the greater part of the skill, dexterity, and judgment with which it is anywhere directed, or applied, seem to have been the effects of the division of labour' (Smith, 1776/1904, p 1). However, Smith also recognised the negative consequences of specialisation:

> The man whose whole life is spent in performing a few simple operations ... has no occasion to exert his understanding or to exercise his invention.... He naturally loses, therefore, the habit of such exertion, and generally becomes as stupid and ignorant as it is possible for a human creature to become.... But in every improved and civilized society this is the state into which the labouring poor, that is, the great body of the people, must necessarily fall, unless government takes some pains to prevent it. (Smith, 1776/1904, p 603)

To prevent such degradation, Smith proposed that governments should educate workers to enable them to flourish outside their restricted employment.

In what has become one of the foundation texts of sociology, *The Division of Labour in Society*,[30] **Émile Durkheim** considered another consequence of specialisation. Durkheim argued that the increased division of labour that characterised modern societies created **organic solidarity** – social cohesion and integration through mutual interdependence. Richard Titmuss developed this idea and argued that welfare states are a collective response to the vulnerability created by the interdependencies of industrialisation, that is, because no one in industrial societies can survive entirely independently, systems of mutual support are required to deal with some of the consequences.[31] Titmuss suggests that everyone in modern societies is dependent upon others at some time; however, only some forms of dependency are provided for through collective social welfare systems. It is also significant that the description 'welfare-dependent' is used to refer to particular welfare service users and not others. Different aspects of this issue are discussed later in this chapter and in Chapter Three.

So, while economic and technological development may have aggregate long-term benefits, they also generate problems. Another example of this is **financial exclusion**, which means not having access to appropriate and affordable banking, credit and savings services.[32] This is a relatively new problem that arises, in part, due to innovations in technology and how services are provided. In the early 1970s, about 60% of British adults did not have a bank account but few suffered any deprivation as a result.[33] However, by 2010, only 7% of adults in Britain had no bank account and this became a serious problem for this small group.[34] Almost 90% of British employees receive their wages and salaries through a bank account, and this will rise to 95% by 2018.[35] A bank account is now essential for daily life in Britain (and many other countries, of course), and those without access to or the capability to use financial services are marginalised and penalised through the higher costs of financial transactions, such as paying bills.

The innovation and technological dynamism of contemporary capitalist societies means that new products and services are continuously created. Many of these improve life and well-being but others generate perhaps less wholesome 'needs'. For example, some feminist critics argue that the cosmetics industry creates aspirations to an unattainable level of attractiveness and evokes feelings of inadequacy that stimulate demand for beauty products.[36] One example of this is Eyelash Hypotrichosis, a condition of insufficiently lush eyelashes for which the pharmaceutical company Alergan developed a treatment (as an accidental by-product for treating Glaucoma) that the US Food and Drug Administration has authorised.[37] This has been marketed as *Latisse* to address a 'problem' that many people would not even have known existed until advertisers informed them that there was a cure.[38] In fact, many products and advertising work in this way. As one critic put it:

> a host of canny advertisers, marketers, investors and politicians is on hand to remind and persuade us to spend money we don't have, on things we don't need, to create impressions that won't last, on people we don't care about.[39]

The result of this system might be a bewildering variety of commodities to choose from (at least for those who can afford them) and economic growth (between cycles of recession), but whether it delivers greater well-being is open to debate.[40]

The social construction of disability

An issue that illustrates both the first idea of social construction (that problems are not inherent, but caused by social practices) and the second use (that problems are defined in particular ways) is the idea of the **social model of disability**. Until quite recently, the dominant view of disability would have been medical: that people with disabilities are incapacitated by physical or mental impairments. This view 'insists on regarding disabled bodies as the source of the problem'.[41] In contrast, disabled rights campaigners have argued that disability is a socially constructed issue. This social model of disability argues that disability is different from illness, which can be treated and perhaps cured by medical science.[42] Advocates of the social model argue that it is not their potentially insignificant differences that disadvantage and marginalise those labelled 'disabled'. Instead, disabilities are created by the social reaction to perceived conditions and by how society is organised so that barriers prevent some people from participating as full and equal members of society (see Chapter Four). People with disabilities are socially excluded by the physical restrictions imposed on them by 'normal' society and also by 'invisible walls' of negative perceptions and ill-informed judgements. From this perspective, disability is not an individual characteristic, but a social reaction to a perceived difference that results in 'social apartheid', segregating disabled people from mainstream society.[43] A particularly important economic and social barrier is the labour market, where people with disabilities face severe discrimination. Only 46% of working-age disabled people were in employment in the UK in 2012 compared to 76% of non-disabled people.[44] As a result, most disabled people in Britain are forced to rely upon welfare benefits, which are not sufficient to meet their needs. Consequently, households with a disabled member are far more likely to live in poverty than those where no one is disabled.[45]

According to the social model of disability argument, people with a disability are not looking for a 'cure'; instead, they regard the discrimination and exclusion they face as a **civil rights** issue. What is required is a change in attitudes and social practices so that disabled people can live independently and access activities and opportunities that able-bodied people take for granted.[46] The campaign for equal rights therefore involves redefining how the issue of disability is perceived, which is why the language used to discuss disability is so significant.[47] The movement to promote an understanding of disability as socially constructed has been quite successful in the UK, and fewer people than before would regard those with mobility or other impairments as incapable and only second-class citizens. This illustrates the power of campaigning and the effect of promoting alternative conceptualisations of issues, but it has not ended the exclusion of disabled people.

Defining social problems

The concept of social construction highlights the potential difference that might exist between perception and reality. However, it is often very difficult to establish what the reality of a social condition actually is. Much of the data used in social science and that inform social policies are not simply found, but socially constructed. This does not mean that they are fabricated lies, but, rather, the product of complex processes of definition, collection, selection, organising, synthesis and interpretation.[48] After going through all these stages, the result may reflect the methods used to gather evidence as much as external reality (as discussed earlier in relation to 'youth crime'). For example, until recently, the level of poverty officially recorded in the US was based on the cost of emergency foods in the 1950s multiplied by three (because in the 1960s, when federal poverty measures was first developed, food represented one third of the budget of an average American family). This definition may have been appropriate for its time and particular purpose, but its limitations beyond this context were obvious and widely known, for example, by 2009, food represented only between one sixth and one seventh of an American family's budget.[49] However, for various political and administrative reasons, this definition remained the official federal poverty measure long after there was any scientific justification for it.

What is defined and counted might shape perceptions and determine policy. Consequently, there can be a lot at stake in debates about how a social issue is measured and recorded, which is why seemingly obscure technical matters of definition and measurement can be very important in Social Policy analysis.

Politics and the measurement of unemployment

Once, when responding to criticisms that his government's policies were less successful in reducing unemployment than those in Britain, the former French President Jacques Chirac argued that 'if unemployment is lower in Britain than in France, it owes no thanks to the virtues of economic liberalism but because the English fiddle their figures'.[50] This dispute highlights the importance of political considerations shaping how some social issues are defined and measured. The level of unemployment is a potent feature of political debate and often used to assess a government's economic performance. It is therefore necessary to be aware of the significance of the different ways of counting unemployment. One measure of unemployment is the **claimant count**: the number of people receiving unemployment benefits (such as Job Seekers Allowance) who can prove that they are actively looking for work. In the UK, unemployment is measured using the *Labour Force Survey*, which counts as unemployed anybody currently without work but available for and seeking work.[51] The claimant count is usually lower than the official unemployment level estimated by the *Labour Force Survey*, and the gap between these two measures has widened at several points since the financial crisis of 2008. This might be a sign that some people are being removed from welfare benefits (because of changes to the eligibility rules) but not actually moving into employment. Instead, they have become **economic inactive**, that is, neither formally employed nor officially unemployed. Some economically inactive people are fully engaged in useful work, such as caring for others, while others may be studying, retired from employment or have a long-term illness that prevents their employment. The alternative ways of defining and measuring unemployment illustrate how the 'facts' about a social issue are not given, but constructed and may be subject to interpretation and dispute.

The word 'count' means both something that is itemised and calculated and also something that matters and is important. To exclude something from a calculation suggests that it is irrelevant and perhaps also unimportant. Such judgements should be subject to critical Social Policy analysis. An example of this is the economic value of voluntary work and caring. The Office of the Third Sector in the UK government includes only formal volunteering in its calculation of **unpaid work**, which it defines as 'giving unpaid help through groups, clubs or organisations which support social, environmental, cultural or sporting objectives'.[52] This definition does not include much informal work and therefore underestimates the scale of volunteering and misrepresents where this takes place and who undertakes it, in particular, the unpaid caring and community work of lower-income groups.[53] It has been estimated that the annual value of the unpaid care provided to adults in the UK amounts to £119 billion.[54] However, although care work is unpaid, it is not free – it involves considerable financial costs for carers, most of whom are women.[55] The decision not to include the contribution of care in national financial accounts is not a neutral, analytical one, but reflects a particular idea of economic and social value.

> ## Perceptions and portrayals of social issues
>
> The British public consistently and significantly overestimates the level of crime and underestimates the severity of court sentences for offences. For example, the *Crime Survey for England and Wales* recorded a 19% fall in crime between 2006/07 and 2012 but 58% of the public did not believe that this had happened.[56] There are several reasons for misplaced public anxiety about crime and the 'systematic public ignorance' that exists about it.[57] According to the Royal Statistical Society, one of the most important reasons is political 'spin': many politicians prefer to 'twist numbers for their own ends rather than discussing statistics even-handedly'.[58] A second factor is how crime is reported by sections of the mass media. What gets covered by the media is what journalists are trained to see and where they look. Journalists select what to report based on their assessment of an issue's **news value**, which leads them to focus on sensational and unrepresentative events. Journalists, in particular, specialist reporters, also have standard news-gathering procedures and familiar sources of information that reinforce their tendency to focus on particular issues and to cover them in conventional ways. The news agenda does not reflect a balanced account of issues. As one experienced journalist explains: 'People tend to suppose journalists are where the news is. This is not so. The news is where journalists are'.[59]
>
> As a result of misrepresentation and selective reporting, some social issues and problems loom larger in the public mind and in political debates than others. This issue of relative visibility is discussed in Chapter Three and the importance of how social issues are perceived is considered in Chapter Six.

How social issues are defined and what indicators are selected to represent them raises a central question of social science research and analysis: validity. **Validity** refers to whether a concept or indicator actually corresponds to what it is trying to grasp and how far it genuinely reflects social reality. It is possible to gather **reliable** social data that is meaningless, in the sense that it bears little resemblance to anything that actually exists. For example, people will politely provide answers to survey questions that they have never seriously considered and on matters that they could not reasonably be said to hold opinions. Such 'evidence' might be technically reliable and **representative** but it is scientifically worthless as it says nothing about social life but has been manufactured by a data-collection process or tool.[60] Devising research processes to collect robust evidence that corresponds to real social processes and events demands considerable methodological skill, which is why university degrees in Social Policy devote so much effort to research methods training.

The language of social policies

Public understanding of social issues might be based not on evidence of real events and conditions, but on how these have been presented. It is important to be aware of the interests that different groups have in promoting their preferred representation of issues and shaping the debate to reflect their particular understanding of society. Policymakers and those with a stake in social issues are competing for media and public attention and trying to prepare the ground for reforms they favour.[61] One policy area that reflects this process is support for unemployed people and, in particular, what has come to be known as **active labour-market** or employability policies. These are programmes where unemployed benefit recipients are supported – and sometimes compelled – to undertake employment or training as a condition of entitlement to benefits in order to increase their chance of getting a job.[62] The use of the word '**employability**' to describe the issue is significant as it suggests that unemployment is caused by the *in*ability of those experiencing it. This implies that unemployment is the responsibility of unemployed people themselves and that policy should therefore correct whatever impairs them. Sometimes, the alleged fault is portrayed – perhaps sympathetically but perhaps also patronisingly – as inadequate or inappropriate skills, which make some people unemployable. In many cases, the unemployed are regarded has having made poor choices or lacking the initiative, motivation or even the moral fibre to get a job. They need **tough love** policies to get them to do what is right, what the former British Prime Minister Tony Blair described as 'a hand up not a hand out'.[63]

The implication that unemployed people are at best incompetent and at worst culpable is often conveyed without the robust and compelling evidence required to substantiate what is a very contestable view. Instead, this assumption is embedded in the rhetoric of policy. For example, the very name of the Personal Responsibility and Work Opportunity Act, passed by the US Congress in 1996, implies that it is the *lack* of personal responsibility among claimants that required a change in law. The term 'active labour-market' policy itself suggests a contrast with what are implied to be 'passive' forms of welfare provision, and evokes the idea that there is a **culture of dependency** that explains the position of some benefit recipients.[64] Whether or not any of this is true is an empirical question for Social Policy analysis and not something that should be implied by rhetoric.

'Othering' the poor

Organisations that campaign against poverty in the UK have objected to using the term 'the poor' to refer to low-income and deprived households.[65] Poverty is an experience, not an identity. For many people, it is neither a permanent nor prolonged condition, so it is misleading to refer to people experiencing poverty as though they are a distinct group. Ruth Lister has argued that using the term 'the poor' portrays lower-income households as homogeneous and also creates a division between 'them' and 'us'. Describing groups in poverty in this way also implies that poverty can be explained by identifying what is different about those who experience poverty. This terminology therefore implies that low incomes and deprivation are characteristics of a deviant **underclass** and that 'the poor' are 'a source of moral contamination, a threat, an undeserving economic burden, failures in the meritocratic race'.[66]

This is why it is important, rather than pedantic 'political correctness', to use alternative terms to refer to poverty, such as 'people experience poverty' or 'lower-income households'.[67] Similar sensitivities to language are important in relation to other groups, such as people with disabilities. The significance of the language of poverty is recognised by governments: throughout the 1980s and 1990s, the UK government went to some lengths to ensure that the word 'poverty' did not appear in its official statements and policy documents.[68] However, this was motivated not by concern for the sensitivities of those experiencing poverty, but because the government at that time denied that genuine poverty existed in Britain.[69]

David Marquand once remarked that in politics, 'the prizes go to those who can "mobilize prejudice" more successfully than their competitors'.[70] These examples show how particular **discourses** are used to try to reframe how social issues are thought about in order to gain support for favoured policy reforms. A discourse is a way of speaking about and representing an issue so that particular assumptions are embedded into how that issue is conceived. If a discourse is sufficiently powerful, then particular ideas are internalised and unquestioned and it becomes impossible to think about it in a different way, let alone persuade others to support alternative policy responses. A dominant discourse can therefore lead to **policy closure**, where alternative ways of thinking about and responding to the subject are precluded.[71]

Many social policy debates therefore involve a war of words and a battle of ideas.[72] Such controversies should not be dismissed as mere talk as they determine what issues are recognised as problems and what actions are taken in response to them.[73] As the journalist and pollster Peter Kellner once noted: 'Language is to politics what DNA is to reproduction. Both carry the codes of evolution.... Anyone who can persuade us to use … words differently has all but persuaded us to think differently'.[74] This is one reason why so many of the interpretive concepts in Social Policy – such as 'justice', 'entitlement', 'need', 'poverty' and so on – are **essentially contested concepts**, that is, continually disputed and debated. Controversy surrounds interpretive concepts as these relate to political ideologies and moral codes. This contrasts with more straightforward descriptive concepts, for which there are agreed definitions.[75]

'Dog whistle' welfare

All political and electoral strategists know about concepts such as the 'dog whistle' phrase, where seemingly innocuous words can be relied upon to produce strong and often negative reactions among those who hear them.[76]

Social Policy analysts must be aware of how potent but implicit signals are used to frame issues and mobilise support for reforms. One example of this in UK social policy was the introduction of a 'benefit cap', which limited the welfare support that a working-age household could receive to no more than median national household income.[77] There was little evidence that such a policy was required as very few households received more than the average national income from benefits. Nor was there evidence that the reform would significantly reduce social security expenditure or improve work incentives. However, the reform sent out a powerful message by implying that there was a widespread and expensive problem that had to be addressed. Irrespective of how much it might save, this policy reaffirmed the concerns of those who believed that social security was a soft touch, and signalled to them that the government was cracking down on benefit claimants. It also legitimised the view that UK welfare expenditure was out of control. The very existence of the policy suggested that there was a problem serious enough to merit action – otherwise, why would the government have introduced it? There was no evident public demand for this policy before it was introduced; in fact, the policy created its own demand for action rather than responding to a known problem.

'The framing of policy is important because it provides the lens that defines the policy problem to be solved and the tenor of the debate that creates the environment in which the policy is embedded and delivered.'[78] Due to this, many welfare issues involve a battle between competing representations, each striving to shape public opinion. These contests do not necessarily take place in the open or involve an explicit exchange of views or the examination of evidence. On many occasions, different interest groups attempts to shape the terms of the debate itself and how the problem is conceptualised at an implicit level. Social Policy analysts must guard themselves against the sway of political rhetoric and be wary of the power of discourses to influence their thinking, including their own discourses and those of other academics.

The dynamics of social problems

The final way in which the concept of social construction is used in Social Policy considered in this chapter is the idea that social problems should not be regarded as conditions or issues, but rather as processes. Some issues become rather than simply *are* social problems, that is, they move from being ignored or accepted to being regarded as problematic. The concept of social construction has been used to analyse this **problematisation** process and investigate how interest groups try to 'construct' social problems by manoeuvring to have their concerns recognised as issues requiring collective action.

One of the most successful examples of this in the second half of the 20th century were campaigns to highlight the environmental damage of industrial production. A landmark contribution to this campaign was Rachel Carson's *The Silent Spring*,[79] published in 1962, which drew attention to the effects of pesticides on ecosystems and moved the problem of pollution into mainstream thinking and onto the policy agenda. The launch of organisations such as Friends of the Earth and Greenpeace in the late 1960s expanded and reinforced what became an international environmental movement, which has pushed environmental issues, particularly climate change, to the forefront of policy debate.

The growth and influence of the environmental movement illustrate several aspects of the dynamics and construction of social problems. According to this variant of the social constructionist perspective, what makes an issue a social problem is not the objective facts about it, but perceptions of and reactions to it. Social problems come about because a social movement has persuaded enough people – or the right kind of people – that something is wrong and action must be taken. There was a time when unemployment was regarded not as a social problem, but a misfortune or failure of particular individuals. Similarly, child labour, domestic violence, racial discrimination, hate speech and many other issues that are today generally regarded as unacceptable and that are firmly established on the social policy agenda were previously disregarded, marginalised or accepted as inevitable. The social constructionist approach explores how what were once overlooked as unimportant or dismissed as unavoidable matters become sufficiently serious concerns for policymakers to take action. Therefore, social constructionism proposes that what is regarded as a social problem is contingent and that analysis should focus on the political and discursive processes that transform issues into recognised social problems.[80] Those who favour this approach recognise that it 'contains some counter-intuitive notions that violate common-sense assumptions'.[81] In particular, the study of social problems is turned around: social conditions are less important than *beliefs* about these conditions.

While new issues may be forced onto the policy agenda by campaigning and lobbying, others can be removed from it, not because the problem has been solved, but because they are no longer recognised as problematic – they have been **delegitimised**. This raises the question of how issues become accepted as authentic and legitimate concerns. Some issues may appear more 'political' than others, reflecting the degree of consensus that surrounds them. For example, until recently, relatively little attention was given to the measures taken by some corporations to minimise their tax liabilities, despite the fact that corporate tax avoidance in the UK is estimated to amount to at least £12 billion a year,[82] and globally, at least $2 trillion is held in offshore tax havens by transnational corporations.[83] In contrast, despite the fact that the amount of money involved is much lower, social security fraud has always been a much higher-profile issue, for example, £1.1 billion of benefit expenditure was lost to fraud in Britain in 2013/14.[84] Of course, the costs or scale of a problem are not necessarily the main determinants of how much attention it receives. Some relatively rare issues may be regarded as so damaging or morally offensive that there is universal agreement over the need for a strong response. However, beyond such conditions, most social problems can be located on a continuum of how relatively 'open' or 'closed' they are. An open issue is one over which there is no agreement that it is a problem, let alone how to define its nature or the best response to it. In contrast, a closed issue is generally accepted as a problem and any debate about it is restricted to technical details of how to respond. An issue can become more or less open or closed depending on the power and persuasiveness of different voices. Social construction theorists have highlighted the role of expert groups in 'enclosing' particular issues and claiming authority to preserve certain areas as their exclusive speciality.[85] The medical profession is one group that has secured considerable scope to enclose a field of issues and restrict debate. Their expertise is powerful enough to give them considerable authority over matters of health and illness, and, as a result, there is no longer serious debate about whether many of the issues with which they deal are really problems at all. In becoming medical matters, these issues have been **depoliticised**.

Depoliticisation is the process where problems become uncontested, often being transferred to the exclusive preserve of qualified experts. **Medicalisation** is a clear example of this process – once a condition is diagnosed as an illness, the range of people who are accepted as qualified to comment on it is restricted. In most cases, only accredited experts are entitled to debate the matter, although, in some cases, other groups, such as patients' organisations, have been able to acquire some influence. Sometimes, patients or other stakeholders collaborate with medical professionals to have their concerns classified as a recognised medical condition as this establishes its credibility to policymakers and the public, and is an important step to ensuring that resources are devoted to the issue. For example, medical insurers in the US require that a condition is a diagnosed medical condition before authorising payment for treatment. In some cases, this creates an incentive for patients and doctors to diagnose as illnesses what might otherwise be regarded as different conditions. This is especially significant for psychological conditions, where there may be considerable scope for interpretation and debate about whether a particular condition is really a problem at all, let alone a medical matter. Concerns have been raised about a process of creeping medicalisation and labelling behaviours and dispositions as forms of mental illness so that what were previously merely differences become forms of sickness or deviance.[86] An example of this tendency is the expansion in the number of conditions classified as illnesses in the *Diagnostic and Statistical Manual of Mental Disorders* (DSM) used by the American Psychiatric Association (APA), which increased from 182 in *DSM-II*, published in 1968, to 365 in the *DSM-IV* edition in 2000.[87] While there are pressures to expand the number and range of medical conditions, there can also be resistance to medicalisation and to differences being classified as deviance. For example, until 1973, the APA defined homosexuality as a psychological illness. The APA board voted to remove this diagnosis from its *DSM-III*, partly in response to pressure from the growing gay rights movement in the US.[88] An ongoing controversy is whether deafness should be regarded as a medical condition or a form of community identity. Since at least the 1980s, a Deaf rights movement has been active in several countries, which has championed Deaf (with a capital 'D') as a cultural identity rather than an affliction.[89] There are obvious parallels and overlaps with the disabled rights movement discussed earlier in the chapter –

these movements resist medicalisation and a 'diagnosis' that imposes upon them a label they reject. Both movements are campaigning to open up and re-politicise debate and promote a *social* understanding of their condition and experiences. Other groups display similar resistance to what they regard as negative labels. For example, few people with low incomes are willing to describe themselves as 'poor',[90] and in the US, those described as a 'welfare mother' make great efforts to distance themselves from the image associated with this label.[91]

Social problems and the policy process

Once an issue is accepted as a genuine problem and a particular understanding of it prevails, policymakers are compelled to respond in some way. If political leaders have no significant stake in the issue and simply being seen to do something will satisfy demands for action, then their response may be mainly symbolic.[92] Even if policymakers genuinely respond to a problem, their options are limited by the resources available and the institutions that already exist to deal with such issues. It is relatively rare for governments to create entirely new systems and institutions to deal with social problems as this can be expensive and time-consuming. Change is always risky as it is disruptive and may provoke resistance from those with an interest in maintaining the status quo.[93] It is possible for political leaders and policymakers to initiate large-scale changes – unprecedented or particularly threatening challenges may require dramatic reforms, and new governments may want to make their mark by setting up new social policy systems. However, grand reforms do not happen frequently, particularly within stable political systems; most policy responses involve relatively minor alterations to existing mechanisms.[94]

Once welfare institutions are in place, the issues they deal with may be reshaped to fit with the systems and processes established to deal with them. This happens because, as Peter Townsend noted, 'bureaucracies … have vested interests in defining problems for which they are largely responsible in forms which … show that these problems are of "manageable" proportions'.[95] Issues that are complex, multidimensional and have blurred edges are much more difficult to deal with than those that are simple, self-contained or technical. Those responsible for developing or delivering policies are inclined to try to convert messy difficulties into routine issues that can be handled by existing systems and procedures. Understandably, policymakers often favour simple technical fixes rather than attempt complex social reforms. For example, it is easier for the UK government to try to limit children's access to pornography by proposing that Internet providers install adult content blockers by default rather than promoting the kind of parental supervision and family communication that might actually be required to achieve this.[96] Similarly, for many years, it was more straightforward for UK governments to adjust the social security system in response to demands from disabled campaigners than to reform equality legislation, although this action was eventually taken. Therefore, welfare systems and bureaucracies may filter out issues that do not fit with how they operate, or 'knock off' the rougher edges of problems and redefine them so that they have to address only those aspects of an issue that are compatible with routine practices.

Existing social policy systems can therefore become institutional barriers to or significantly reform social issues. Redefinition and filtering processes also operate at an individual level. Psychological studies have shown that people limit the consideration they devote to familiar and routine issues but when a task is presented as difficult, they apply more mental energy to it. Even something as simple as using a typeface that makes a document more difficult to read, or asking people to furrow their brows when tackling a challenge, can make them consider it more carefully.[97] The implication for social policies is that welfare professionals and those delivering services may limit how much consideration they give to standardised procedures and routine decisions. In such cases, they draw upon rather than question familiar categories and convenient stereotypes. It is inevitable that any system that deals with many thousands and perhaps millions of service users treats most in a standardised way rather than as distinct individuals, but the result is that the particular needs of each may be lost as their unique situation is processed to comply with system requirements.

In addition to the impact of institutional and individual perceptions, the techniques used to organise and collect data can shape how policies are designed and implemented. Many welfare policies are monitored by performance measurement systems and these influence the behaviour of those who are being assessed as they devote more attention to issues on which they are judged. This can lead to **game playing** – where those delivering welfare services do whatever is necessary to meet their performance measures even if this does not benefit the service user; a process described as 'hitting the target and missing the point'.[98] If the performance of an active labour-market policy is assessed by the number of clients who get jobs, rather than by increasing their skills and 'employability', then there is an incentive for service providers to concentrate their efforts on those who are most likely to get jobs rather than those who need most support. This is known as 'creaming and parking', where clients who are easiest to deal with are selected for help while the most difficult are sidelined.[99] The requirement to demonstrate the impact of a policy focuses attention on what can be measured rather than what might actually matter, and policy can be dictated by what can be shown rather than what is important but more difficult to see. In such cases, the performance measure shapes how the problem is defined and the action taken to address it.[100] Social constructionist theorists argue that, paradoxically, the response to a policy may exist prior to and determine what 'the problem' is rather than the other way around.[101]

The social constructionist perspective proposes that social problems do not necessarily exist as objective conditions in the outside world, but may actually be produced by the systems that are supposed to solve them. What counts as a social problem, how it is defined, its causes and the policy response are all shaped by social processes and political institutions. An important example of these processes is the Children Act 1989 in the UK.[102] The Act obliged local authorities to protect children against the risk of abuse, and established Child Protection Registers to assist social work departments to identify children considered at greatest risk.[103] In addition to overt behaviours and visible signs of abuse, among the potential risk factors on the register checklist were several social and demographic characteristics. These included children living in unemployed families, children living in lone-parent households, children from a lower working-class background and children living in poverty. While abuse may be statistically more likely in particular social groups and types of household, this may become a self-fulfilling prophecy – problems are more likely to be found wherever attention is focused. Child abuse and neglect are more likely to be identified among those who score highly on the checklist while it may be overlooked elsewhere, in the same way that crime is detected wherever the police focus resources and 'news' is whatever journalists choose to report. Some critics have argued that such checklists and similar risk assessment techniques stigmatise particular socio-economic groups and increase the surveillance and social control to which they are subjected.[104] Deviance becomes whatever is identified by the technology, and particular groups themselves become the social problem to be monitored.

The ways in which professional expertise, technology and welfare institutions actually create the problems that they were supposedly developed to deal with is central to the work of **Michel Foucault** (1926–84).[105] Foucault has been one of the most influential social theorists in the last 50 years, but he is just one of many analysts to propose radical critiques of the damaging effects of welfare professionals and institutions and who have challenged the authority of professionals and experts to determine what is defined as normal and deviant.[106] Several critical theorists argue that groups who are vulnerable to the power of welfare surveillance need to be protected from the institutions that are supposed to help them, and call for reforms to allow service users greater control over social policy decisions and resources. The fact that many welfare professionals themselves might agree with this, and are familiar with the ideas of social construction and the work of Foucault through their Social Policy training, raises further intriguing questions about the contribution of critical theory to understanding social problems. This is an issue considered in Chapter One and returned to in the Chapter Seven.

Conclusions

This chapter asked a basic question of Social Policy analysis: what actually *is* a 'social problem'? It is clear that the answer is far from simple. Social problems are not simply conditions, but also ideas and propositions, and they are determined not only by the facts, but also by political ideologies and values. What might be a problem for one group could be a matter of indifference or even a benefit to others. The concept of social construction offers several insights that assist the analysis of social problems. It is a valuable corrective to simple-minded assumptions about issues and policies and demonstrates that what are sometimes accepted as 'facts' in the social world and in policy are really artefacts, conventions and sometimes convenient fictions (for some).

Taken to an extreme, this perspective raises the question of whether any objective understanding of social problems is possible at all, and might even question the possibility of a discernible external reality. Such a **Perspectivist** view is expressed in Friedrich Nietzsche's proposition: 'There are no facts, only interpretations'.[107] Although this is a more complex position than it might initially appear, the relativism that it implies, and that follows from an extreme interpretation of the social constructionist perspective, is not persuasive. Social constructionism offers practical insights when applied to social practices and norms, but there are obvious problems when it is extended to suggest that there are no facts and conditions that are independent of beliefs.[108] The fallacy that 'reality' can be willed or is purely a matter of perception was shown by the hubris of a senior adviser to President George W. Bush (believed to be his Deputy Chief of Staff Karl Rove), who had a revealing conversation reported by a journalist:

> The aide said that guys like me were 'in what we call the reality-based community,' which he defined as people who 'believe that solutions emerge from your judicious study of discernible reality.... That's not the way the world really works anymore,' he continued. 'We're an empire now, and when we act, we create our own reality. And while you're studying that reality – judiciously, as you will – we'll act again, creating other new realities, which you can study too, and that's how things will sort out. We're history's actors ... and you, all of you, will be left to just study what we do.'[109]

In his minority report on the inquiry into the failure of the Challenger space shuttle, the physicist Richard Feynman remarked that 'nature cannot be fooled'. It is clear from the experience of the Bush administration – for example, in prematurely declaring 'mission accomplished' in the Iraq War – that social reality cannot simply be willed away either.

The idea of social construction suggests that what might be addressed by a social policy is not the 'real' problem itself, but a particular idea or representation of it. In fact, interest groups and policymakers may devote more energy to promoting their preferred understanding of what the problem is than in actually trying to solve it. The concept of social construction reinforces the multidisciplinary nature of Social Policy analysis by highlighting the political competition that takes place between alternative definitions of social issues. A historical awareness of how ideas about social issues and what is regarded as normal or deviant change over time is also valuable in understanding social problems.

Social Policy analysis involves challenging social problems, not only in the sense of trying to change problematic conditions, but also questioning why something ought to be regarded as a problem at all, and who says that it is? Social Policy analysts have played an important role in establishing some of the institutions and systems created to deal with social problems, and in informing the policies that they implement. However, analysts must retain their critical independence of these measures and always question the ideas that inform them and what impact they have.

Notes

[1]   Williams, R. (1983) *Keywords* (rev edn). London: Fontana, p 332.

[2]   Temple, W. (1941) *Citizen and Churchman*. London: Eyre & Spottiswoode. Although, as noted in Chapter Four, some state welfare policies were developed in authoritarian societies, such as Germany in the late 19th century, and the Vichy government in France, which collaborated with Nazi Germany.

[3]   There are older German terms similar to the English concept of 'welfare state', for example, '*Wohlfahrtsstat*' and '*Sozialstaat*'. See Béland, D. and Peterson, K. (2014) 'Introduction', in Béland, D. and Peterson, K. (eds) *Analysing Social Policy Concepts and Language: Comparative and Transnational Perspectives*. Bristol: The Policy Press, pp 1–2. Wincott challenges the Anglocentric assumptions about some of the language of Social Policy – Wincott, D. (2014) 'Original and Imitated or Elusive and Limited? Towards a Genealogy of the Welfare State Idea in Britain', in Béland, D. and Peterson, K. (eds) *Analysing Social Policy Concepts and Language: Comparative and Transnational Perspectives*. Bristol: The Policy Press, pp 127–8.

[4]   Titmuss, R.M. (1963) 'The Welfare State: Images and Realities', *Social Service Review*, xxxvi(1), pp 3–4.

[5]   Hobsbawm, E. (1994) *The Age of Extremes: The Short Twentieth Century, 1914–1991*. London: Michael Joseph, p 8.

[6]   Olson, P. and Champlin D. (1998) 'Ending Corporate Welfare as We Know It: An Institutional Analysis of the Dual Structure of Welfare', *Journal of Economic Issues*, 32(3). Klein et al note that 'in US political discourse, the concept of "welfare state" has long proved highly contentious, and it is frequently associated with negative connotations': Klein, J., Béland, D. and Peterson, K.N. (2014) 'Social Policy Language in the United States', in Béland, D. and Peterson, K. (eds) *Analysing Social Policy Concepts and Language: Comparative and Transnational Perspectives*. Bristol: The Policy Press, p 285.

[7]   Clery, E., Lee, L. and Kunz, S. (2013) *Public Attitudes to Poverty and Welfare, 1983–2011: Analysis Using British Social Attitudes Data*. York: Joseph Rowntree Foundation.

[8]   Quoted in Tierney, J. (2010) *Criminology Theory and Context* (3rd edn). Abingdon: Routledge, p 14.

[9]   Scott, W.R. and Meyer, J.W. (1994) *Institutional Environments and Organizations*. London: Sage.

[10] McMillan, L. (2013) 'Sexual Victimisation: Disclosure, Responses and Impact', in Lombard, N. and McMillan, L. (eds) *Violence Against Women: Current Theory and Practice for Working with Domestic Abuse, Sexual Violence and Exploitation*. London: Jessica Kingsley.

[11] There are even documented cases of crime statistics being deliberately manipulated by the authorities to meet certain targets. See Eterno, J.A. and Silverman, E.B. (2012) *The Crime Numbers Game: Management by Manipulation*. Boca Raton: CRC Press.

[12] Boghossian, P. (2001) 'What is Social Construction?', *Times Literary Supplement*, 23 February, pp 6–8.

[13] Marx, K. (1968) '"Preface" to "A Contribution to the Critique of Political Economy"', in Marx, K. and Engels, F., *Selected Works in One Volume*. London: Lawrence and Wishart, p 181.

[14] Marx, K. and Engels, F. (1874) *The German Ideology: Part One* (2nd edn) (ed Arthur, C.J.). London: Lawrence and Wishart, p 64.

[15] See, for example, Lukács, G. (1971 [1923]) *History and Class Consciousness* (trans Livingstone, R.). Boston, MA: MIT Press. Gramsci, A. (1971) *Selections from Prison Notebooks* (ed and trans Hoare, Q. and Smith, G.N.). London: Lawrence & Wishart. Althusser, L. (1969) *For Marx* (trans Brewster, B.). Harmondsworth: Penguin.

[16] Mannheim, K. (1936) *Ideology and Utopia: An Introduction to the Sociology of Knowledge* (trans Wirth, L. and Shils, E.). London: Routledge & Kegan Paul.

[17] Berger, P.L. and Luckmann, T. (1967) *The Social Construction of Reality: A Treatise in the Sociology of Knowledge*. Harmondsworth: Penguin.

[18] Berger and Luckmann (1967), p 27.

[19] Berger and Luckmann (1967), p 15.

[20] This maxim (also known as the 'definition of the situation' principle) first appeared in Znaniecki, F. and William, W.I. (1917) *The Polish Peasant in Europe and America*. Boston: R.D. Badger/Gorham Press. However, the actual quote that is most frequently used is taken from Thomas, W.I. and Thomas, D.S. (1928) *The Child in America: Behavior Problems and Programs*. New York, NY: Knopf, p 572.

[21] Hofstadter, D. (1982) 'Default Assumptions', *Scientific American*, 247(4).

[22] Although it is important to note that heuristics are (short-cut) mental *processes*, while default assumptions are interpretative frameworks of meaning, dispositions and deep-lying outlooks.

[23] Gouldner, A.V. (1970) *The Coming Crisis of Western Sociology*. London: Heinemann, p 32.

[24] Becker, H.S. (1963) *Outsiders: Studies in the Sociology of Deviance*. Glencoe, IL: Free Press.

[25] Becker, H.S. (1970) 'Whose Side Are We On?', in Douglas, J.D. (ed) *The Relevance of Sociology*. New York, NY: Appleton-Century-Crofts, p 103. See also Mills, C.W. (1943) 'The Professional Ideology of Social Pathologists', *American Journal of Sociology*, 49(2).

[26] Engels, F. (1844) 'The Condition of the Working-Class in England', p 40. Available at: http://www.gutenberg.org/files/17306/17306-h/17306-h.htm

[27] See, for example, Boo, K. (2102) *Behind the Beautiful Forevers: Life, Death and Hope in a Mumbai Slum*. London: Portobello Books.

[28] Mathias, P. (1969) *The First Industrial Nation: An Economic History of Britain, 1700–1914*. London: Methuen.

[29] Smith, A. (1776) *An Inquiry in the Nature and Causes of the Wealth of Nations*. London: Methuen (1904 edition).

[30] Durkheim, É. (1984) *The Division of Labour in Society*. Basingstoke: Macmillan (original 1893).

[31] Titmuss, R.M. (1958) *Essays on 'the Welfare State'*. London: George Allen & Unwin.

[32] Sinclair, S. (2001) *Financial Inclusion: An Introductory Survey*. Edinburgh: Centre for Research into Socially Inclusive Services.

[33] Stewart, T. (2010) 'Addressing Financial Exclusion Among Families Living in Poverty', *Journal of Poverty and Social Justice*, 18(2).

[34] Kempson, E. and Collard, S. (2012) *Developing a Vision for Financial Inclusion*. Dorking: Friends Provident Foundation, p 12.

[35] Payments Council (2010) *The Way We Pay, 2010: The UK's Payment Revolution*. London: Payments Council.

[36] Wolf, N. (1991) *The Beauty Myth: How Images of Beauty Are Used Against Women*. London: Vintage.

[37] Alergan have stated that their product meets a cosmetic rather than a medical condition, but by publicising Latisse as approved by the Food and Drug Administration, they might be interpreted as implying that it serves a health need. See Walker, R. (2009) 'Eyelash of the Beholder', *New York Times*, 31 July.

[38] Bennet, C. (2009) 'The Beauty Industry Is at It Again… It's Not a Pretty Sight', *The Observer*, 18 January. The Latisse example follows the model of the more famous case of Listerine, which became hugely successful after the company that developed it persuaded millions of people to be concerned about the problem of Chronic Halitosis; see Levitt, S.D. and Dubner, S.J. (2005) *Freakonomics: A Rogue Economist Explores the Hidden Side of Everything*. London: Penguin, p 91.

[39] Jackson, T. (2013) 'New Economic Model Needed not Relentless Consumer Demand', *The Guardian*, 17 January. A character in the film *Fight Club* makes a similar point: 'we buy things we don't need with money we don't have to impress people we don't like'.

[40] Hamilton, C. (2004) *Growth Fetish*. London: Pluto.

[41] Gibbs, D. (1995) 'The Law Giveth and the Law Taketh Away', *The Observer*, 7 May.

[42] Barnes, C. (1991) *Disabled People in Britain and Discrimination: A Case for Anti-Discrimination Legislation*. London: Hurst and Company.

[43] Cooper, G. (1998) 'Disabled Demand End to "Apartheid"', *The Independent*, 27 May.

[44] Office for Disability Issues/Department for Work and Pensions (2014) 'Disability Facts and Figures'. Available at: https://www.gov.uk/government/publications/disability-facts-and-figures/disability-facts-and-figures

[45] Heslop, P. (2013) *Disabled People and their Relationship with Poverty*. Working Paper – Methods Series No. 23. Bristol: Poverty and Social Exclusion in the UK.

[46] Barnes, C. and Mercer, G. (2005) 'Disability, Work, and Welfare: Challenging the Social Exclusion of Disabled People', *Work Employment & Society*, 19(3).

[47] Corker, M. (2005) *Disabling Language: Analysing the Discourse of Disability*. London: Routledge.

[48] Sinfield, A. (1993) 'Introduction: Reviving Debate on Poverty and Inequality', in Sinfield, A. (ed) *Poverty, Inequality and Justice*. Social Policy Series No 6. Edinburgh: New Waverley Papers, p 2.

[49] StamfordPlus.com (2009) 'Dodd Introduces Bill to Modernize Poverty Measurement', 10 August. Available at: http://www.stamfordplus.com/stm/information/nws1/publish/News_1/Dodd-introduces-bill-to-modernize-poverty-measurement_printer.shtml (accessed 31 December 2014).

[50] Nickell, S. and Van Ours, J. (2000) 'Mirage or Miracle? Labour Market Performance in Britain and the Netherlands', *CentrePiece*, 5(1), p 7.

[51] Office for National Statistics (no date) 'Unemployment and the Claimant Count'. Available at: www.ons.gov.uk/ons/guide-method/method-quality/specific/labour-market/articles-and-reports/unemployment-and-the-claimant-count.pdf (accessed 1 August 2015). See also Economics Online (no date) 'Measuring Unemployment'. Available at: http://www.economicsonline.co.uk/Managing_the_economy/Measuring_unemployment.html (accessed 31 December 2014).

[52] Office of the Third Sector (2008) *Participation in Regular Volunteering*. Briefing Note for Local Strategic Partnerships, No 16. London: Cabinet Office.

[53] Oxfam (2010) 'Something for Nothing: Changing Negative Attitudes to People Living in Poverty'. Available at: http://policy-practice.oxfam.org.uk/publications/something-for-nothing-changing-negative-attitudes-to-people-living-in-poverty-114046 (accessed 31 December 2014).

54 Buckner, L. and Yeandle, S. (2011) *Valuing Carers, 2011 – Calculating the Value of Carer's Support*. London: Carers UK.

55 Himmelweit, S. and Land, H. (2008) *Reducing Gender Inequalities to Create a Sustainable Care System*. York: Joseph Rowntree Foundation.

56 Ipsos MORI (2013) 'Perceptions Are Not Reality – The Top 10 We Get Wrong'. Available at: https://www.ipsos-mori.com/researchpublications/researcharchive/3188/Perceptions-are-not-reality-the-top-10-we-get-wrong.aspx (accessed 31 December 2014).

57 Hough, M. and Park, A. (2011) 'How Malleable Are Attitudes to Crime and Punishment? Findings from a British Deliberative Poll', in Roberts, J. and Hough, M. (eds) *Changing Attitudes to Punishment: Public Opinion, Crime and Justice* (3rd edn). Abingdon: Rouledge, p 163.

58 Chalabi, M. (2013) 'Crime, Teen Pregnancy and Job-seekers: What Do We Overestimate?', *The Guardian*, 9 July.

59 Marr, A. (2005) *My Trade: A Short History of British Journalism*. London: Pan, p 292.

60 Bourdieu, P. (1979) 'Public Opinion Does Not Exist', in Mattelart, A. and Sugelaub, S. (eds) *Communication and Class Struggle, Vol. 1*. New York, NY: International General.

61 Wilson, S., Meagher, G. and Hermes, K. (2012) 'The Social Division of Welfare Knowledge: Policy Stratification and Perceptions of Welfare Reform in Australia', *Policy & Politics*, 40(3).

62 Robinson, P. (2000) 'Active Labour-Market Policies: A Case of Evidence-Based Policy-Making?', *Oxford Review of Economic Policy*, 16(1).

63 Beveridge Lecture, Toynbee Hall London, 18 March 1999.

64 A typical example of this is a speech made by the then Minister for Employment and Welfare Reform Jim Murphy on 27 February 2007 to the Work Foundation. See also Murphy, J. (2007) 'Progressive Self-Interest – The Politics of Poverty and Aspiration', in Rossiter, A., Murphy, J., Blanden, J., Harker, L., Gregg, P., Macmillan, L., Sainsbury, R., Phillips, T., Sacks, J., Batmanghelidjh, C. and Hutt, D. (eds) *The Politics of Aspiration*. London: Social Market Foundation.

65 See, for example, UK Coalition Against Poverty (2008) *Communicating Poverty*. Liverpool: UK Coalition Against Poverty. Available at: http://www.tuc.org.uk/sites/default/files/extras/communicatingpoverty.pdf. Poverty Truth Commission (no date) *Nothing About Us without Us Is for Us: Findings of the Poverty Truth Commission, March 2009–April 2011*. Glasgow: Poverty Truth Commission. Available at: http://www.faithincommunityscotland.org/wp-content/themes/charitas-wpl/files/doc_14401207062012_30031_Poverty_Truth_Commission_A5_report_-_small.pdf

66 Lister, R. (2008) 'Povertyism and Othering: Why They Matter', presentation delivered at TUC Conference, 'Challenging Povertyism', 17 October. See also Lister, R. (2004) *Poverty*. Cambridge: Polity Press.

67 McKendrick, J.H. (2011) *Writing and Talking about Poverty – Briefing Paper 26*. Edinburgh: Scottish Government.

68 Oppenheim, C. and Harker, L. (1996) *Poverty: The Facts* (3rd edn). London: Child Poverty Action Group, pp 12–13.

69 Moore, J. (1989) *The End of the Line for Poverty*. London: Conservative Political Centre.

70 Quoted in Hennessey, P. (1996) 'The Glories and Blemishes of the British Governing Class', *Fabian Review*, 108(1), p 9.

[71] Veit-Wilson, J. (2000) 'Horses for Discourses: Poverty, Purpose and Closure in Minimum Income Standards Policy', in Gordon, D. and Townsend, P. (eds) *Breadline Europe: The Measurement of Poverty*. Bristol: The Policy Press.

[72] Edelman, M. (1977) *Political Language: Words that Succeed and Policies that Fail*. New York, NY: Academic Press.

[73] As George Orwell said: 'Political language … is designed to make lies sound truthful and murder respectable, and to give an appearance of solidity to pure wind'. Orwell, G. (1946) 'Politics and the English Language', in Orwell, G., *The Collected Essays, Journalism and Letters of George Orwell, Volume 4 – In Front of Your Nose* (ed Orwell, S. and Angus, I.). Harmondsworth: Penguin, p 170.

[74] Quoted in Miller, S. and Peroni, F. (1992) 'Social Politics and the Citizen's Charter', in Manning, N. and Page, R. (eds) *Social Policy Review 4*. Canterbury: Social Policy Association, p 243.

[75] Dworkin, R. (2011) *Justice for Hedgehogs*. Cambridge, MA: Harvard University Press.

[76] Stoller, T. (2013) 'Antipoverty Debate Needs to be Conducted with the Right Language', Joseph Rowntree Foundation Blog, 3 May. Available at: http://www.jrf.org.uk/blog/2013/05/antipoverty-debate-right-language (accessed 31 Decemebr 2014).

[77] See: https://www.gov.uk/benefit-cap

[78] Walker, R. and Chase, E. (2014) 'Adding to the Shame of Poverty: The Public, Politicians and the Media', *Poverty*, 148(Summer), p 11.

[79] Carson, R. (1962) *The Silent Spring*. Boston: Houghton Mifflin.

[80] Spector, M. and Kitsuse, J.I. (1995) 'The Definition of Social Problems', in Rubington, E. and Weinberg, S. (eds) *The Study of Social Problems: Seven Perspectives* (5th edn). Oxford: Open University Press.

[81] Spector, M. and Kitsuse, J.I. (1987) *Constructing Social Problems*. New York, NY: Aldine de Gruyter, p 170.

[82] Business in the Community (2014) 'The World's First Fair Tax Mark Launched with Support from Pioneer Businesses', 25 February. Available at: http://www.bitc.org.uk/news-events/news/world%E2%80%99s-first-fair-tax-mark-launched-support-pioneer-businesses (accessed 31 December 2014).

[83] Palan, R., Murphy, R. and Chavagneux, C. (2010) *Tax Havens: How Globalization Really Works*. Ithaca, NY: Cornell University Press, p 63.

[84] Department for Work and Pensions (2014) *Fraud and Error in the Benefit System: Preliminary 2013/14 Estimates (Great Britain)*. London: DWP Information, Governance and Security Directorate.

[85] Haines, H.H. (1979) 'Cognitive Claims Making, Enclosure and the Depoliticisation of Social Problems', *Sociological Quarterly*, 20(1).

[86] Furedi, F. (2008) 'Medicalisation in a Therapy Culture', in Wainwright, D. (ed) *A Sociology of Health*. London: Sage.

[87] Carlat, D. (2010) *Unhinged: The Trouble with Psychiatry – A Doctor's Revelations about a Profession in Crisis*. New York, NY: Free Press.

[88] Conrad, P. and Angell, A. (2004) 'Homosexuality and Remedicalization', *Society*, 41(5).

[89] See: http://wfdeaf.org/human-rights

[90] Dean, H. and Taylor-Gooby, P. (1992) *Dependency Culture: The Explosion of a Myth*. Hemel Hempstead: Harvester Wheatsheaf.

[91] McCormack, K. (2004) 'Resisting the Welfare Mother: The Power of Welfare Discourse and Tactics of Resistance', *Critical Sociology*, 30(2).

[92] Edelman, M. (1964) *The Symbolic Uses of Politics*. Urbana, IL: University of Illinois Press.

[93] Niccolo Machiavelli warned leaders against the hazards of innovation in 1532: 'there is nothing more difficult to plan or more uncertain of success or more dangerous to carry out than an attempt to introduce new institutions, because the introducer has as his enemies all those who profit from the old institutions, and has as lukewarm defenders all those who profit from the new institutions'. Machiavelli, N. (1972) *The Prince, Selections from the Discourses and Other Writings* (ed Plamenatz, J.). London: Fontana/Collins, pp 71–2.

[94] Pierson, P. (1996) 'The New Politics of the Welfare State', *World Politics*, 48(2).

[95] Townsend, P. (1976) *Sociology and Social Policy*. Harmondsworth: Penguin, p 307.

[96] McVeigh, T. (2015) 'Net Porn Filters Block Sex Abuse Charity Sites', *The Observer*, 25 January. In similar fashion, in the 1990s, President Bill Clinton proposed that television manufacturers install devices to block violent broadcasts rather than become embroiled in debates about the depiction and effects of violence, social norms, parental responsibilities and questions of censorship and freedom of speech. See Purdum, T.S. (1995) 'Clinton Takes on Violent Television', *New York Times*, 11 July.

[97] Alter, A. (2103) 'Can't Follow This Column? Try Changing the Typeface', *Wired*, October, p 60.

[98] Hood, C. (2006) 'Gaming in Targetworld: The Targets Approach to Managing British Public Services', *Public Administration Review*, 66(4), p 516.

[99] Rees, J., Whitworth, A. and Carter, E. (2013) *Support for All in the UK Work Programme? Differential Payments, Same Old Problem*. Working Paper 115. Birmingham: Third Sector Research Centre.

[100] Power, M. (1994) *The Audit Explosion*. London: DEMOS.

[101] Manning, N. (ed) (1985) *Social Problems and Welfare Ideology*. Aldershot: Gower.

[102] I am indebted to my colleague Peter Kennedy for drawing my attention to this example.

[103] Feàt, J. (2012) 'Current Legal Framework and Relevant Legislation' in Hooper, C., Thompson, M., Laver-Bradbury, C. and Gale, C. (eds) *Child and Adolescent Mental Health: Theory and Practice* (2nd edn). London: CRC Press, p 79.

[104] Parton, N. (2006) *Safeguarding Childhood: Early Intervention and Surveillance in a Late Modern Society*. Basingstoke: Palgrave Macmillan.

[105] Burchell, G., Gordon, C. and Miller, P. (eds) (1991) *The Foucault Effect: Studies in Governmentality*. London: Harvester Wheatsheaf.

[106] See, for example, Illich, I. (1973) *Tools for Conviviality*. New York, NY: Harper & Row.

[107] See Babich, B.E. (1994) *Nietzsche's Philosophy of Science: Reflecting Science on the Ground of Art*. Albany, NY: State University of New York Press, p 47. It is worth noting that Nietzsche chose not to publish this statement; it appears in his notebooks and was published posthumously.

[108] See Boghossian (2001), p 11.

[109] Suskind, R. (2004) 'Faith, Certainty and the Presidency of George W. Bush', *The New York Times Magazine*, 17 October.

THREE

Who benefits from welfare?
The social division of welfare

> **Social division of welfare: key points**
> - The social division of welfare (SDW) challenges conventional ideas of what counts as a 'welfare' service.
> - A simple division between public and private welfare services is misleading.
> - The SDW identifies three forms of welfare provision: public, fiscal and occupational.
> - Recognising the different ways in which welfare is provided has implications for understanding who finances and uses welfare.
> - Domestic welfare, largely provided unpaid by women, does not feature in many calculations of the costs and benefits of welfare.

Introduction

A characteristic of societies with a **liberal**[1] political tradition (such as the UK and the US) is that many people are rather ashamed to admit to receiving particular forms of welfare support. Such societies attach great importance to the idea of self-sufficiency, and relying on state support is regarded by many as a sign of failure. There is also some suspicion of certain welfare claimants in such societies. For example, 54% of respondents to the 2014 British Social Attitudes survey believed that 'most unemployed people could find a job if they really wanted one', and 49% felt that the government should spend less on supporting unemployed people, while only 15% thought that more should be spent.[2] However, not all forms of support are associated with this negative idea of **welfare dependency**. In the UK, for example, receiving a state pension or using National Health Service medical care are generally regarded as acceptable. There are several reasons for such distinctions. Among the most important are what people consider to *be* a 'welfare' service, and who they think uses different services. These are not straightforward issues. For example, should the criminal justice system be regarded as a welfare service? There might be good reasons for thinking so. Among the functions of the criminal justice system are protecting the public from harm and rehabilitating offenders, including, in many cases, providing those convicted with education and training. If education provided in state schools is a welfare service, is similar provision in prisons or institutions for young offenders not also welfare? If the criminal justice system *is* regarded as a welfare service, who are its users or beneficiaries: convicted prisoners, rehabilitated ex-offenders or the public who are protected by the system? Different answers could be given to these questions, and this is important because there is more at stake than semantics. What is regarded as a 'welfare' service and who is believed to benefit from it will determine answers to fundamental Social Policy questions, such as who receives and who pays for welfare? Do welfare services redistribute from richer to poorer groups? Has state welfare gone too far and become an unaffordable burden? Such contentious questions show that many Social Policy debates that seem to be about political or moral ideas also involve complex technical issues.

One of the most influential concepts developed within Social Policy (rather than being borrowed or adapted from another social science) provides valuable insights into these questions. This is the idea of the **social division of welfare** (SDW), developed initially by Richard Titmuss in 1955.

Richard Titmuss, 1907–73

Richard Titmuss was Professor of Social Policy at the London School of Economics between 1950 and 1973. Among his most influential publications were *Problems of Social Policy*, *Essays on 'The Welfare State'* and *The Gift Relationship*.[3] It has been said that 'More than anyone else, Titmuss established social administration as a subject of academic study and as a worthwhile intellectual activity. He exerted an enormous influence on the subject in its formative academic years',[4] and what has been described as the 'Titmuss School' of Social Policy analysis 'reigned unchallenged over the construction of social policy' in Britain from the 1940s until the 1970s.[5] His essay on SDW has been described as 'perhaps the most important post-war comment on social policy'.[6]

What is the 'social division of welfare'?

Titmuss's lecture (later published as an essay) on 'The Social Division of Welfare: Some Reflections on the Search for Equity'[7] is regarded as 'a milestone in the analysis of welfare state policies',[8] and 'probably ... the most cited paper' in both British and American studies of welfare provision.[9] However, if it is such an important contribution to Social Policy, why is it so unfamiliar outside the discipline? One reason is that some of Titmuss's insights have since become absorbed and part of the general understanding of welfare, so that while the term 'social division of welfare' itself might not be familiar to many, some of Titmuss's innovative ideas are now accepted. However, there remain some aspects and implications of the idea of an SDW that are still not recognised.

The impact and influence of Social Policy analysis

The idea of an SDW is an interesting example of the nature of the influence and *impact* of social science. There is currently considerable interest in the impact of research and the economic and social contribution of academic subjects.[10] However, influence and impact can take several forms. The direct use of research evidence to inform policies does happen but is most likely where findings confirm what policymakers already believe, or they are uncontroversial, require fairly limited change and can be implemented within existing systems.[11]

A deeper and often more significant influence that social science has on policy is informing how issues are understood and shifting debates over time. It is difficult to measure this kind of impact but it can be profound. Sir Peter Middleton, a former Permanent Secretary at the UK Treasury, suggested that overt **power** is less important than more subtle **influence** as power dies with whoever holds it but influence can carry on through generations. This echoes a famous statement by John Maynard Keynes:

> The ideas of economists and political philosophers, both when they are right and when they are wrong, are more powerful than is commonly understood. Indeed the world is ruled by little else. Practical men, who believe themselves to be quite exempt from any intellectual influence, are usually the slaves of some defunct economist.[12]

Changing how issues are thought of can often be more important than directly changing policies (see Chapter Two). However, this influence can be hidden, as what were once original and sometimes controversial ideas and insights from social science become absorbed as common-sense knowledge. Giddens describes this process as the 'slippage' of social science into everyday thinking and behaviour, where 'the concepts constructed in sociology ... are appropriated by those whose conduct they were originally coined to analyse, and hence tend to become integral features *of* that conduct'.[13]

The significance of the concept is that it highlights the different ways in which welfare support can be provided and the effects of these alternatives. Titmuss wrote his essay in response to criticisms that the British welfare state of the 1950s had gone too far, levied too much tax from middle-class households and unfairly favoured lower-income groups. Titmuss challenged the accusation of excessive redistribution by pointing out that it all depended on what was meant by 'welfare'. He argued that a welfare service should be defined by its objectives rather than associated with particular administrative systems and practices. A social security system or a care home for infirm older people are simply ways of delivering welfare and means to further ends. Titmuss argued that a welfare service should be defined by what it aims to do, not how it does it. This seemingly simple point 'represented a paradigmatic shift in thinking about social policy'.[14]

Developing this point, Titmuss identified three forms of welfare provision: social or public welfare; fiscal welfare; and occupational welfare. Titmuss argued that all three of these were different ways of transferring resources to supplement household incomes and should therefore be recognised as forms of social welfare support. The first form – social or **public welfare** – refers to direct transfers in the form of state benefits. This is a familiar type of welfare and what many people in the UK understand by the term.

Fiscal welfare refers to tax allowances, exemptions and rebates. Although tax reliefs do not involve an actual cash payment, reducing tax liability still involves a transfer of resources and has an effect on public accounts and what is available to spend on other activities.[15] As one British commentator explained:

Every citizen in these island [sic] pays higher taxes than they otherwise would to compensate for the lack of tax coming from tax-sheltered pensions. The contributions to build up personal pension funds are allowable against tax and the funds, once acquired, pay no capital gains tax and no income tax on dividends. Up to 40% of the value of any pension fund is thus created through the construction of a watertight tax-free zone.[16]

Titmuss described tax reliefs as a 'sacrifice of revenue' by the government,[17] and other Social Policy analysts and economists have suggested that it would be more appropriate to call them **tax expenditures** or 'tax benefits'.[18] Until quite recently, the cost of these fiscal welfare expenditures were not easily available from the UK government published accounts, but they involve considerable sums of money. Figures require careful interpretation as different expenditures have different functions, but to provide some context, there were 1,128 different tax reliefs in the UK in 2013, and the total cost of tax expenditure was estimated to be £101 billion – equivalent to about 21% of UK gross domestic product (GDP).[19] Tax relief on employers' National Insurance contributions to pension schemes in the UK alone cost £10.8 billion in 2013/14.[20] In comparison, the UK social security budget – including spending on unemployment, Income Support (and Universal Credit), Housing Benefit and disability allowances, but excluding pensions – amounted to about 13% of GDP in 2012/13.[21]

The third form of welfare that Titmuss identified is **occupational welfare**. These are benefits and supplements provided by employers, such as pensions or subsidised health insurance. Although sometimes described as 'fringe benefits', these can be worth a great deal and add considerably to some employees' incomes. It might seem that such perks are purely private contractual matters between an employer and employees. However, many forms of occupational welfare receive tax reliefs and subsidies, that is, they are supported by fiscal welfare. In addition, the costs of occupational welfare are ultimately paid for by customers through higher prices.

Implications of the social division of welfare #1: unifying welfare

The identification of an SDW has been described as 'a milestone in the analysis of welfare state policies' as it led to a 'radical reconceptualization of the boundaries of the welfare state'.[22] It showed that a simple distinction between public and private forms of welfare is misleading. Instead, welfare services can be categorised using several dimensions:

- Provision – is the service provider a public, private or third sector organisation (ie a voluntary or community association, or a not-for-profit social enterprise), or perhaps some combination of these?[23]

- Finance – does the public pay for the service, either directly thorough subsidy or indirectly through benefits and tax relief (fiscal welfare), or is it privately financed?
- Decision-making – do individual service users choose for themselves which provider to use or the amount of the service they receive?[24]

Welfare services are not simply either public *or* private services, but may have a multidimensional character and involve a combination of elements. This means that there is a range of different ways to fund and deliver welfare services. By demonstrating the variety of social policy options, Titmuss challenged assumptions about the scope and nature of the 'welfare state'.[25] Restricting the idea of a welfare state to direct state provision has implications for political and Social Policy debates, such as how large the welfare state is in different countries, when and why welfare services first emerged or expanded, and whether a particular welfare reform should be regarded as 'privatisation'. Limiting analysis of welfare to only services directly funded and provided by the state underestimates the full scale and costs of welfare, both in terms of the actual revenue spent and the alternatives forgone as a result (what economists call **opportunity costs**). It also creates a misleading impression of which groups benefit from welfare provision, as discussed later.

The different ways in which welfare services can be provided (ie funded, decided upon and delivered) have been portrayed as a diamond, with four points representing public sector, private market, voluntary or third sector, and household provision.

Figure 3.1: The welfare diamond

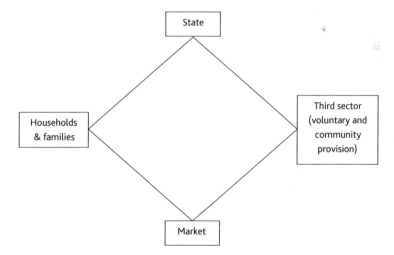

Source: Adapted from Evers, A., Pilj, M. and Ungerson, C. (eds) (1994) *Payments for Care*. Aldershot: Avebury.

One implication of analysing the SDW is to recognise the significance of occupational welfare. Including employer-provided welfare transforms the welfare diamond into a pentagon.

Figure 3.2: The welfare pentagon

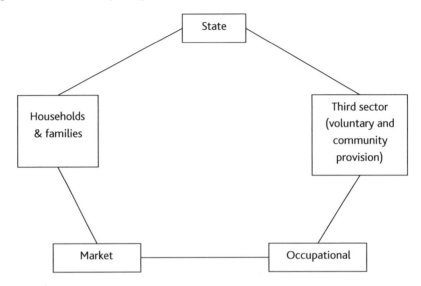

The balance of provision between these alternative options varies between different societies and across different welfare issues. National welfare systems can be grouped together into welfare types or 'regimes' according to how they combine these alternatives (see 'Rethinking the nature of welfare regimes' in Chapter One). For example, care and welfare provision within families is central to what has been described as the **Southern welfare model**, which characterises social policy in Mediterranean countries such as Italy, Spain, Portugal and Greece.[26] These systems also have more localised welfare services, often provided by voluntary associations and professional organisations, and rely less on national schemes provided by central government. Other national welfare models would produce different pentagon shapes, illustrating the variety of approaches available to deliver welfare services.

Titmuss's argument that a welfare service should be defined by its aims rather than the means used to deliver them also highlights the different functions that welfare can perform. These include relieving social problems (such as poverty), reducing inequality, promoting social cohesion and supporting economic activity (eg by investing in education and training), among others. Welfare services – including directly provided state services – may therefore perform functions that are not particularly 'progressive' or 'left-wing' (however these terms might be interpreted).[27] Among the first and most extensive state welfare systems were those developed by authoritarian governments and fascist dictatorships in Europe. The Prussian Chancellor Otto von Bismarck (1815–98) is usually credited with introducing the first national social insurance scheme in 1883, and his government banned the opposition Social Democratic Party around the same time. The aim of both measures was to consolidate an authoritarian political and social system in a period of rapid industrialisation and social change.[28] Similarly, the Vichy regime, which collaborated with the Nazis after the defeat of France in 1940, introduced an extensive system of social welfare, including old-age pensions, a minimum wage and access to medical care.[29] The current association between what are regarded as 'right-wing' or conservative political movements and minimal state welfare provision is a recent development. Many conservative regimes have favoured extensive welfare provision to preserve their legitimacy, maintain national unity and promote economic productivity.

Titmuss outlined some of the different roles that welfare systems perform and the various principles that underpin alternative approaches[30]:

- Residual welfare model – needs should be met within families or purchased in the market and delivered by private providers; the state should only step in if either of these sources fails to deliver.
- Industrial achievement-performance model – social welfare services should support economic production; needs are 'met on the basis of merit, work performance and productivity'.
- Industrial redistributive model – social welfare provision promotes social integration and egalitarian principles; universal services are used to redistribute resources and are provided to all those in need.

These different models clarify some of the key principles that shape welfare systems, but while national welfare states may favour one approach over another, in practice, they usually combine aspects of several models. In the UK, for example, the main function of social security is to provide a basic level of income to alleviate poverty, but any provision beyond this is regarded as an individual responsibility. This is why Britain has relatively large private and occupational welfare sectors catering mainly for better-off households and subsidised by fiscal welfare.

Bismarckian and Beveridgean welfare systems

There are different ways of financing state welfare, determining eligibility to receive services and the level of benefits provided. One model can be traced to the first national social security system, established in Germany in 1883 by the Chancellor Otto von Bismarck. This created a **contributory social insurance** system funded by earnings-related payments deducted from employees' wages and levied from employers. The benefits that claimants received were dependent upon their contributions and related to their earnings.

From the beginning of the 20th century, the UK developed an alternative approach that became central to one of the foundations of British social policy: the 1942 *Beveridge Report on Social Insurance and Allied Services*. This proposed a single rate of National Insurance contributions paid by all employees and **flat-rate** benefits set at a subsistence income level, rather than benefits that reflected previous earnings. Beveridge argued that state benefits should 'not stifle incentive, opportunity, responsibility ... [and] should leave room and encouragement for voluntary action' and for anyone who wanted to purchase additional private cover.

Many European countries that developed social insurance schemes in the 20th century adopted the German contributory model. However, several English-speaking countries copied the flat-rate subsistence British scheme. The result is that national welfare systems are often grouped together into various 'regime types' or 'families'.[31]

Social security systems redistribute income, but not always in the way that many people assume. What Titmuss called social or public welfare operates, in part, by redistributing an individual's or household's income *horizontally* over their lifecycle rather than *vertically* between different income groups and classes. This means that individuals and households pay contributions while employed and receive these as benefits when they are no longer earning, due to unemployment, retirement or some other reason. In this way, welfare smoothes out personal income between the highs and lows that occur over a lifetime, and functions as a kind of compulsory collective savings bank. It is estimated that in the UK, about 75% of welfare is self-financed and operates across lifecycles in this way, rather than redistributing from richer to poorer groups.[32]

Implications of the social division of welfare #2: divisive welfare

Titmuss commented that the three forms of welfare provision he identified 'operate as virtually distinct stratified systems', and that particular forms of welfare have tended to benefit different groups.[33] The reason why Titmuss referred to a 'social *division* of welfare' is because similar needs are met differently in these three forms of provision. Specifically, fiscal and occupational welfare are often of greater value and more highly regarded than direct social security benefits. As a later commentator observed: 'The stark reality is that those who can gain access to occupational and fiscal welfare almost invariably receive more benefits and a better service', while less affluent groups struggle as best they can on 'the most visible and stigmatised benefits which provide the least security'.[34]

The SDW therefore provides insights into who pays for and who benefits from different types of welfare provision, and also 'requires that we consider very carefully in whose welfare decisions are taken'.[35] The public generally assumes that most welfare support is targeted towards lower-income groups. However, once the costs of the fiscal and occupational sectors are included in calculations, it becomes clear that a very large volume of public resources primarily benefit middle- and higher-income groups.[36] In the UK, the total cost of tax relief on pension contributions in 2007/08 was £37 billion, 60% of which went to higher-rate taxpayers, with 25% (almost £10 billion per year) going to the top 1% of earners (those with annual incomes above £150,000).[37] According to one estimate, the top 0.1% of UK taxpayers receive 86 times the amount of tax relief as those on average incomes.[38] In terms of tax contributions, the top 1% of earners pays about one third of all UK income tax, but while this is undoubtedly important, income tax only contributes about 25% of all UK tax revenue. About 45% of UK tax is raised by Value Added Tax, Excise Duty and National Insurance and these counteract the redistributive effects of income tax.[39]

A similar pattern is evident in the US: the top fifth of households ranked by income receive more from the government in taxes and benefits than the bottom fifth.[40] Considering tax expenditure alone, in 2011, the top fifth of US households received 66% of these benefits, and the top 1% in the income distribution received 23.9% – more than eight times as much as the bottom fifth of the population, which received 2.8% of tax-expenditure benefits.[41]

Gender divisions of welfare

One particular division illuminated by the SDW concept is how the costs and benefits of welfare are distributed between men and women. Feminist Social Policy analysts have argued that Titmuss's threefold division of welfare ignored unpaid 'domestic' care, which is largely provided by women and that has a significant impact on their life chances and well-being compared to those of men.[42] Most care and support is provided in private within families, but while this **domestic welfare** is largely unseen and uncounted, the public scale and cost of welfare would be far greater if it was not provided freely.[43] However, this public saving may impose considerable financial costs on those providing care. In many welfare systems, the right to use services is not inherent, but depends upon having paid contributions, reflecting the idea of social security as a lifetime savings bank. The ability to make sustained contributions to social welfare systems through taxation is closely related to employment, but those who provide unpaid care and domestic welfare – raising children or looking after older or otherwise vulnerable people – are unlikely to be continuously employed and build up a regular contributions record. The result is that in the UK, as well as several other countries with employment-related and contributory welfare systems, women are less likely than men to be eligible for full and equal benefits and other welfare support.[44] This is particularly evident in access to public, occupational and private pensions, where disruptions to employment can have significant consequences for entitlements and the value of pensions.[45] Career breaks (to have children or for any other reason) reduce the contributions made and are often associated with downward occupational mobility (ie those temporarily leaving work return at a lower grade), which reduces the salary used to calculate pension payments. It is not always the case that women rather than men will have these breaks in employment, but it still remains more likely, even in more equal societies.

The result is that women are generally more likely than men to have a fluctuating pattern of contributions to pension schemes. It is broadly similar to men at a younger age before they have children, it falls below that of men during the years of bearing and raising children, before recovering somewhat in mid–career phase and then declining again before retirement (see Figure 3.3). As a result, the care responsibilities assumed by or imposed upon women during their working lives lead to lower incomes in retirement.

Figure 3.3: Women's fluctuating employment and pension entitlements

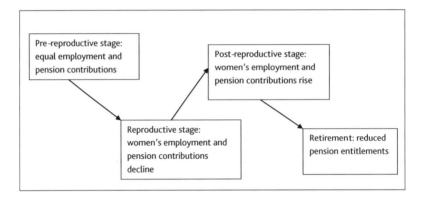

Women's ability to build up equal pension and other welfare entitlements is also shaped by their relative opportunities and position in the labour market and the occupational segregation that still characterises this in many societies.

Occupational segregation

In most countries, women's average income from employment is lower than the average income received by men. For example, in the UK in 2012, the difference between the median earnings of women and men working full-time was 9.6% for hourly earnings (excluding overtime) and 17.8% for gross weekly earnings (including overtime).[46]

Part of the reason for this is occupational gender segregation, which takes two forms:

1. Horizontal segregation refers to differences in the kinds of jobs that men and women do, that is, women are much more likely than men to be employed in particular labour-market sectors. Gender occupational divisions are usually measured by various 'dissimilarity' indices, which use several indicators to summarise the relative proportion of men and women in different jobs. For example, in 2005, almost 36% of women in employment in the European Union were employed in just six (out of the 130) occupational categories, while the top six occupations for men accounted for only 25% of those in employment. The top six occupations for women were: shop salesperson and demonstrators; domestic and related helpers, cleaners, and launderers; personal care and related workers; office clerks; administrative associate professionals; and housekeeping and restaurant services workers.[47]
2. Vertical or hierarchical segregation describes how women are less likely to occupy senior positions (even in sectors of the labour market where they are a majority) and

more likely to be employed in lower-paid occupations. Women's relative lack of access to the very top occupational positions has long been described as a 'glass ceiling'. More recently, it has been suggested that many women are not promoted beyond a 'marzipan layer' below the most senior positions, which are dominated by men (see Table 3.1).[48] The UK Equality and Human Rights Commission has estimated that at the current rate of progress, it will take 70 years to achieve an equal number of women directors in FTSE 100 companies, and 14 elections before there are an equal number of female and male Westminster MPs.

Table 3.1: Vertical gender segregation: percentage of women in senior UK occupations, 2003–11

	2003	2004	2007/08	2010/11
	% of positions held by women			
Members of the UK Parliament	18.1	18.1	19.3	22.2
Directors of FTSE 100 companies	8.6	9.7	11.0	12.5
Senior armed forces officers	0.6	0.8	0.4	1.0
Senior police officers	7.5	8.3	11.9	16.8
Senior judges	6.8	8.3	9.6	12.9
Secondary school head teachers	30.1	31.8	36.3	35.5

Source: Equality and Human Rights Commission (2011) 'Sex and Power, 2011'. Available at: http://www.equalityhumanrights.com/publication/sex-and-power-2011

If access to social protection is based on the assumption of typical male patterns of employment and contributions, rather than rights being inherent or credited, then welfare systems may reproduce and reinforce gender inequalities.[49] Therefore, in order to understand women's position in relation to divisions of welfare, it is necessary to recognise the close relationship between the public worlds of welfare rights and employment and the **private sphere** of the family, and to understand that the assumption that domestic care should be unpaid is neither neutral nor natural.

The SDW also highlights the ideological (and often implicitly sexist) nature of the concept of 'dependence'. This term is rarely used in a positive way, as shown by such phrases as **dependency culture** and 'welfare-dependent'; even the idea of a 'dependency ratio' in Demographics has negative implications.[50] Dependence is implicitly contrasted with the ideal (promoted by neoclassical economic theory) of an autonomous and independent agent who is not a 'burden' to others.[51] However, this ideal ignores the fact that everyone is dependent upon others at some point, for example, in childhood, during periods of ill-health or unemployment, or when retired.[52] In complex modern economies, it is also impossible to live without depending upon products and services provided by others; to some extent, everyone is mutually interdependent (see 'Dependence and the division of labour' in Chapter Two). Rather than the fiction of unattached independent agents, it is more accurate to think of units of care and provision (usually but not exclusively families) embedded within wider networks of exchange and support (eg extended families, friends, neighbours and communities), which provide and draw upon care at different times. However, domestic welfare is not an infinite or free resource, and any reduction in public or social welfare provision may increase the demand for unpaid care that falls upon families and still, above all, upon women. Extending the idea of the SDW and the analysis that it enables in this way can therefore highlight the implications of significant but often hidden shifts in who pays and who benefits from different forms of welfare.

Visibility, awareness and opinions about welfare

Most members of the British and American public equate the welfare state with direct public provision. Fiscal and occupational welfare receive much less media and public attention than social or public welfare. Consequently, many people are unaware of the true scale and impact of tax expenditures and underestimate the benefits flowing to higher-income groups. For this reason, fiscal and occupational welfare have been described as the **hidden welfare state**.[53] However, public attention is not random, but directed towards particular social issues and social policies:

> social visibility is not merely an inherent quality of phenomena; it relates also to what people are looking for, and what is brought to their attention by the media…. The evidence is that public attention to particular areas of social activity, and public definitions of certain social phenomena as problems, do not occur spontaneously; they result from identifiable social institutions and social processes. 'Public opinion', it could be said, is socially produced.[54]

In addition to relative visibility, opinions on welfare are influenced by the personal proximity of a service, that is, how much someone uses or is familiar with it – 'citizens pay most attention to policies that apply to them and would have less experience, even knowledge, about what happens to people with different lifecourses and interests'.[55] In general, those with little contact or familiarity with a welfare service are least likely to support it.[56] Altruism and social solidarity play some part in shaping support for different welfare services, but there is also a strong dose of self-interest.[57]

The higher visibility of direct public expenditure means that it appears more 'political' than tax expenditure, in that it receives more scrutiny and criticism and is more contentious. Titmuss was initially prompted to analyse the SDW because allegations of excessive welfare provision focused on public rather than fiscal or occupational welfare. Tax credits have been introduced in both the UK and US with far less controversy than more visible cash benefits. They have generally been more favourably received, if noticed at all, despite their significant cost and the fact that tax credits that support the incomes of low-waged employees are effectively subsidies to the wage bill of employers, and therefore involve taxpayers supplementing private profits.

The varying visibility of different forms of welfare shapes the options and actions of governments: less controversy is provoked in expanding the hidden welfare state of tax expenditures and benefits than extending direct cash transfers. The expansion and contraction of social welfare provision is less clear-cut than often supposed, and shifts between different forms of provision may go largely unnoticed but can have a significant impact on which groups receive most from the welfare state.[58] Applying the concept of an SDW makes such shifts more visible and highlights how there may be alternative routes to the same end – and various ways to subsidise different groups – which would otherwise not be apparent. Understanding the SDW therefore opens up new ways of classifying policies and widening the range of options available.

Conclusions

As was explained in Chapter One, the question of who pays for and benefits from welfare services is central to Social Policy analysis. The SDW concept illustrates that studying the distributional effects of social policies requires going far beyond the boundaries of conventional ideas of the welfare state.[59] As Townsend noted: 'Government policy is no more synonymous with social policy than Government behaviour is synonymous with social behaviour'.[60] The SDW shows that to answer the question posed in this chapter (Who benefits from welfare?) requires first considering several other questions: 'What counts as a 'welfare' service?'; 'Which service is being considered?'; 'What are the purposes of a service?'; and 'What are the different policy options available to reach a particular outcome?' The SDW illuminates the alternative aims and means of welfare services and prevents us becoming entrapped by familiar mechanisms and conventions.

The SDW also challenges ideas of dependency. It highlights the complex mutual interdependencies that contemporary societies create and how the costs of meeting these needs and providing care is not shared equally, particularly between men and women. In this way, the SDW reveals important aspects of how some social and economic inequalities are reproduced. This is a useful reminder that welfare services do not necessarily operate according to different principles from other aspects of society and should not be regarded as some kind of social 'Robin Hood': taking from the rich to give to the poor and righting injustices. Social welfare services can reinforce solidarity and pool risks in a system of shared citizenship, but they may also be divisive by reflecting divisions and reproducing inequalities.[61]

The SDW reminds us that it is necessary to analyse the implications of any welfare reform for relatively privileged and disadvantaged groups because 'One man's social security can become another man's social insecurity – and another woman's too'.[62] In this sense, the SDW is one of the richest and most suggestive concepts in Social Policy as it opens up new ways to analyse inequality by asking who gets what, by what means and why.

Notes

[1] A 'liberal' welfare system is one in which the state plays a relatively limited role in directly providing services and there is greater requirement upon individuals to purchase private provision.

[2] Nat Cen Social Research (no date) 'British Social Attitudes, 31'. Available at: http://www.bsa-31.natcen.ac.uk/read-the-report/benefits/public-attitudes-to-the-benefits-system-are-they-changing.aspx (accessed 18 January 2015).

[3] Titmuss, R.M. (1950) *Problems of Social Policy*. London: H.M. Stationery Office; Titmuss, R.M. (1958) *Essays on 'The Welfare State'*. London: George Allen & Unwin; and Titmuss, R.M. (1970) *The Gift Relationship: From Human Blood to Social Policy*. London: Penguin.

[4] Wilding, P. (1995) 'Titmuss', in George, V. and Page, R. (eds) *Modern Thinkers on Welfare*. London: Prentice Hall/Harvester Wheatsheaf, p 149.

[5] Rose, H. (1981) 'Rereading Titmuss: The Sexual Division of Welfare', *Journal of Social Policy*, 10(4), p 284.

[6] Townsend, P. (1976) *Sociology and Social Policy*. Harmondsworth: Penguin, p 261.

[7] Titmuss, R.M. (1958) 'The Social Division of Welfare: Some Reflections on the Search for Equity' in *Essays on 'The Welfare State'*. London: George Allen & Unwin.

[8] Wilding (1995), p 156.

[9] Sinfield, A. (1978) 'Analyses in the Social Division of Welfare', *Journal of Social Policy*, 7(2), p 129.

[10] 'Impact' is an important factor in the Research Excellence Framework used to rank the quality of and allocate resources to British universities, see: http://www.ref.ac.uk/

[11] Davies, H. and Nutley, S. (2002) *Evidence-Based Policy and Practice: Moving from Rhetoric to Reality*. Discussion Paper. St Andrews: Research Unit for Research Utilisation.

[12] Keynes, J.M. (1936) *The General Theory of Employment, Interest and Money*. Cambridge: Cambridge University Press, p 383.

[13] Giddens, A. (1976) *New Rules of Sociological Method: A Positive Critique of Interpretative Sociologies*. London: Hutchinson, p 162, emphasis in original.

[14] Walker, A. (1997) 'The Social Division of Welfare Revisited', in Robertson, A. (ed) *Unemployment, Social Security and the Social Division of Welfare: A Festschrift in Honour of Adrian Sinfield*. Social Policy Series No 13. Edinburgh: New Waverley Papers, p 2.

[15] McKay, A. (1998) 'Social Security Policy', in Ellison, N. and Pierson, C. (eds) *Developments in British Social Policy*. Houndmills: Macmillan, p 113.

[16] Hutton, W. (2014) 'This Pensions "Freedom" Will Be a Long-Term Disaster', *The Observer*, 23 March.

[17] Titmuss, R.M. (1962) *Income Distribution and Social Change: A Study in Criticism*. London: George Allen & Unwin, p 166.

[18] Surry, S.S. (1973) *Pathways to Tax Reform: The Concept of Tax Expenditures*. Cambridge, MA: Harvard University Press. Sinfield, A. (2000) 'Tax Benefits in Non-State Pensions', *European Journal of Social Security*, 2(2).

[19] National Audit Office (2014) 'Tax Reliefs', p 8. Available at: http://www.nao.org.uk/wp-content/uploads/2014/03/Tax-reliefs-summary.pdf (accessed 29 January 2015).

[20] HM Revenue & Customs (2014) 'Estimated Costs of the Principal Tax Expenditure and Structural Reliefs'. Available at: https://www.gov.uk/government/uploads/system/uploads/attachment_data/file/302317/20140109_expenditure_reliefs_v0.4published.pdf (accessed 29 January 2015).

[21] Department for Work and Pensions (2014) 'Social Security Expenditure in the United Kingdom, including Scotland', p 6. Available at: https://www.gov.uk/government/uploads/system/uploads/attachment_data/file/305371/social-security-spending-in-UK-including-scotland.pdf (accessed 29 January 2015).

[22] Wilding (1995), pp 156–7.

[23] Teasdale, S. (2011) 'What's in a Name? The Construction of Social Enterprise', *Public Policy and Administration*, 27(2).

[24] Burchardt, T. and Hills, J. (1999) *Private Welfare and Public Policy*. York: Joseph Rowntree Foundation.

[25] Walker, A. (1984) *Social Planning: A Strategy for Socialist Welfare*. Oxford: Basil Blackwell, p 28.

[26] Ferrera, M. (1996) 'The "Southern Model" of Welfare in Social Europe', *Journal of European Social Policy*, 6(1).

[27] See: http://www.politicalcompass.org/

[28] Hennock, E.P. (2007) *The Origin of the Welfare State in England and Germany, 1850–1914: Social Policies Compared*. Cambridge: Cambridge University Press.

[29] Paxton, R.O. (2013) 'Vichy Lives! In a Way', *New York Review of Books*, 25 April.

[30] Titmuss, R.M. (1974) *Social Policy: An Introduction*. London: George Allen & Unwin, pp 30–1.

[31] Bonoli, G. (1997) 'Classifying Welfare States: A Two-Dimension Approach', *Journal of Social Policy*, 26(3).

[32] Hills, J. (2004) *Inequality and the State*. Oxford: Oxford University Press. See also Office for National Statistics (2013) 'The Effects of Taxes and Benefits on Household Income, 2011/12'. Available at: http://www.ons.gov.uk/ons/rel/household-income/the-effects-of-taxes-and-benefits-on-household-income/2011-2012/index.html (accessed 31 January 2015).

[33] Titmuss (1958), p 42. See also Titmuss (1974), p 137.

[34] Mann, K. (1992) *The Making of an English 'Underclass': The Social Divisions of Welfare and Labour*. Milton Keynes: Open University Press, p 164. The various tax credits introduced since the late 1990s have reduced some of the division between different social, fiscal and occupational welfare.

[35] Sinfield (1978), p 144.

[36] Foote, G. (1997) *The Labour Party's Political Thought: A History* (3rd edn). Houndmills: Macmillan, p 217.

[37] Trades Union Congress (2009) 'Decent Pensions for All: Why Public Sector Pensions Are Affordable and the Real Challenge Is the Collapse of Private Sector Pensions', p 3. Available at: http://publicservicepensioners.org.uk/pdfs/TUC%20Decent%20Pensions%20for%20All.pdf (accessed 31 January 2015).

[38] Sinfield, A. (2014) 'How Can We Reduce Poverty Without Improving its Prevention?', *Poverty*, 147, p 16.

[39] Hutton, W. (2014) 'Capitalism Simply Isn't Working', *The Observer*, 13 April.

[40] Micklethwait, J. and Wooldridge, A. (2014) *The Fourth Revolution: The Global Race to Reinvent the State*. London: Penguin.

[41] Sherman, A., Greenstein, R. and Ruffing, K. (2012) 'Contrary to "Entitlement Society" Rhetoric, Over Nine-Tenths of Entitlement Benefits Go to Elderly, Disabled, or Working

Households', Center on Budget and Policy Priorities. Available at: http://www.cbpp.org/cms/?fa=view&id=3677 (accessed 31 January).

[42] Rose, H. (1981) 'Re-Reading Titmuss: The Sexual Division of Welfare', *Journal of Social Policy*, 10(4).

[43] Pascal, G. (1986) *Social Policy: A Feminist Analysis*. London: Routledge.

[44] Himmelweit, S. and Land, H. (2008) *Reducing Gender Differences to Create a Sustainable Care System*. York: Joseph Rowntree Foundation.

[45] Ginn, J. and Arber, S. (1993) 'Pension Penalties: The Gendered Division of Occupational Welfare', *Work, Employment & Society*, 7(1).

[46] Perfect, D. (2012) *Gender Pay Gaps, 2012*. London: Equality and Human Rights Commission, p 3.

[47] European Commission's Expert Group on Gender and Employment (2009) *Gender Segregation in the Labour Market: Root Causes, Implications and Policy Responses in the EU*. Luxembourg: European Commission Directorate-General for Employment, Social Affairs and Equal Opportunities, p 30.

[48] Equality and Human Rights Commission (2011) 'Sex and Power, 2011', p 1. Available at: http://www.equalityhumanrights.com/publication/sex-and-power-2011

[49] Luckhaus, L. (2000) 'Equal Treatment, Social Protection and Income Security for Women', *International Labour Review*, 139(2).

[50] A dependency ratio is the proportion of the population of working age relative to those not in employment, for example, because they are too young or retired. It is used as a measure of the economically productive population.

[51] Chang, H.-J. (2014) *Economics: The User's Guide*. London: Pelican, pp 120–6.

[52] Marçal, K. (2015) *Who Cooked Adam Smith's Dinner?* London: Portobello.

[53] Howard, C. (1999) *The Hidden Welfare State: Tax Expenditures and Social Policy in the United States*. Princeton, NJ: Princeton University Press.

[54] Hyman, R. (1972) *Strikes*. Glasgow: Fontana/Collins, p 143.

[55] Wilson, S., Meagher, G. and Hermes, K. (2012) 'The Social Division of Welfare Knowledge: Policy Stratification and Perceptions of Welfare Reform in Australia', *Policy & Politics*, 40(3), p 324.

[56] Gilens, M. (1999) *Why Americans Hate Welfare: Race, Media, and the Politics of Antipoverty Policy*. Chicago, IL: University of Chicago Press.

[57] Reeskens, T. and Van Oorschot, W. (2013) 'Equity, Equality, or Need? a Study of Popular Preferences for Welfare Redistribution Principles Across 24 European Countries', *Journal of European Public Policy*, 20(8).

[58] Bauer, W., Jordan, A., Green-Pedersen, C. and Héritier, A. (eds) (2012) *Dismantling Public Policy: Preferences, Strategies and Effects*. Oxford: Oxford University Press.

[59] Walker (1984), p 39.

[60] Townsend (1976), p 3.

[61] Sinfield (1978), p 154.

[62] Sinfield, A. (1989) *Social Security and its Social Division: A Challenge for Sociological Analysis*. Social Policy Series No 2. Edinburgh: New Waverley Papers, p 8.

FOUR

Who is a member of society?
Social inclusion and exclusion

Social inclusion and exclusion: key points
- Social inclusion and exclusion are not simply alternative terms for poverty.
- Social inclusion means the ability to participate in mainstream social life.
- Social exclusion is a dynamic and multidimensional process involving a lack of access to material resources and essential services, non-participation in social and cultural activities, and a lack of effective political involvement.
- Understanding the interactions between the dimensions of social exclusion enables policies to target key risk points.

Introduction

In 2009, the mother of a pupil attending a primary school in Inverness threatened to take the local authority to court for breaching disability rights legislation. Her daughter had Muscular Dystrophy and would have been unable to participate in a planned school trip to an adventure park. She objected that her daughter was being excluded from joining in an activity available to every other pupil. Some of the parents of other children in the school argued that simply because one pupil was not able to enjoy this activity was no reason to deny it to everyone. In the end, the local authority and school proposed an alternative event in which all pupils could participate.[1]

Although the 'thought is often expressed that "social exclusion" is no more than a relabelling of what used to be called "poverty"',[2] this case shows how the idea of inclusion raises issues beyond low income and how some people may be excluded from everyday activities by a variety of barriers. Social inclusion and exclusion mean more than poverty – they are concerned with participation and rights, what it means to be a member of society and how involvement may be limited or denied. The case of the Inverness school pupil raises several questions in relation to social exclusion – was this mother justified in claiming that her daughter's rights had been denied? What is required for **social inclusion**? What are the normal social activities in which everyone has the right to engage? If some people cannot participate in mainstream social activities for various reasons, how much reasonable adjustment should the majority make to enable them to do so? Was this girl unable to participate because of her condition, or should her school have anticipated her needs, or should the facility that would host pupils have accommodated and adapted to her requirements? Does it matter that this was a publicly funded school trip – should public and welfare services be expected to be more inclusive than private ones?

Social inclusion means the capacity to participate in normal social life. Access and social participation are particular concerns for people with disabilities (see Chapter Two).[3] Article 19 of the United Nations Convention on the Rights of Persons with Disabilities commits signatories to provide the means and mechanisms that enable **independent living** for people with disabilities:

> Parties to the present Convention recognize the equal right of all persons with disabilities to live in the community, with choices equal to others, and shall take effective and appropriate measures to facilitate full enjoyment by persons with disabilities of this right and their full inclusion and participation in the community.

To ensure social inclusion, the Convention requires that 'Community services and facilities for the general population are available on an equal basis to persons with disabilities and are responsive to their needs'.[4] Inclusion and social participation are also central Social Policy concerns in a wider sense. Social inclusion is closely related to the idea of citizenship – the rights and duties attached with full membership of society (see Chapter Five). Many welfare services are intended to promote inclusion and shared citizenship by providing common rights and reducing social divisions and potentially exclusionary differences. Welfare services are often developed to promote integration in the face of social upheaval, which is why they have been favoured by conservative and authoritarian regimes (see Chapter Three). However, developing and implementing policies that enable social integration and participation raises moral dilemmas and practical challenges. For example, should social inclusion involve equal treatment of citizens with significant differences, or is differential provision justified to compensate for unequal conditions (and, if so, which conditions)? Does ensuring social inclusion for some mean constraining others' freedom of choice? How can policies promote social solidarity while respecting difference and allowing people to express their individuality? Although not initially developed to answer these questions, the concepts of social exclusion and inclusion do shed light on them. However, to show how they do this, it is first of all necessary to consider how these ideas have been used and developed and how both relate to more familiar concepts, including poverty and freedom.

Poverty, capability and freedom

Poverty might initially appear a straightforward concept – not having enough money to live on seems a simple enough notion. However, as with many of the central concepts in Social Policy, poverty is a contested idea. People can be said to experience poverty when they have an income below what is required to live at a minimum accepted standard of living in society. This raises the question of what counts as a minimum acceptable standard, which is a matter of judgement. A distinction often drawn in discussing poverty is between absolute and relative definitions. **Absolute poverty** means the level of resources required for subsistence, that is, the income needed for basic physical survival. The United Nations defined absolute poverty as 'a condition characterised by several deprivations of basic human needs, including food, safe drinking water, sanitation facilities, health, shelter, education and information. It depends not only on income but also access to social services'.[5] Seebohm Rowntree, one of the pioneers in the scientific measurement of poverty, defined 'primary poverty' as 'the minimum necessaries for the maintenance of merely physical efficiency'.[6] Rowntree described the very austere standard of living that this definition of poverty entailed in his original 1901 study:

> let us clearly understand what 'mere physical efficiency' means. A family living upon the scale allowed for in this estimate must never spend a penny on railway fare or omnibus. They must never go to the country unless they walk. They must never purchase a half-penny newspaper or spend a penny to buy a ticket for a popular concert. They must write no letters to absent children for they cannot afford to pay the postage. They must never contribute anything to their church or chapel, or give any help to a neighbour which costs them money. They cannot save nor can they join a sick club or Trade Union because they cannot pay the necessary subscriptions. Their children must have no pocket money for dolls, marbles or sweets. The father must smoke no tobacco, and must drink no beer. The mother must never buy any pretty clothes for herself or for her children, the character for the family wardrobe as for the family diet being governed by the regulation 'Nothing must be bought but that which is absolutely necessary for the maintenance of physical health, and what is bought must be of the plainest and most economical description'.... Finally, the wage-earner must never be absent from his work for a single day.

Rowntree defined 'secondary poverty' as an income that might provide enough to survive but some money was spent on things that were not essential for subsistence. He calculated that 9.9% of the population of York were in primary poverty and 17.9% were in secondary poverty at the time of his first study.

Rowntree chose this minimal definition of poverty, in part, because he wanted to avoid accusations of exaggerating the scale of the problem. His choice was therefore partly motivated by political concerns, as well as technical considerations. However, this definition also expresses a moral judgement. Deciding that poverty should refer only to very meagre conditions of subsistence is a statement about what an acceptable standard of living is. By the time of his second survey of York in 1936, Rowntree felt that a primary poverty line should allow for expenditure on **social necessities** that are not strictly necessary for survival, such as newspapers.

Rowntree's inclusion of such items reflects the fact that human needs are partly social. This is the key feature of the idea of **relative poverty**. The relative approach to defining poverty is based on the argument that what counts as a 'necessity' varies according to social standards and expectations. The Social Policy analyst most associated with this approach was **Peter Townsend** (1928–2009), who argued that all definitions of poverty, including those described as absolute, are actually relative to the norms and standards of a particular society.[7] Townsend defined poverty as 'the absence or inadequacy of those diets, amenities, standards, services and activities which are customary or common in society'; he proposed that 'Individuals, families and groups in the population can be said to be in poverty when they lack the resources to obtain the types of diet, participate in the activities which are customary, or at least widely encouraged or approved, in the societies which they belong'.[8] One implication of this approach is that as societies vary and change over time, so too does the poverty line, for example, as living standards rise, what might have been a luxury becomes regarded as a social necessity and must be included in calculating poverty. Equally, some things may no longer be regarded as essential and are dropped from the poverty calculation. As was noted in Chapter One, this is one reason why this approach is controversial: those opposed to it argue that ideas about social 'necessities' will inevitably be subjective, and that defining poverty in relation to fluctuating living standards confuses genuine poverty with inequality.[9] Critics also argue that a relative approach means that poverty will always exist as new items are added to calculations of supposedly 'minimum' living standards.[10]

The terms 'absolute' and 'relative' poverty may be convenient ways to distinguish different technical approaches to measuring poverty but the standard distinction between them is simplistic. The Nobel Prize-winning economist **Amartya Sen** suggested that poverty has both absolute and relative components, and any alleged opposition between these approaches is based on a misunderstanding.[11] Sen argues that one flaw in definitions that only relate poverty to social norms and general living standards is that they imply that there would be no poverty in a society where everyone was starving equally. He therefore concludes that any plausible definition of poverty must include a core element of subsistence. However, there is also a relative aspect to poverty beyond the level of basic needs and survival. Sen argues that 'There is a difference between achieving *relatively less than others*, and achieving *absolutely less because of falling behind others*'.[12] The former situation is inequality, but the latter condition is poverty. To appreciate Sen's point, it helps to consider the implications of a passage from Adam Smith's *Wealth of Nations*, which is often quoted in discussions of how poverty should be defined and what counts as a necessity:

> By necessaries I understand, not only the commodities which are indispensably necessary for the support of life, but whatever the custom of the country renders it indecent for creditable people, even of the lowest order, to be without. A linen shirt, for example, is, strictly

speaking, not a necessary of life.… But in the present times, through the greater part of Europe, a creditable day-labourer would be ashamed to appear in public without a linen shirt.… Custom, in the same manner, has rendered leather shoes a necessary of life in England. The poorest creditable person of either sex would be ashamed to appear in public without them.[13]

Smith's argument summarises a key feature of relative approaches to defining poverty – that humans are social beings and our basic needs are socially conditioned. Another famous quotation in discussions of poverty comes from Molly Orshansky, who developed the first federal measures of poverty in the US in the early 1960s, who wrote that 'poverty, like beauty, lies in the eye of the beholder'.[14] This is usually taken to mean that poverty evokes subjective values, but another interpretation is that poverty involves an element of social judgement. As Adam Smith says, those who are too ashamed to participate in social life because they cannot afford whatever is required to appear acceptable without shame and stigma are in a condition of poverty, even if they are not destitute. Further implications of this point are discussed later, but the main issue is that the socially relative aspect of poverty is not simply about some having less than others, it means being cut off from society by not reaching a basic minimum: 'Inequality is concerned solely with the comparison between groups. Relative poverty adds to the comparison the notion of the incapacity to meet certain needs, broadly defined to include participation in society'.[15] Just because someone is not currently suffering from a terminal illness does not mean that they are 'healthy'. Similarly, having enough calories or basic clothing to survive does not mean that someone has avoided poverty; beyond subsistence, there is a threshold of social decency that people must reach to avoid poverty.

Capability

The level of poverty in society is usually calculated using income thresholds, for example, an income less than 60% of median household income (equivalised for different types of household).[16] This is a convenient measure because it is often easier to gather data on income than to collect information on other factors. However, income is only a means to an end. What really matters is the absence of the outcomes that income is used to purchase, and these may be accomplished using means other than income, for example, public welfare services may support living standards without directly transferring money to households (see Chapter Three). Income is therefore an **indirect** proxy measure of poverty. An alternative more **direct** approach is to look at what people actually *do* rather than how much money they have, that is, measure their living standards or consumption.[17] Expenditure and consumption are still proxy measures of outcomes but they are more direct than calculating income. Although it sounds more severe and is a more commonly used term in Social Policy analysis, poverty is actually a less fundamental issue than **deprivation**. Income is a means to acquire necessities but deprivation is the absence of these necessities themselves: 'poverty means not having enough financial resources to meet need. Deprivation on the other hand refers to unmet need, which is caused by a lack of resources of all kinds, not just financial'.[18] Deprivation may be a consequence of low income and a lack of other resources, so income is important, but not for its own sake – only for what it enables people to do.

Focusing on what people can actually do is a central feature of the **Capability** approach to analysing poverty and deprivation. This approach was also developed by Amartya Sen and reflects his view that economic development should be concerned with enhancing the genuine freedom that people can enjoy rather than merely expanding the economy or increasing average annual income.[19] This is one reason why Sen was involved in creating the Human Development Index, used by the United Nations as a measure of social progress, in contrast to the exclusively economic focus on gross domestic product and similar indices.[20] The Capability approach is characterised by a complex thicket of concepts that require careful consideration, but it provides interesting ways of thinking about poverty, deprivation and social exclusion. Sen argues that well-being is made up of **functionings**. These are the things that someone can achieve – what they can do and be, the actual outcomes or states of affairs that they accomplish.[21] Sen sometimes refers to them as *realised* functionings.[22] Important examples of functionings include being 'adequately nourished, being in good health … being happy, having self-respect, and taking part in the life of the community'.[23] In addition to these actually realised functionings, individuals also have outcomes that they *could* achieve should they choose to, that is, opportunities and options. An individual's **capability set** consists of the combination of functionings that they could achieve (if they wanted to) and what they have actually achieved. The capability set describes an individual's effective life options.[24] The capability approach is therefore interested in people's genuine or substantive opportunities to realise their potential. Sen describes poverty as 'capability deprivation' – a level of resources so low that it significantly limits the range of an individual's possible and achievable functionings.

An individual's quality of life depends not only upon the outcomes that they achieve, but also upon the options that they have. Therefore, the capability approach is concerned with the conditions in which people make choices and their opportunities to make genuinely free ones.[25] As Sen explains: 'we have to examine … the extent to which people have the opportunity to achieve outcomes that they value and have reason to value'.[26] This requires understanding the conditions in which people form their preferences, rather than taking these as given, as neoclassical economics does with the concept of utility.[27] Sen illustrates this by contrasting famine and fasting – understanding this difference requires looking beyond someone's outcomes and accomplished functionings to consider their choices. Sen does not itemise which capabilities or functionings he thinks are essential, although other theorists have expressed views on this.[28] This silence is consistent with Sen's emphasis on the importance of individual agency and freedom of choice.[29] People have their own ideas about the good life and this is neither universal nor fixed, 'pure theory cannot "freeze" a list of capabilities for all societies for all time to come, irrespective of what the citizens come to understand and value'.[30]

The capability approach aligns with the idea of **positive freedom**. Isaiah Berlin described this as the condition of being in control of one's own fate, of possessing the freedom *to* accomplish things. This contrasts with the idea of **negative freedom**, which means being able to act as one prefers without interference (except when this would curtail the freedom of others). Negative freedom means 'not being prevented from choosing as I do', or freedom *from* constraints.[31] From a capabilities perspective, genuine freedom means the opportunity to realise the life that one has freely chosen. Such freedom may be inhibited by various incapacities, including a lack of resources. As J.K. Galbraith put it: 'Nothing ... sets a stronger limit on the liberty of the citizen than a total absence of money'.[32] From a capabilities perspective, promoting positive freedom requires removing barriers that prevent people from achieving the life that they have freely chosen for themselves. The capability approach therefore supports measures that enhance social inclusion, if necessary by providing the resources to ensure that freedom is genuine and rights are effective rather than an existing only on paper.[33] Thinking of freedom and social inclusion in terms of capability challenges narrow ideas of economic growth and development, and requires considering growth *for what* and *for whom*. Sen argues that inclusive development ought to enhance capabilities and reduce unfreedoms, particularly those imposed upon women and children.[34] Other commentators have outlined further implications of this approach: 'a politics of capabilities would endow people ... with adequate, fair and efficient resources: with effective rights to social deliberation and participation, with benefits and collective services focused on the development of personal and collective capabilities'.[35] This does not just apply to the developing world. The capability approach provides a way of conceptualising the social and economic barriers that particular individuals and groups encounter and that can lead to their exclusion, including people with disabilities.[36]

Defining social exclusion

'Social exclusion' is undoubtedly a contested term. Its chequered history and flexibility has encouraged widespread use but also a variety of definitions. The range of possible interpretations has led some to criticise it as too elastic to be useful[37]: 'exclusion appears to be a very vague term – loaded with numerous economic, social, political and cultural connotations and dimensions ... the expression is so evocative, ambiguous, multidimensional and elastic that it can be defined in many different ways'.[38]

The history of 'social exclusion'

The first use of the term 'social exclusion' in Social Policy is generally attributed to René Lenoir, the Secretary of State for Social Action in the French Government, who, in 1974, identified 10% of the French population as 'the excluded'.[39] This referred to destitute and extremely marginal groups outside mainstream society, such as problem drug users, abused children, multi-problem households and what Lenoir described as 'delinquents' and 'social misfits'.[40] This concern reflected the principle in the French Republican political tradition that there is a collective responsibility for citizens.[41] It also related to the influential ideas of solidarity, *conscience collective* and anomie central to the theories of Émile Durkheim (1858–1917), France's greatest sociologist.[42]

The term became more common in the UK and throughout Europe in the 1980s and 1990s, largely due to the influence of the European Union, as it was considered less controversial than the word 'poverty'.[43] One of the attractions of the term 'social exclusion' throughout this time was its vagueness, which allowed politicians from many different countries and opposing political outlooks to agree on a succession of National Action Plans on Social Inclusion. Indeterminate terms can be politically convenient, and the vagueness of 'social exclusion' at that time strengthened its acceptability.[44] The term was attractive because it was 'imprecise, but nonetheless worthy-sounding', and 'its introduction can be seen as an example of policy making by subterfuge'.[45]

The capacity of the term to slide between different meanings may have accelerated its uptake but it did not help clarification, which was only attempted after it had already become widely used in debates and policy reforms. The result is that there is a 'series of overlapping national discourses of exclusion rather than a pan-European consensus', and the concept became 'a curious amalgam of a liberal, Anglo-Saxon concern with poverty and a more conservative continental concern with moral integration and social order'.[46]

The Labour government elected in Britain in 1997 enthusiastically adopted the phrase 'social exclusion', with one of the leading government figures describing it as 'one of the great scourges of modern times' and stating that the government's 'vision is to end social exclusion'.[47] The concept was given greater prominence by the creation of the Social Exclusion Unit within the UK Cabinet Office. However, over the course of its time in office, the Labour government increasingly focused on a narrower version of social inclusion – defined by participation in the labour market (discussed further in the following).

It is clear that social exclusion is more than simply a euphemism for poverty and is a much richer multidimensional idea.[48] Social exclusion is used to understand the various barriers that limit the ability of some to participate effectively in social life and how these interrelate. Low income is a particularly important factor, but 'Social exclusion is a broader concept than poverty, encompassing not only low material means but the inability to participate effectively in economic, social, political and cultural life, and, in some characterisations, alienation and distance from the mainstream society'.[49] Poverty means deprivation due to low income but social exclusion goes beyond this; the distinction is between:

> *poverty* as a lack of material resources, especially income, necessary to participate in British society and *social exclusion* as a more comprehensive formulation which refers to the dynamic process of being shut out, fully or partially, from any of the social, economic, political and cultural systems which determine the social integration of a person in society. Social exclusion may, therefore, be seen as the denial (or non-realisation) of the civil, political and social rights of citizenship.[50]

Social exclusion can occur as a result of a lack of resources or a lack of access to the rights, goods or services that most people regard as essential.[51] The UK National Centre for Social Research described social exclusion as 'living in society, but not having the opportunity to participate in the normal activities of citizens in that society'[52] – or even more simply: exclusion means involuntary non-participation in social life.

Social exclusion is not a metaphor, but can be a quite literal experience, as economic deprivation in particular can lead to **social isolation** and disengagement. In *The Other America* – a study of poverty in the early 1960s that influenced President Lyndon Johnson's 'War on Poverty' programme – Harrington argued that those experiencing poverty become invisible as they fall from the sight of mainstream society. Low income, in particular, can lead to social withdrawal as many activities involve unaffordable expenses. For example, unemployed benefit recipients experiencing prolonged poverty can become housebound, as they:

> become 'locked into poverty' so that their home becomes a prison. When they had a job, it was somewhere that most were glad to return to; but poor and out of work they find that their home is 'a mouth that eats up' their money before they start to buy food for themselves. In their attempt to cope, they cut themselves off from others.[53]

The capability to mix with others and 'participate in the activities of the community' are important aspects of full membership of society.[54] Poverty can prevent this, and the concept of social exclusion captures this effect and also less tangible aspects of deprivation, including 'loss of status, power, self-esteem and expectations'.[55] This relates to the earlier point about the shaming effects of poverty and exclusion. Sen notes that Adam Smith's view of poverty as including not being able to appear in public without shame 'is a good example of a capability deprivation that takes the form of social exclusion'.[56] The sting of stigma and humiliation felt by those unable to maintain self-respect due to low income has been documented in international studies and is a common experience across diverse countries at different stages of economic development.[57] This shame undermines self-esteem and causes people to retreat socially as they try to conceal their deprivation.[58] Studies of people struggling to get by on inadequate incomes found that they 'often spoke of avoiding settings in which they might be "outed" or otherwise shamed, such as family gatherings, community events or social outings'.[59] Poverty and deprivation may therefore be hidden by the very people it marginalises, leading others to be unaware of its scale and effects.[60]

Social exclusion also results in powerlessness and a lack of voice as excluded groups feel unable to change institutions that they cannot access or influence processes in which they do not participate, such as political systems or how services upon which they may rely operate.[61] Lower-income groups are less likely to vote or engage in other organised political activities, which leads to a 'class gap' in political participation. For example, voting turnout in the 2010 UK general election was about 50% among the lowest income groups compared to over 70% among higher-income voters.[62] Political disengagement is partly due to the constraints that life on a low income impose, such as unaffordable transport costs. However, it also reflects a deeper sense of alienation and corrosive resignation.[63] Prolonged deprivation is also stressful and alienating, which is one reason that it is strongly associated with lower levels of physical and mental health.[64] The experience of poverty and exclusion undermines people's sense of agency and their personal and **political efficacy**, that is, belief in their capacity to change their circumstances and their level of faith in political institutions. Deprivation causes people to feel trapped and powerless and their struggle to cope places them under relentless pressure. Such people are not often heard, but when listened to, they are able to describe their experience eloquently: 'you feel like life's doing things to you, you're not in control of life'.[65]

The broader meaning of social exclusion reflects, in part, its intellectual origin in European Christian Democrat and Republican political theory, in contrast to the more Anglo-American liberal tradition associated with the idea of poverty.[66] However, some commentators have warned against overstating the contrast between the concepts of poverty and social exclusion as there are overlaps between them.[67] Townsend's account of relative poverty is a strand of the English-speaking tradition that resembles Continental ideas of social exclusion.[68] Townsend argued that poverty means where 'resources are so seriously below those commanded by the average family or individual that they [the poor] are in effect excluded from ordinary living patterns, customs and activities'.[69] Social exclusion and poverty might not be the same, but they are connected 'with an umbilical link: low income'.[70]

Measuring social exclusion

The multidimensional nature of social exclusion makes it challenging to measure its scale and chart trends over time. A vital initial step in measuring any social issue is **operationalisation**, which is the process of converting ideas into empirical concepts and variables on which information can be gathered. Operational definitions use *indicators* as proxy measures of a concept. These are pointers or signposts used to identify the issue. Indicators are often rough markers of the item of interest and should not be confused with the phenomenon itself.[71] For example, low birthweight might be a convenient aggregate indicator of variations in deprivation between groups but it does not measure it directly. It is an indirect pointer – poverty can exist without this factor and the relationship between low birthweight and deprivation is mediated by other factors at an individual level. It is also important to distinguish between **risk factors** associated with an outcome or issue and the causes of that condition.[72] Risk factors indicate the relative chances of some outcome occurring but they do not bring it about, for example, old age is generally associated with but does not itself cause poverty, as shown by the fact that not all older people are income-deprived.

One example of conflating indicators, symptoms and causes is the UK government's Troubled Families programme. This programme targeted families that the government claimed 'have problems and cause problems to the community around them, putting high costs on the public sector'.[73] The government estimated that there were 120,000 such families in Britain and that they cost the UK taxpayer £9 billion per year through the demands they place on social welfare and public services. However, it has been suggested that the figure of 120,000 troubled families 'turns out to be a factoid – something that takes the form of a fact, but is not'.[74] This figure was derived from analysis of the Family and Children Study undertaken by the Social Exclusion Task Force for the previous UK government, which found that 2% of families were 'severely multiply disadvantaged' as they had five or more characteristics (out of a maximum of seven) associated with social exclusion.[75] The purpose of the Task Force's *Families at Risk* report was to identify families in greatest need of intensive support; there was no evidence that they were particularly 'troublesome', for example, involved in crime or anti-social behaviour. However, this analysis was turned upside down for the Troubled Families programme, which used research aimed at identifying families who *experienced* multiple disadvantages to identify them as the *cause* of a different set of problems. By confusing the relationships between social conditions and associated features (ie risk factors) with causes – based on alleged characteristics – families *with* troubles came to be portrayed as 'troublesome families'.

The decisive quality of any concept or measure is its validity, that is, whether the definition and indicators used genuinely correspond to and capture the phenomenon (see Chapter Two). Devising legitimate and accurate operational definitions of complex social phenomena requires expert understanding of the issue and considerable intellectual craft. Operationalisation is a skill requiring specialised methodological training and one reason why formal research remains indispensable for Social Policy analysis, alongside participatory, community-based and user-led research.

A range of conditions and experiences must be considered to identify and measure social exclusion. What these should be and which indicators are most suitable to capture them is a matter of judgement, but they would need to include factors that express the relative capacity to participate in economic, social, political and cultural life, as well as less tangible sentiments and attitudes relating to efficacy and alienation. This means that a battery of indicators and multiple sources of evidence are required to measure social exclusion. For example, the New Policy Institute used 50 indicators to capture and track changes in the first of its annual analyses of social exclusion in Britain in 1998, while the social inclusion strategy launched by the UK government in 1999 used 59 indicators.[76] Table 4.1 summarises the principal dimensions of two alternative operational frameworks developed in the UK to measure social exclusion. Each outlines a small number of broad dimensions that comprise several sub-fields and indicators.

Table 4.1: Alternative dimensions of social exclusion

Centre for Analysis of Social Exclusion[a]		Bristol Social Exclusion Matrix[b]	
Dimension	*Indicators*	*Dimension*	*Domain and Indicators*
Consumption – capacity to acquire and use goods and services	• Income below half of national mean	Resources	• Material and economic (income, necessities, home ownership, assets/savings, debt, perceived poverty) • Service access (public services, utilities, transport, private services, financial services) • Social resources (confined to institutions, social support, family contact)
Production and economic participation	• Not employed • Not in education or training	Participation	• Economic (paid work, unpaid work and care, employment status, quality of work) • Social (social participation, social roles) • Cultural and educational (skills, educational attainment, educational access, leisure access, Internet access) • Political and civic (citizenship status, voting, civic efficacy, voluntary activities)
Political engagement	• Voting • Membership of a political organisation	Quality of life	• Health and well-being (physical condition, mental health, disability, personal development, self-esteem and efficacy, stigma, self-harm, substance abuse) • Environment (housing quality, neighbourhood safety and satisfaction, access to open spaces) • Crime (victimisation risk, perceived safety, bullying and harassment, discrimination, criminal record, anti-social behaviour, imprisonment)
Social interaction and community integration	• Lacking social support		

Sources: [a] Burchardt, T., Le Grand, J. and Piachaud, D. (2002) 'Degrees of Exclusion', in Hills, J., Le Grand, J. and Piachaud, D. (eds) *Understanding Social Exclusion*. Oxford: Oxford University Press, p 34. [b] Levitas, R., Pantazis, C., Fahmy, E., Gordon, D., Lloyd, E. and Patsios, D. (2007) *The Multi-Dimensional Analysis of Social Exclusion*. Bristol: Department of Sociology and School for Social Policy, Townsend Centre for the International Study of Poverty and Bristol Institute for Public Affairs, pp 86–96.

The purpose of the elaborate and technically challenging process of defining and operationalising social exclusion is to ensure that justice is done to its complex and multidimensional nature, and to improve understanding of how factors combine to create different paths to exclusion. For example, there are complex relationships between the economic participation, resources and consumption dimensions of social exclusion. Over half of those experiencing poverty in the UK in 2013 (ie in households whose income was below 60% of median national income) lived in a household where are least one person was employed.[77] Such households are not necessarily socially isolated or disengaged from civic and political life. It is also possible that any shame or stigma that may be attached to poverty applies less to those in employment, whatever other deprivations they may experience. A high proportion of those classified as self-employed in the UK have spells of low income, but their economic status may provide a degree of respect that other forms of poverty do not.[78] It is therefore important to recognise the multiple components of social exclusion that extend beyond income, and examine their interconnections carefully.

The dynamics of social exclusion

Some theorists argue that the conceptual value of social exclusion is that it refers to 'an ongoing process, as opposed to a timeless state' and that this dynamic aspect is more insightful than the more static condition implied by the term 'poverty'.[79] A particular dynamic feature that distinguishes social exclusion from poverty is duration – a prolonged experience of low income increases the risk of other deprivations and longer-term damage. One factor that has encouraged the use of the concept of social exclusion has been an improvement in longitudinal data, which enables exploration of the dynamics of households' incomes and circumstances.[80] These analyses have found that poverty is not a permanent condition: there is considerable movement into and out of poverty over time, and households have different 'exit rates' reflecting their distinctive composition, needs and capacity to earn.[81] It is important to understand these different income trajectories as some conditions and circumstances are more likely than others to lead to social exclusion, and each requires distinct policy responses.[82] For example, the risk of social exclusion is relatively low for those whose poverty is temporary and passing, as is the case for most higher education students. In contrast, groups that experience persistent poverty (ie lasting two or more years) or chronic deprivation – repeated and frequent spells of poverty – are more vulnerable to compounded exclusions and require particular types of support. Older people who have retired from the labour market have fewer options to increase their incomes compared to those of working age and may require social protection in the form of direct transfers (ie pensions) or social services and in-kind support, sometimes collectively described as the **social wage**.[83] In contrast, unemployment insurance might be the most effective way to help those whose poverty is transient and due to short-term unemployment. This was the assumption of the 1942 Beveridge

Report, one of the foundations of the British social welfare system (see Chapter Three). The social insurance scheme that this report recommended was based on the assumption that claimants would only be unemployed for a short period and that the overall level of unemployment would be kept low through a policy of maintaining full employment.[84]

One low-income group that has become a recent focus of concern is working-age households vulnerable to recurrent poverty. About 20% of those in poverty at any time in the UK are caught in a **low-pay–no-pay cycle**.[85] Their poverty may be short-term but it is also repeated and an ever-present threat as they move through a revolving door of unemployment and short-term low-paid jobs. Some of the reasons for this low-pay–no-pay cycle are illustrated in Figure 4.1, which shows how personal and household circumstances, structural factors, and labour-market conditions interact to shape access to and exits from employment. Households with limited opportunities to increase their income and/or lacking in savings and assets are vulnerable to any changes that disrupt their capacity to earn (eg ill-health, caring for others) or that create additional needs (eg having children, the breakdown of informal childcare arrangements).[86] Such disruptions and demands make it difficult for them to escape from poverty by a long way or for a long time.

This situation can also lead to longer-term problems as those with low-paid and insecure employment are less able to save, more likely to experience problem

Figure 4.1: Factors shaping the low-pay–no-pay cycle

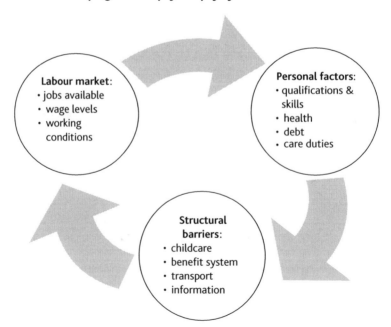

Source: Adapted from Goulden, C. (2010) *Cycles of Poverty, Unemployment and Low Pay*. York: Joseph Rowntree Foundation, p 7.

debt and will face lower incomes and greater vulnerability when they retire from the labour market as they have not been able to accumulate pension entitlements or other assets (see Chapter Three). Although households that are vulnerable to recurrent poverty would be helped by additional cash benefits, this is not in itself enough to improve their longer-term prospects. This requires enhancing their capacity to earn by investing in skills training and improving the quality of jobs available in terms of wages, security and opportunities to progress.

Another significant finding from analysing the dynamics of income and poverty is that there is no permanent or distinct unemployed 'underclass' in Britain and that 'two generations of extensive or permanent worklessness in the same family is a rare phenomenon' (see Chapter Six).[87] In most cases, poverty is temporary, but it is also widespread – between 50% and 60% of the British population are at risk of experiencing a period of poverty at some point in their lives.[88] It has also been estimated that by 2030, 80% of American adults will have experienced at last one period of economic insecurity.[89] In neither country will all those who experience poverty become socially excluded. The evidence shows that neither the British nor American populations can be divided into 'included' and 'excluded' groups. Instead, the concept of social exclusion enables a more nuanced and dynamic analysis of the circumstances and processes that lead into and out of different types of deprivation. Deprivation in one area can lead to multiple forms of exclusion in others and understanding these processes is an important feature of social exclusion analyses. For example, persistent income deprivation places considerable stress on households, contributing to the break-up of relationships, which, in turn, leads to further vulnerabilities: two fifths of the children in lone-parent households in Britain live in families whose income is in the lowest 20%, compared to only 22% of children living in families headed by couples.[90] Struggling on a persistent low income increases the likelihood of experiencing other deprivations, particularly living in lower-quality housing and having less access to quality educational and training services, which could enhance capabilities. Analysing the intersections between household circumstances, the labour market, the social environment and institutions is essential to identify the key junctures and points in the lifecycle where policy interventions may be most required and effective. Sen argues that the major achievement of the literature on social exclusion is that it enriches 'the analysis of processes that lead to capability deprivation … the literature on social deprivation has helped us to understand better the multidimensional nature of deprivation as well as the importance of causal – and often dynamic – connections'.[91]

Interpretations of social exclusion

One final feature of the concept of social exclusion is that, according to some uses, it relates to factors and processes that are features of the social system rather than aspects of individual behaviour or character.[92] For analysts who favour **methodological individualism** – the principle that 'society' is an aggregate and abstract concept and that only individuals *really* exist – this would be a reason to be suspicious of the idea of social exclusion.[93] However, for analysts who focus on social-structural forces, the concept of social exclusion suggests that many forms of deprivation occur for reasons beyond individual control, that is, exclusion 'is the fault of "society" as a whole ... something that is done by some people to other people'.[94] Whether any such exclusion might be deliberate is considered in Chapter Five.[95]

Some commentators have identified different interpretations of social exclusion that centre on this question of **structure** and **agency**, that is, whether social outcomes are determined by collective societal-level patterns and institutions (ie macro-social structures) or are the result of individual choices and actions (ie micro-social agency). Veit-Wilson distinguished between 'weak' and 'strong' uses of the idea of social exclusion.[96] The strong version focuses on the actions of powerful exclusionary groups and social practices, and examines structural forces that lead to exclusion, for example, the physical, economic and social barriers that marginalise people with disabilities. In contrast, the weak interpretation highlights the alleged 'handicapping characteristics' of those who become excluded and considers how they can be helped or compelled to improve themselves and their situation.

The existence and implications of alternative and perhaps even contradictory ideas of social exclusion is one reason why some Social Policy analysts have criticised and rejected the concept.[97] Some are troubled by 'its profound ambiguity' and attribute its popularity – which has waned in the UK since the early 2000s – to its flexibility rather than its analytical clarity.[98] Others have suggested that it adds little to understanding social policy issues not already provided by the idea of poverty, and that it actually promotes individualist or behavioural explanations for deprivation.[99] Some of these criticisms depend upon how the concept is defined and applied. Levitas identified three broad uses – or discourses – of social exclusion in British social policy, each offering alternative accounts of the nature and causes of exclusion.[100] The first is the redistributive (or 'RED') approach to social exclusion, associated with the relative conception of poverty, as outlined by Townsend. In this case, social exclusion means a level of poverty too low to enable social participation, but it also recognises that income is not the only type of resource and that there are other dimensions to social inclusion. This interpretation of the concept also reflects the dynamic nature of social exclusion as a process rather than a permanent condition.[101]

The second version of social exclusion is the 'social integration' approach (or 'SID'). This interprets integration narrowly by equating it with participation in the labour market and paid employment. The SID approach is preoccupied with unemployment and economic inactivity, with little interest in the many other forms of integration and social participation, except in so far as they impact upon employment. The view that economically productive activity is what really matters, and that this means only paid employment, also ignores the value and contribution of unpaid care work.[102] This approach fails to consider how employment might not be enough in itself to enable full social inclusion (eg if it is low-paid) and, in fact, may even limit it in some ways, for example, through the stresses that insecure employment and working anti-social hours place upon household relationships and the limits that they can impose on other social activities.

The final discourse of social exclusion that Levitas identifies is the 'moral underclass' conception (or 'MUD'). This focuses on the alleged deviant values and deficient behaviour of excluded households and communities. Social exclusion is seen as attributable to the breakdown of the traditional family, personal irresponsibility and a lack of moral values, particularly a commitment to work and a misplaced sense of entitlement to welfare support. Supporters of this view argue that such dysfunctional behaviour can become concentrated in particular neighbourhoods, where it contaminates entire communities. As one UK government report put it:

> A 'culture of worklessness' or 'poverty of aspirations' can develop in such areas, generating a vicious and self-perpetuating cycle leading not only to high levels of worklessness but also to crime, deprivation, and social exclusion. It is important that these cycles are broken and these concentrations addressed.[103]

This focus on concentrations of workless households, 'broken' families and benefit dependency repeats long-standing ideas about a dangerous underclass.[104] It is also reflected in some of the statements made in support of the UK government's Troubled Families programme and similar measures.[105] From this perspective, a potential attraction of 'social exclusion' is that it suggests that poverty and a lack of material resources are less important than dysfunctional behaviour in explaining how exclusion occurs. This belief seems to underlie the UK government's proposal to redefine child poverty to focus on behavioural factors rather than household income.[106]

The potential association between the idea of social exclusion and the moral condemnation of those criticised as responsible for their own deprivation is one reason for the reluctance of some Social Policy analysts to adopt and apply this concept. Another concern has been the predominance of the SID version, which recasts exclusion as an essentially economic issue defined by an individual's or group's relationship to the labour market.[107] The equation between social inclusion and labour-market integration is one reason for the popularity of employability, active labour-market and **workfare** programmes (see Chapter Two). This narrow approach strips the concept of much of its analytic value and insight – as a way of exploring the shifting interconnections between different dimensions of social participation.[108] It also reinforces individualist and behavioural explanations that focus on what is supposedly different (and deficient) about those who are excluded rather than the barriers preventing them from fulfilling their capabilities. The more positive idea of social *inclusion* did not achieve the prominence given to social exclusion by successive UK governments and many commentators.[109] Furthermore, 'weaker' versions of social exclusion have dominated policy discussion in the UK, with little consideration given to the exclusionary practices that help create such outcomes (discussed in Chapter Five). As with many contested concepts in Social Policy, social inclusion and exclusion can be applied to either expand or contract analysis and understanding. These concepts come with baggage but also with potential, and must be used conscientiously and with care.

Conclusions

This chapter discussed the question of what it means to be a member of society. In one sense, this is a legal question – societies have regulations that specify membership and the rules of citizenship. However, being part of a society involves far more than a legal status. In British nationality law, there is a status of having 'indefinite leave to remain', which grants people the right to reside and work in the UK. This is a formal and passive idea of citizenship; merely having the right to stay in a place is far from living a full life there or belonging somewhere. Being part of society in a meaningful sense goes beyond a minimal legal right of residence and includes being able to join in the life of the community. The concepts of social inclusion and exclusion express this richer sense of membership and show both what it entails and how it can be impeded.

Social exclusion means not having the full and effective rights of a citizen – the 'denial of civil, political, social, economic and cultural rights' – and the concept enriches the understanding of deprivation by going beyond a concern with low income and lack of resources, vitally important though they are.[110] Understanding social exclusion brings home the multiple forms, processes and consequences of deprivation – of what it is to go without rather than be within the social mainstream. This is evident in Adam Smith's description of deprivation as exclusion from social interaction: the inability to interact freely with others and take part in community life.[111] This is why the case of the Inverness schoolgirl outlined at the beginning of this chapter is an example of social exclusion. In this case, it may not have been poverty that prevented her participating in an activity available to every other pupil, but it is an example of institutions failing to take the measures necessary to ensure that everyone is granted respect and treated equally, which is a requirement of inclusion.[112]

Poverty has been described as a 'corrosive social relation'.[113] Stigma and shame are some of the hidden injuries of exclusion, but it can also create a social distance and segregation that undermines empathy. A degree of interaction and shared understanding between people is required to underpin many social policies, and social exclusion can undermine these bonds.[114] When the physical and social distances between people become too great and people become regarded as 'others' who are different from 'us', then the psychological foundations of empathy are weakened (see 'Othering the poor' in Chapter Two) . This has been demonstrated in neuro-imaging experiments, which show that many people regarded those who are homeless as 'mindless objects [rather] than as fully mindful people' like themselves.[115] Social inclusion counteracts this by implying unity and togetherness; it is based on an idea of a shared commonwealth. The principle of social inclusion could be the basis for insisting on the right to participate as a citizen, while exclusion means a society that fails to provide the support and resources that people with different needs require to do and be what society considers to be normal. Exclusion and inclusion are therefore not merely technical, but also moral, issues, concerned with rights and social justice.[116]

Social exclusion highlights the various ways in which some people can be marginalised and denied effective participation. The multidimensionality of the concept enables the interconnections between different factors to be analysed and to examine which deprivations are connected with poverty directly, which are mediated through other factors and processes, and which are not connected all. For example, some low-income groups, such as students, are not excluded from the social mainstream. Similarly, a young unemployed person from a minority ethnic community is not necessarily socially excluded if they can rely upon supportive networks. One dimension of social exclusion cannot simply be 'read off' from another. Different forms of exclusion interact in distinctive ways and the relations between life events, economic circumstances and policy must be investigated carefully.[117] Having said that, it still remains the case that 'the poor are more likely to be socially excluded and the poorer you are the more socially excluded you are likely to be, but not on all dimensions'.[118]

Social exclusion is a valuable concept because it reflects the genuine complications of deprivation and poverty. It may seem counter-intuitive to commend a concept for introducing greater complexity, but defining and discussing poverty and related issues is not simple, and if a concept replaces a simplistic misinterpretation with a more complicated but more valid account, then it has advanced our understanding.

Notes

1. 'Disabled Girl's Mother Defends School Trip Legal Action Threat', *Inverness Courier*, 30 December 2009. Available at: http://www.inverness-courier.co.uk/Home/Disabled-girls-mother-defends-school-trip-legal-action-threat-5477387.htm. The case was also reported on the BBC's *Reporting Scotland* programme on 23 December 2009.

2. Barry, B. (1998) *Social Exclusion, Social Isolation and the Distribution of Income*. CASEpaper12. London: LSE/CASE, p 1.

3. Independent Living in Scotland (2010) 'Human Rights and Self-Directed Support'. Glasgow: ILiS Policy Briefing 3.

4. United Nations (no date) 'Enable: Development and Human Rights for All'. Available at: http://www.un.org/disabilities/default.asp?id=279 (accessed 31 December 2014).

5. United Nations (1995) 'World Summit for Social Development, Chapter 2: Eradication of Poverty'. Available at: http://www.un.org/esa/socdev/wssd/text-version/agreements/poach2.htm (accessed 1 February 2015).

[6] Rowntree, B.S. (1901) *Poverty: A Study of Town Life*. London: Macmillan, p 134.

[7] The terms 'absolute' and 'relative' poverty are used in rather different and specific ways in discussions of UK measures and policy, and this can lead to some confusion. The UK government uses the term 'absolute poverty' to refer to a baseline in a particular year against which changes in the numbers in poverty over time are compared, for example, in the definition of child poverty, the 'absolute' measure is the number of households who fall below the 2010/11 poverty standard (ie following the election of the Conservative–Liberal Democrat Coalition government). 'Relative poverty', on the other hand, is defined as income less than 60% of the UK median household income in the current year. See Department for Work and Pensions (2012) *Measuring Child Poverty: A Consultation on Better Measures of Child Poverty*. Cm 8483. London: Department for Work and Pensions.

[8] Townsend, P. (1979) *Poverty in the United Kingdom*. London: Penguin, pp 915, 31.

[9] Lanchester, J. (2014) 'There's Poverty in the UK, but We Are Better Off Calling It Inequality', *The Guardian*, 5 September.

[10] Niemietz, K. (2011) *A New Understanding of Poverty: Poverty Measurement and Policy Implications*. London: Institute of Economic Affairs.

[11] Sen, A. (1983) 'Poor, Relatively Speaking', *Oxford Economic Papers*, 35.

[12] Sen (1983), p 155 (emphases in original).

[13] Smith, A. (1776) *An Inquiry in the Nature and Causes of the Wealth of Nation*. London: Methuen (1904 edition).

[14] Orshansky, M. (1969) 'How Poverty Is Measured', *Monthly Labor Review*, 92(2), p 37.

[15] Lister, R. (2004) *Poverty*. Cambridge: Polity, p 23.

[16] Equivalisation involves adjusting the calculation of minimum income by taking into account the needs of different types of household, for example, families with dependent children generally have greater demands on their income than single-person household and so have a higher minimum income requirement. See Office for National Statistics (2012) 'Equivalised Income', in Office for National Statistics, *Family Spending, 2012 Edition*. London: ONS, ch 3. Available at: http://www.ons.gov.uk/ons/rel/family-spending/family-spending/family-spending-2012-edition/art-chapter-3--equivalised-income.html

[17] Ringen S. (1988) 'Direct and Indirect Measures of Poverty', *Journal of Social Policy*, 17(3).

[18] Noble, M., Wright, G., Dibben, C., Smith, G.A.N., McLennan, D., Anttila, C., Barnes, H., Mokhtar, C., Noble, S., Avenell, D., Gardner, J., Covizzi, I. and Lloyd, M. (2003) *The English Indices of Deprivation, 2004 (Revised)*. London: Office of the Deputy Prime Minister/Neighbourhood Renewal Unit, p 9.

[19] Sen, A. (1999) 'The Ends and Means of Development', in Sen, A., *Development as Freedom*. Oxford: Oxford University Press.

[20] See: http://hdr.undp.org/en/content/human-development-index-hdi. Sen was also a member of the Commission invited by President Sarkozy of France to devise alternatives to GDP in measuring national economic and social development, see Report by the Commission on the Measurement of Economic Performance and Social Progress (2009). Available at: http://www.stiglitz-sen-fitoussi.fr/documents/rapport_anglais.pdf

[21] Unterhalter, E. (2003) 'Crossing Disciplinary Boundaries: The Potential of Sen's Capability Approach for Sociologists of Education', *British Journal of Sociology of Education*, 24(5), p 666.

[22] Sen, A. (1997) *Resources, Values and Development*. Cambridge, MA: Harvard University Press.

23 Sen, A. (1992) *Inequality Re-Examined*. Oxford: Clarendon Press, p 40.

24 Sen, A. (1999) *Development as Freedom*. Oxford: Oxford University Press, pp 3–15.

25 Sen, A. (1999) *Commodities and Capabilities*. Oxford: Oxford University Press, p 45.

26 Sen, A. (1999) *Development as Freedom*, p 291.

27 Chang, H.-J. (2014) *Economics: The User's Guide*. London: Pelican, p 121.

28 Nussbaum, M.C. (2011) *Creating Capabilities: The Human Development Approach*. Cambridge, MA: Harvard University Press.

29 Srinivasan, S. (2007) 'No Democracy without Justice: Political Freedom in Amartya Sen's Capability Approach', *Journal of Human Development*, 8(3), p 457.

30 Sen, A.K. (2005) 'Human Rights and Capabilities', *Journal of Human Development*, 6(2), p 158.

31 Berlin, I. (1969) 'Two Concepts of Liberty', in Berlin, I., *Four Essays on Liberty*. Oxford: Oxford University Press, p 31.

32 Galbraith, J.K. (1994) 'The Good Society Has No Underclass', *The Guardian Weekly*, 6 February, p 23.

33 Fukuda-Parr, S. (2003) 'The Human Development Paradigm: Operationalizing Sen's Ideas on Capabilities', *Feminist Economics*, 9(2/3), p 303.

34 Sen, A. (2003) 'Development as Capability Expansion', in Fukuda-Parr, S. and Shiva Kumar, A. K. (eds) *Readings in Human Development*. New York, NY: Oxford University Press.

35 Salais, R. and Villeneuve, R. (eds) (2004) *Europe and the Politics of Capabilities*. Cambridge: Cambridge University Press, p 9.

36 Burchardt, T. (2004) 'Capabilities and Disability: The Capabilities Framework and the Social Model of Disability', *Disability and Society*, 19(7).

37 'Conceptual stretching' is the distortion of a concept beyond cases to which it can be applied with validity. It is an issue particularly relevant in comparative political analyses, and to the question of whether categories and ideas that are appropriate in one location are relevant and applicable elsewhere. Stretching is distinct from 'conceptual travelling', which is the legitimate application of the concept to new cases. Sartori, G. (1970) 'Concept Misformation in Comparative Politics', *The American Political Science Review*, 64(4).

38 Silver, Ü.H. (1994) 'Social Exclusion and Social Solidarity: Three Paradigms', *International Labour Review*, 133(5/6), p 536.

39 Lenoir, R. (1974) *Les Exclus: Un Francais sur Dix*. Paris: Editions du Seuil.

40 See Alcock, P. (2005) 'From Social Security to Social Inclusion: The Changing Policy Climate', *Benefits: The Journal of Poverty and Social Justice*, 43(2). Sen, A. (2000) *Social Exclusion: Concept, Application, and Scrutiny*. Social Development Papers No 1. Manila: Office of Environment and Social Development, Asian Development Bank.

41 Axford, N. (2010) 'Is Social Exclusion a Useful Concept in Children's Services?', *British Journal of Social Work*, 40(3), p 740.

42 Levitas, R. (1996) 'The Concept of Social Exclusion and the New Durkheimian Hegemony', *Critical Social Policy*, 46.

43 Room, G. (1995) 'Poverty and Social Exclusion: The New European Agenda for Policy and Research', in Room, G. (ed) *Beyond The Threshold: The Measurement and Analysis of Social Exclusion*. Bristol: The Policy Press.

44 Lee, P. and Murie, A. (1999) *Literature Review of Social Exclusion*. Edinburgh: The Scottish Office Central Research Unit, p 13.

[45] Marsh, A. and Mullins, D. (1998) 'The Social Exclusion Perspective and Housing Studies: Origins, Applications and Limitations', *Housing Studies*, 13(6), p 751.

[46] Levitas, R. (1998) *The Inclusive Society? Social Exclusion and New Labour*. London: Macmillan, p 22.

[47] Mandelson, P. (1997) *Labour's Next Steps: Tackling Social Exclusion*. Pamphlet 581. London: Fabian Society.

[48] Hills, J. (1997) 'A CASE for Investigation', *LSE Magazine*, 9(2).

[49] Duffy, quoted in Oppenheim, C. and Harker, L. (1996) *Poverty: The Facts* (3rd edn). London: Child Poverty Action Group, p 18.

[50] Walker, A. (1997) 'The Strategy of Inequality', in Walker, A. and Walker, C. (eds) *Britain Divided: The Growth of Social Exclusion in the 1980s and 1990s*. London: Child Poverty Action Group, p 8 (emphases in original).

[51] Levitas, R., Pantazis, C., Fahmy, E., Gordon, D., Lloyd, E. and Patsios, D. (2007) *The Multi-Dimensional Analysis of Social Exclusion*. Bristol: Department of Sociology and School for Social Policy, Townsend Centre for the International Study of Poverty and Bristol Institute for Public Affairs, p 9.

[52] Hinds, K. (2000) *Social Exclusion: What Is It, and How Can We Measure It in a Meaningful Way?* 15 November. Edinburgh: Royal Statistical Society/Social Research Association.

[53] Sinfield, A. (1985) 'Being Out of Work', in Littler, C. (ed) *The Experience of Work*. Aldershot: Gower, p 203.

[54] Sen, A. (1983) 'Poor, Relatively Speaking', *Oxford Economic Papers*, 25(2), p 162.

[55] Choitz, V. (1998) *An Inclusive Society: Strategies for Tackling Poverty*. London: Institute for Public Policy Research, p 2, 'Summary'.

[56] Sen (2000), p 7.

[57] Gubrium, E.K, Pellissery, S. and Lødemel, I. (eds) (2013) *The Shame of It: Global Perspectives on Anti-Poverty Policies*. Bristol: Policy Press. See also Reyles, D.Z. (2007) *The Ability to Go About without Shame: A Proposal for Internationally Comparable Indicators of Shame and Humiliation*. Working Paper No 03. Oxford: Oxford Poverty & Human Development Initiative.

[58] Jo, Y.N. (2012) 'Psycho-Social Dimensions of Poverty: When Poverty Becomes Shameful', *Critical Social Policy*, 33(3), p 514.

[59] Walker, R. and Chase, E. (2014) 'Adding to the Shame of Poverty: The Public, Politicians and the Media', *Poverty*, 148(Summer), p 10.

[60.] Beresford, P., Green, D., Lister, R. and Woodward, K. (1999) *Poverty First Hand: Poor People Speak for Themselves*. London: Child Poverty Action Group.

[61] Becker, S. (1991) 'Introduction: From Enterprise to Opportunity', in Becker, S. (ed) *Windows of Opportunity: Public Policy and the Poor*. London: Child Poverty Action Group, p 2. See also Ignatieff, M. (2013) *Fire and Ashes: Success and Failure in Politics*. London: Harvard University Press, pp 104–6.

[62] Skelton, D. (2013) 'Reviving the Tory Tradition of Social Reform', in Derbyshire, J. (ed) *Poverty in the UK: Can It Be Eradicated?* London: Prospect Publishing, p 47.

[63] Clark, T. and Health, A. (2014) *Hard Times: The Divisive Toll of the Economic Slump*. Newhaven, CT: Yale University Press.

[64] Percy-Smith, J. (2000) 'Introduction: The Contours of Social Exclusion', in Percy-Smith, J. (ed) *Policy Responses to Social Exclusion: Towards Inclusion*. Maidenhead: Open University Press, p 10.

See also Burns, H. (2012) *Kilbrandon's Vision – Healthier Lives, Better Futures. The Tenth Kilbrandon Lecture*. Edinburgh: Scottish Government, pp 28–31.

[65] Cohen, R., Coxall, J., Craig, G. and Sadiq-Sangster, A. (1992) *Hardship Britain: Being Poor in the 1990s*. London: Child Poverty Action Group, pp 11, 28.

[66] Room (1995), pp 5–6.

[67] Rosenfield, J. (2010) '"The Meaning of Poverty" and Contemporary Quantitative Poverty Research', *British Journal of Sociology*, 61, p 106.

[68] Poverty and Social Exclusion Survey (no date) 'Social Exclusion'. Available at: http://www.poverty.ac.uk/definitions-poverty/social-exclusion (accessed 1 February 2015).

[69] Townsend (1979), p 31.

[70] Dean, M. (1997) 'Haunted by the Breadline', *The Guardian*, 1 October, p 2.

[71] Spicker, P. (2004) 'Developing Indicators: Issues in the Use of Quantitative Data About Poverty', *Policy and Politics*, 32(4).

[72] Veit-Wilson J. (2013) 'Measuring Child Poverty: A Response to the Consultation', 12 February. Available at: https://northeastchildpoverty.wordpress.com/2013/02/12/measuring-child-poverty-a-response-to-the-consultation/ (accessed 1 February 2015).

[73] Department for Communities and Local Government (2012) 'Helping Troubled Families Turn Their Lives Around'. Available at: https://www.gov.uk/government/policies/helping-troubled-families-turn-their-lives-around (accessed 1 February 2015).

[74] Levitas R. (2012) *There May be 'Trouble' Ahead: What We Know About Those 120,000 'Troubled' Families*. Policy Working Paper 3. Bristol: Poverty and Social Exclusion in the UK.

[75] Social Exclusion Task Force (no date) *Families at Risk: Background on Families with Multiple Disadvantages*. London: Cabinet Office. The seven characteristics identified by the Social Exclusion Task Force were: (1) no parent in the family is in work; (2) family lives in poor-quality or overcrowded housing; (3) no parent has any qualifications; (4) mother has mental health problems; (5) at least one parent has a long-standing limiting illness, disability or infirmity; (6) family has low income (below 60% of the median); and (7) family cannot afford a number of food and clothing items.

[76] Howarth, C., Kenway, P., Palmer, G. and Miorelli, R. (1999) *Monitoring Poverty and Social Exclusion, 1999*. York: Joseph Rowntree Foundation/New Policy Institute. The 2013 report used 38 indicators, see MacInnes, T., Aldridge, H., Bushe, S., Tinson, A. and, Born, T.B. (2014) *Monitoring Poverty and Social Exclusion, 2014*. York: Joseph Rowntree Foundation. Department for Work and Pensions (2007) *Opportunities for All: Indicators Update 2007*. London: Department for Work and Pensions, Family, Poverty and Work Division.

[77] MacInnes, T., Aldridge, H., Bushe, S., Kenway, P. and Tinson, A. (2013) *Monitoring Poverty and Social Exclusion 2013*. York: Joseph Rowntree Foundation.

[78] The increase in self-employment in the UK in recent decades is not necessarily a sign of entrepreneurialism or new businesses being created, but a sign of those who were previously employees being hired on a freelance basis in a general shift towards more precarious employment. See Hatfield, I. (2015) *Self-Employment in Europe*. London: Institute for Public Policy Research.

[79] Byrne, D. (1999) *Social Exclusion*. Buckingham: Open University Press, p 1.

[80] Alcock, P. (2004) 'The Influence of Dynamic Perspectives on Poverty Analysis and Anti-Poverty Policy in The UK', *Journal of Social Policy*, 33(3).

[81] Kemp, P.A. (2005) 'Escape Routes from Poverty', *Benefits*, 13(3).

[82] Walker, R. (1999) 'Lifetime Poverty Dynamics', in Hills, J. (ed) *Persistent Poverty and Lifetime Inequality: The Evidence*. CASEreport 5. London: Centre for Analysis of Social Exclusion/HM Treasury.

[83] Sefton, T. (2002) *Recent Changes in the Distribution of the Social Wage*. CASEpaper 62. London: Centre for Analysis of Social Exclusion.

[84] Jones, K. (1991) *The Making of Social Policy in Britain, 1830–1990*. London: Athlone, pp 129–30.

[85] Fuertes, V. and McQuaid, R. (2012) 'Recurrent Poverty and the Low-Pay–No-Pay Poverty Cycle', *Scottish Anti-Poverty Review*, 15(Winter), p 10.

[86] Tomlinson, M. and Walker, R. (2010) *Recurrent Poverty: The Impact of Family and Labour Market Changes*. York: Joseph Rowntree Foundation.

[87] Shildrick, T., MacDonald, R., Furlong, A., Roden, J. and Crow, R. (2012) *Are 'Cultures of Worklessness' Passed Down the Generations?* York: Joseph Rowntree Foundation.

[88] Spicker, P. (2002) *Poverty and the Welfare State: Dispelling the Myths*. Working Paper. London: Catalyst. Available at: http://www.rightsnet.org.uk/pdfs/catalystaugust2002.pdf (accessed 1 February 2015). See also Kemp, P.A. (2005).

[89] Aghai, V. (2014) *America's Shrinking Middle Class*. Bloomington, IN: AuthorHouse, p 218.

[90] Skelton (2013), p 47.

[91] Sen (2000), p 26.

[92] Axford (2010), p 743.

[93] Lukes, S. (1968) 'Methodological Individualism Reconsidered', *British Journal of Sociology*, 19(2).

[94] Byrne (1999), p 2.

[95] Atkinson, A.B. (1998) 'Social Exclusion, Poverty and Unemployment', in Atkinson, A.B. and Hills, J. (eds) *Exclusion, Employment and Opportunity*. CASE paper 4. London: Centre for Analysis of Social Exclusion, pp 7–8.

[96] Veit-Wilson, J. (1998) *Setting Adequacy Standards*. Bristol: The Policy Press, p 45.

[97] Oyen, E. (1997) 'The Contradictory Concepts of Social Exclusion and Social Inclusion', in Gore, C. and Figueiredo, J.B. (eds) *Social Exclusion and Anti-Poverty Policy*. Geneva: International Institute of Labour Studies, p 63. Winlow, S. and Hall, S. (2013) *Rethinking Social Exclusion: The End of the Social?* London: Sage.

[98] Cameron, A. (2005) 'Geographies of Welfare and Exclusion: Initial Report', *Progress in Human Geography*, 29(2), p 194. Levitas (1998) *The Inclusive Society?*, p 178.

[99] Bradshaw, J. (2004) 'How Has the Notion of Social Exclusion Developed?', in Cookson, R., Sainsbury, R. and Glendininng, C. (eds) *Jonathan Bradshaw on Social Policy: Selected Writings 1972–2001*. York: York Publishing Services, p 236.

[100] Levitas (1998) *The Inclusive Society?*.

[101] Levitas, R. (1998) 'Social Exclusion and the New Breadline Britain Survey', in Bradshaw, J., Gordon, D., Levitas, R., Middleton, S., Pantazis, C., Payne, S. and Townsend, P. (eds) *Perceptions of Poverty and Social Exclusion*. Bristol: Townsend Centre for International Poverty Research, p 39.

[102] Marçal, K. (2015) *Who Cooked Adam Smith's Dinner? A Story About Women and Economics*. London: Portobello Books.

[103] HM Treasury and Department for Work and Pensions (2003) *Full Employment in Every Region*. London: Office of the Deputy Prime Minister, para 5.5.

[104] Welshman, J. (2013) *Underclass: A History of the Excluded since 1880* (2nd edn). London: Bloomsbury.

[105] The Troubled Families programme bears some resemblance to the Family Pathfinder programme, launched in 2007. See York Consulting (2010) *Turning Around the Lives of Families with Multiple Problems: An Evaluation of the Family and Young Carer Pathfinders Programme*. Research Report DFE-RR154. London: Department for Education.

[106] Wintour, P. (2015) 'Government to Scrap Child Poverty Target Before Tax Credits Cut', *The Guardian*, 1 July.

[107] Powell, M., Boyne, G. and Ashworth, R. (2001) 'Towards a Geography of People Poverty and Place Poverty', *Policy & Politics*, 29(2), p 245.

[108] Lister, R. (1997) *Citizenship: Feminist Perspectives*. Basingstoke: Macmillan, p 196.

[109] See Cameron (2005). This applies less to some of the devolved UK administrations, for example, the Scottish Executive (as it was then known) initially emphasised social inclusion before this concept was replaced by 'social justice' and subsequently 'solidarity' after the Scottish National Party assumed office in 2007. See Scottish Executive (2004) *Social Justice: A Scotland Where Everyone Matters*. Edinburgh: Scottish Executive.

[110] Oppenheim, C. and Harker, L. (1996) *Poverty: The Facts* (3rd edn). London: Child Poverty Action Group, p 19.

[111] Sen (2000), pp 4, 7.

[112] Witcher, S. (2013) *Inclusive Equality: A Vision for Social Justice*. Bristol: The Policy Press.

[113] Lister (2004), p 7.

[114] Jo (2012), p 516.

[115] Epley, N. (2014) *Mindwise: How We Understand What Others Think, Believe, Feel and Want*. London: Allen Lane, p 48. This is not a blindness that is unique to American university students, in *The Road to Wigan Pier*, George Orwell (1937, London: Gollancz/Left Book Club) considers how many well-educated people at the time assumed that those who had the misfortune to live in slums were somehow inured to the experience: 'It struck me then that we are mistaken when we say that "It isn't the same for them as it would be for us," and that people bred in the slums can imagine nothing but the slums. For what I saw in her face was not the ignorant suffering of an animal. She knew well enough what was happening to her – understood as well as I did how dreadful a destiny it was to be kneeling there in the bitter cold, on the slimy stones of a slum backyard, poking a stick up a foul drain-pipe'.

[116] Sen, A. (2010) *The Idea of Justice*. London: Penguin.

[117] Percy-Smith, J. (2000) 'Introduction: The Contours of Social Exclusion', in Percy-Smith, J. (ed) *Policy Responses to Social Exclusion: Towards Inclusion*. Maidenhead: Open University Press, p 11.

[118] Bradshaw (2004), p 236.

FIVE

How does inequality persist?
Social closure

Social closure: key points
- Income and wealth inequalities have widened and social mobility has declined in the UK and US, mostly due to large increases in the incomes of higher earners.
- Social closure refers to the various ways in which groups restrict access to scarce resources and opportunities.
- Advantages are maintained by opportunity-hoarding within exclusive networks and controlling different forms of capital.

Introduction

Inequalities of income and declining social mobility are troubling many people and shaping the political agenda as never before. President Barack Obama expressed his concern about a 'relentless, decades-long trend' in the US: 'a dangerous and growing inequality and lack of upward mobility that has jeopardized middle-class America's basic bargain – that if you work hard, you have a chance to get ahead'.[1] Similarly, all of the major British political parties express their commitment to promoting social mobility and claim to be concerned about growing inequalities of income and wealth. The former British Prime Minister John Major stated that his ambition was to make Britain a 'classless society'.[2] His successor, Tony Blair, declared that his mission was 'to break down the barriers that hold people back, to create real upward social mobility, a society that is open'.[3] These sentiments were echoed by the UK Coalition government elected in 2010, with Prime Minister David Cameron and his Deputy Nick Clegg stating: 'We both want a Britain where social mobility is unlocked; where everyone, regardless of background, has the chance to rise as high as their talents and ambitions allow them'.[4]

Types of inequality
It is important to distinguish between different forms of equality. In his 1754 *Discourse on the Origin and Basis of Inequality*, Jean-Jacques **Rousseau** distinguished between 'natural' inequalities, which individuals are born with, and 'moral' or 'political' inequalities, which are socially generated, such as inherited wealth. He argued that the former are unavoidable and add to the variety of life, but the latter might be objectionable if they involve unjustifiable advantages or discrimination.[5]

There are also several forms of social inequality:

- **Equality of persons** (or *ontological equality*) is the view that all human beings are fundamentally equal and share certain innate properties and inherent human rights. This is expressed in the American Declaration of Independence and enshrined in the United Nations Convention of Human Rights. This position would also require equal treatment of similar cases, so that social systems (such as the law) operate without favour or prejudice.
- **Equality of opportunity** 'means that access to important social institutions should be open to all on universalistic grounds, especially by achievement and talent'.[6] This is the idea that there should be a 'level playing field' in competition for particular positions – a position closely associated with support for social mobility.[7]
- **Equality of conditions** is the view that a genuinely level playing field between competitors requires an equal starting point, which means removing unfair advantages, such as the effects of inherited wealth or other unearned privileges. Creating equal starting conditions might require transforming the circumstances and social forces that generate inequality in the first place. This approach is associated with egalitarian ideas and accused by critics of favouring a levelling down and social uniformity.
- **Equality of outcomes** or result might require applying different policies to particular social groups to compensate for past inequalities of treatment or the denial of equal opportunities. An example of this would be positive discrimination measures designed to redress systemic disadvantages.

Few social reformers or Social Policy analysts advocate complete social uniformity.[8] However, achieving equal treatment in welfare services (based on the belief in equal value) might require accommodating significant differences (eg removing barriers encountered by people with disabilities), which means that standardised provision for all might not be suitable.

Whether or not inequality is regarded as wrong also depends on judgements about rights (and principles of social justice) and fairness, which reflect beliefs about how society operates and what causes social outcomes.

The extent of social mobility is often taken as a measure of the equality of economic and social opportunity. High degrees of social mobility suggest an open and **meritocratic** society, where achievements reflect ability and effort rather than unfair advantages, such as inherited privilege or favouritism.[9] There are also believed to be economic benefits to enabling competition for higher occupations. It has been estimated that if the UK had the same level of social mobility as the most open societies in the developed world, national income would increase by £150 billion each year, equivalent to gross domestic product (GDP) growth of 4%.[10]

However, there is growing evidence of widening inequalities and declining social mobility in several developed nations. It appears likely that, for the first time in decades, younger generations in many developed countries may have lower standards of living than their parents.[11] This has led to resentment and a questioning of the legitimacy of social and economic systems that do not seem to improve well-being, as shown by the Spanish *Indignados* protests, the sporadic Occupy movement and the emergence of radical and extremist political movements in several European countries.[12] It is important to consider how these developments relate to welfare policies and systems. The concept of 'social closure' is particularly useful to analyse these issues and illuminate how social inequalities are sustained and widened. However, it is first of all necessary to establish that there are, in fact, substantial and growing inequalities in income and opportunities in many societies.

Inequalities of income and opportunity

To understand and interpret the evidence on inequality, it is necessary to distinguish between income and wealth and also the situation at a particular point and trends over time. In assessments of equality, **income** refers to earnings from employment and other sources, such as dividends from stocks, shares or other investments, interest from deposits and bonds, rents received, and business profits. Income also includes state transfers, such as social protection benefits and tax credits. **Marketable wealth** includes assets that can be sold or converted into cash, such as stocks, shares and property. The largest marketable asset that most people own is residential property, usually their own home. Non-marketable wealth refers to assets that cannot be sold, the most important of which are pension entitlements. Including non-marketable assets in calculations of the distribution of wealth significantly influences estimates of inequality. For example, occupational pensions – often subsidised by tax exemptions – can widen inequality between higher- and lower-income households (see Chapter Three).

There are two striking features of inequality in recent years: first, the variation between countries in both the overall levels and trends over time in inequality; and, second, the particularly high levels of income and wealth inequality in both the UK and the US and the increase in both countries in recent decades. It is important to consider the reasons for these differences and developments, but the fact that there are variations and changes over time suggests that there is nothing inevitable about the scale or direction of inequality.

The richest 1% of individuals took 15% of all income in the UK in 2012, compared to 6% in 1979.[13] Income inequality has risen faster in the UK than in any other developed country since the mid-1970s.[14] Between 1977 and 2010/11, the share of income going to the top fifth of households in the UK (known as a quintile) increased by 40% while that going to the bottom fifth fell by 60%.[15] A similar pattern has been evident in the US, where the top 10% of workers (known as a decile) received 35% of all growth in national income between 1975 and 2007 (and by 2012, received half of all pre-tax income) while the bottom 90% received only 18%. In contrast, in Denmark, the top decile received only 2.5% of income growth over the same period.[16] Between 1979 and 2007, the average income of the bottom 50% of Americans grew by 6% while the income of the top 1% increased by 229%.[17] Figure 5.1 illustrates these national variations in which groups benefited most from economic growth since the mid-1970s.

Figure 5.1: Relative share of income growth in different countries, 1975–2007

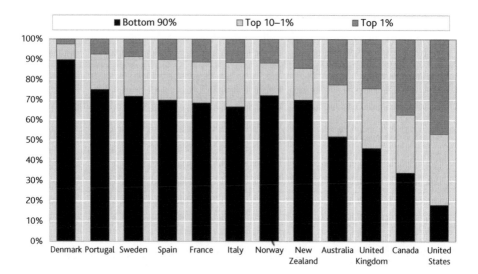

Source: Organisation for Economic Co-operation and Development (2014) 'Focus on Top Incomes and Taxation in OECD Countries: Was the Crisis a Game Changer?' Available at: http://www.oecd.org/els/soc/OECD2014-FocusOnTopIncomes.pdf (accessed 1 February 2015).

Countries that have experienced the greatest increase in inequality over the past 30 years have seen the largest surge take place in the incomes of those at the very top of the distribution. For example, in the US, the top 1% of earners now receives over 20% of total income, double the share they received in the late 1970s. This top 1% is estimated to have captured 95% of the gains from the economic growth that the US experienced between 2009 and 2012.[18] This is part of a longer-term trend: between 1993 and 2013, the incomes of the top 1% in the US grew by 86.1%. Alongside widening inequalities has been an even more dramatic concentration of income – the top 0.1% of US taxpayers received 11.3% of overall income in 2012, up from 2.6% in 1978, and the super-rich top 0.01% received 5%. There is now a chasm between the incomes of the richest and poorest in the US: the average income of the top 0.01% of Americans in 2012 was 859 times that of the bottom 90%; in 1973, this ratio was less than 80, still large but not the gulf that now divides the US.[19]

Wealth is generally even more unequally distributed than income in many countries (most notably, in Britain and the US), particularly if housing and non-marketable wealth are excluded from calculations. Globally, the wealthiest 1% of individuals owned about 48% of the world's assets in 2014; at the same time, the least wealthy 80% owned only 5% of global wealth.[20] The 85 wealthiest individuals in the world own as much as the poorest half of the world's population.[21]

Why has income and wealth inequality grown?

There are several reasons for the growth in inequality in particular countries. These include changes to tax policy and rules on inheritance and the transfer of wealth, but a particularly important factor has been increasing wages at the higher end of the labour market. The average salary of chief executives in the top 100 US corporations was £8.3 million in 2014 (US$13.9 million).[22] In 1960, the average wage (after tax) of chief executives in the largest US corporations was 12 times greater than the average wage of factory workers; by 1974, chief executives' average salaries had risen to 35 times that of an average worker, and 42 times as much by 1980. However, since the 1980s, this pay gap has become vastly greater: it increased to 84 times as much in 1990 and 400 times as much in 1999. By the turn of the century, US corporate chief executives were receiving on average 531 times as much as average wage-earners in the US, although the ratio has since reduced slightly.[23] A similar trend has been evident in the UK: average salaries for the senior executives of the UK's largest companies (listed in the FTSE 100 index) trebled in the 10 years to 2013 to £4.8 million, equivalent to 185 times average pay in Britain.[24]

Some economists (in particular, those from a neoclassical perspective[25]) and political ideologies have argued that increasing income and wealth for the richest would lead to a '**trickle down**' effect, which would raise the incomes of the less well-off. An alternative analogy to express the same theory is that 'a rising tide lifts all boats'.[26] Whichever image is used, the evidence is clear that the opposite happened – not only did income and wealth not trickle down, but there was an increase in inequality and a relative decline in living standards at the bottom of the income scale in those countries that pursued this strategy.[27] For example, the UK economy doubled in the 30 years to 2014 but the proportion of people in poverty rose from 14% to 33% over the same period.[28] Economic growth and productivity in the US also did not benefit lower-income groups: between 1973 and 2012, per capita economic production in the US increased by 93% but the real income of the median US household rose by only 12%.[29] The value of real wages for typical workers in the US in 2000 was below the 1988 level, and in 2013, real median weekly earnings were no higher than in 1979.[30] In both the US and UK, median wages have become decoupled from productivity growth, and this is mainly due to the increased share of productivity gains that have been absorbed by higher salaries and pensions for top earners.[31]

Mean versus median measures

The apparent anomaly of economic growth and increased productivity alongside stagnant or declining living standards for many is also explained by the difference between average (mean) and median incomes.[32] These are useful measures to summarise information, but if misinterpreted, they can obscure as much as they enlighten.[33] Mean and median are alternative *measures of central tendency*, which provide a simple overview of a range of different cases. The **mean** (what is commonly called the 'average') is calculated by adding up the value of all the cases (eg all of the incomes earned by either individuals or households in a society) and then dividing this total by the size of the population. The **median** is the midpoint that divides the entire population into two equal halves. It is important to consider how the distribution or spread of whatever is being considered can have different effects on the mean and the median. Average (mean) income could rise without any significant rise in the median if this is driven by large wage increases at the top of the scale.[34]

This is what happened to incomes in Britain and the US: the top decile absorbed most of the increases from economic growth and rising national income, which pushed up the average without significantly benefiting lower earners. A similar pattern has also been evident in India, where rapid aggregate economic growth has led to a very large increase in the incomes of the richest and wealthiest groups but has had much less impact on the very poorest.[35]

While the highest earners in the US and the UK have enjoyed large income increases, many of those at the lower-paid end of the job market have experienced declining living standards and working conditions.[36] Low pay is not necessarily a significant problem for those working in entry-level positions taking the first step in a sustained career leading to higher wages. However, more people than before in the UK have become locked into these positions, or find themselves shuttling between short-term and low-paid jobs and spells of unemployment (see Chapter Four).[37] This is reflected in the fact that three quarters of those in low-paid jobs in Britain in 2002 were still receiving low pay 10 years later, and one quarter of them remained in this position every year throughout the decade.[38]

The widening division between the top and bottom incomes reflects how some employers and governments have responded to structural changes in the labour market, and also reflects changes in the outlooks and expectations of higher-income groups. Globalisation and technological development have changed demand for labour and the nature of many jobs. There has been a **polarisation** of job opportunities in the UK, with new technologies enhancing the work and raising the productivity of higher-skilled workers, while increased international competition has lowered the wages offered for low-skilled jobs that cannot be easily mechanised, such as employment in services and retail.[39] There are fewer middle-ranking jobs in the UK than before and competition for them has become more intense, so that employers can demand higher qualifications and more skills and experience from applicants for what would previously have been entry-level positions.[40] In addition, many jobs are less secure than before: about half of the increase in earnings inequality in the UK is due to changes in self-employment, as self-employed workers generally earn less than full-time employees.[41] This is not a sign of entrepreneurialism, but a result of employers lowering their labour costs by reducing the terms and conditions of jobs, creating a new class of insecure workers.[42] Zero-hour contracts have been the most controversial form of this new **flexible labour market**, but they are only the most high-profile example of a wider trend.[43] Insecure and low-paid employment is not only an immediate problem; it also has long-term implications for people's ability to save and maintain contributions to retirement pensions. The underpaid and insecure workers of today will be tomorrow's poor pensioners.

Worsening pay and conditions at the bottom of the British and US labour markets contrast with large increases in salaries at the top. The performance of senior executives and the companies they run have not improved over the past 30 years anything close to the extent required to match the salary increases that they have enjoyed. Neither are the skills and expertise of top executives so scarce that international competition to recruit them pushes up salaries. As the Organisation for Economic Co-operation and Development (OECD) pointed out:

> if this was the main driver, we should have observed the surge in the share of top income across all market economies, but this is not the case; top income shares have grown only modestly in countries such as Japan or France even though these countries were affected by these global changes as much as the English-speaking countries.[44]

Hutton suggests that the 'super-salaries' of chief executives and senior managers:

> have almost nothing to do with performance and everything to do with CEOs [chief executive officers] keeping up with each other in a status race ... one of the best determinants of any CEO's pay in the US was the size of his or her social network. The more examples of highly paid members in one's network, the more generous a remuneration committee felt it had to be.[45]

The inflated salaries of senior executives reflect what sociologists call their **reference group**, that is, the comparisons they make with those they regard as similar to themselves.[46] This is not the only factor contributing to the large increases in the rewards granted to higher-income groups, but it is striking that the incomes of some of the most vocal supporters of the rationality and efficiency of free markets and economic laws of supply and demand are so strongly influenced by the **moral economy** of their cultural group, that is, the customs, values, practices and expectations of a particular social arrangement.[47] A recent and distinctive feature of this elite culture is that fewer high earners than in the past feel that their incomes should be limited by social considerations. This acceptance and justification for large and widening income gaps 'reflects the collapse of a whole set of old ideas of justice and injustice'.[48]

Neither the increased job insecurity and low pay at the bottom end of the labour market nor the ballooning salaries and bonuses at the top were inevitable or universal developments – they reflect political choices and economic policies. In particular, they are the product of the economic doctrine that became known as the **Washington Consensus**.[49] This promoted privatisation, market deregulation, tax cuts and reducing public services to produce 'creative imbalances' in order to stimulate the economy.[50] While this approach widened inequalities of income and wealth, it did not create the economic growth hoped for: growth and productivity rates in Britain were a third lower and unemployment five times higher in the 30 years after 1980 than in the post-war era, a period usually dismissed by neoclassical economists and political conservatives as one of economic stagnation.[51]

Social mobility

To understand the relationship between social inequality and social mobility, it is first of all necessary to clarify what social mobility means and how it is measured. Mobility can be measured either intra- or intergenerationally. This first analyses the movement of an individual during their employment career, that is, comparing their first to their last job. Intergenerational social mobility compares an individual's final class position to that of their parents. **Absolute social mobility** refers to the number of people who move through the class system over time. **Socio-economic class** is usually measured by occupation and income, and the level of absolute social mobility is calculated by comparing an individual's class origin (ie their parents' occupation and income) to their destination, that is, the occupation and income that they have achieved themselves as an adult.[52] **Relative social mobility** considers how opportunities relate to different starting positions and class backgrounds. Relative mobility considers 'the extent to which people's future prospects are determined by the families they are born into'.[53] Relative mobility (sometimes called **social fluidity**) is measured by comparing the chances of someone born into a lower-class background moving up to a higher occupational position compared with the chances of someone born into a higher position staying there throughout their lives.

Measuring social mobility presents several technical challenges. The first is how different occupations should be classified and ranked.[54] A second challenge is that an individual's occupational outcome (their social class destination) cannot be known until they have been in the labour market some time; in effect, when they have reached middle age. This means that it is only possible to know what has happened to social mobility in the past rather than current or very recent developments.[55] Therefore, evidence on social mobility cannot be used to assess the policies of a contemporary government as current data will reflect the effects of government policies and socio-economic circumstances of 20 or more years earlier. However, it may be possible to offer hypotheses about the likely effects of current government policies based on previous trends or the experiences of other countries.

Most policymakers and commentators are interested in relative intergenerational social mobility, which is the opportunity people have to progress and reach higher occupations irrespective of their parents' incomes and employment. This is what the UK government's social mobility strategy is concerned with.[56] Absolute social mobility can reflect structural labour-market changes without any significant change in equality of opportunity; for this reason, it is sometimes called **structural mobility**. For example, high levels of upward social mobility but little downward mobility suggest that a change in the nature of the jobs available accounts for much of the movement rather than a more open competition for higher-level occupations. This is what happened in Britain and several other developed societies after the Second World War. In the UK, in the period up to the 1980s, upward mobility rose due to increased demand for middle-class, white-collar technical and professional occupations and a decline in the number of blue-collar manual jobs. To illustrate this: in 1911, about three quarters of the British labour force were employed in manual occupations, by 1991, this had fallen to 38%, with a corresponding increase in administrative, managerial, technical and professional occupations.[57] An increase in relative mobility and social fluidity would require not just an expansion in higher occupational positions, but an exchange between classes, with some people moving down the occupational and class hierarchy. In these terms, there was little **exchange mobility** in Britain in the post-Second World War period.[58] Similar stability was evident in several developed countries: fewer than 30% of those in the richest 1% in the US, Canada and France fall from this position from one year to the next; in contrast, approximately two fifths of the top 1% in Australia and Norway exit from this group over the course of a year. Stability and consolidation of advantage are particularly strong in the US, where the probability of staying in the top 1% has not changed significantly since the 1970s.[59] Figure 5.2 shows the varying strengths of the connection between parents' income and that of their male offspring in different countries.

Unlike the rest of Europe, where relative mobility increased, social mobility declined in Britain in the late 20th century.[60] For example, fewer men born in 1970 had moved as far from their class origin as those born in 1958.[61] There are several reasons for this, but one of the most important is that large inequalities in incomes and wealth appear to reduce the level of relative intergenerational mobility.[62] As one summary analysis of the evidence put it: 'moving up a ladder is harder if its rungs are further apart'.[63] However, evidence from the US suggests that the vast increases in wages at the top of the job market have not had a direct effect in reducing social mobility – intergenerational mobility has remained relatively consistent over the period when the incomes of the top 1% raced away.[64] The effect of this extreme enrichment on mobility is more indirect: making the rewards of occupational success greater and therefore intensifying the competition for higher positions. The simultaneous reduction in middle-ranking jobs has reinforced the motivation of 'those who start higher up [to] fight harder to ensure their children do not slip down' and to pull up the ladder behind them to preserve their advantages and pass them on to their children.[65] The result is that economic and other advantages reinforce themselves across generations, particularly in the UK.[66] This gap between official and public support for meritocracy and social mobility and the reality of widening inequality and social rigidity requires explanation.

Figure 5.2: Strength of the link between individual and parental earnings in selected developed countries

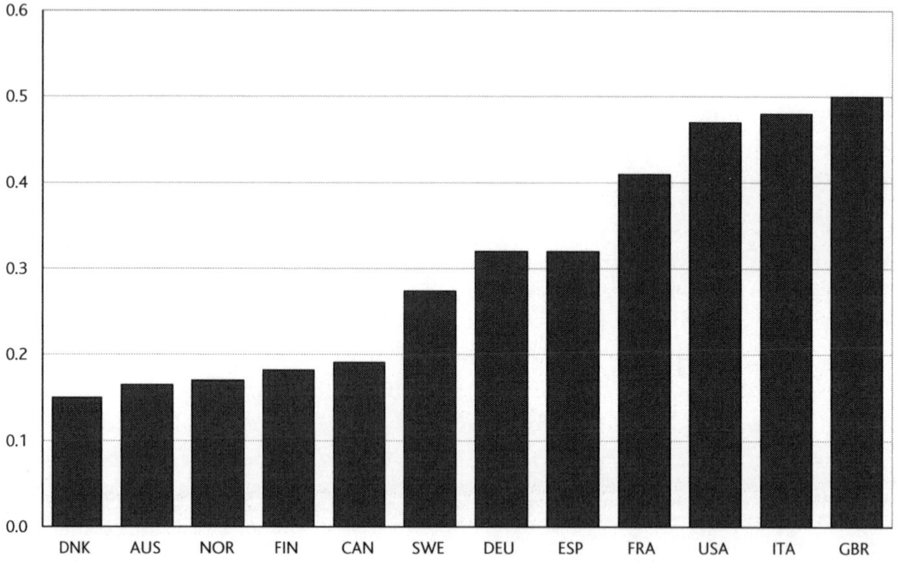

Note: The height of each column represents the extent to which a son's earnings reflects those of their father. The higher the value, the greater the persistence of earnings across generations and the lower the level intergenerational mobility.

Source: OECD (2010) 'A Family Affair: Intergenerational Social Mobility Across OECD Countries', p 185. Available at: http://www.oecd.org/tax/public-finance/chapter%205%20gfg%202010.pdf

Social closure

Social closure refers to any practice that a group uses to restricts access to resources.[67] The concept was initially developed by Max Weber to describe the 'appropriation of social and economic opportunities'.[68] This idea was developed and applied more extensively by Frank Parkin, who defined it as 'the process by which social collectivities seek to maximise rewards by restricting access to resources and opportunities to a limited circle of eligibles'.[69] Closure involves a group ensuring exclusive possession of particular assets or resources. This may involve legal ownership or some other way of restricting access. Monopolising scarce resources enables a group to secure and maintain relative advantages. Weber argued that 'Any cultural trait, no matter how superficial, can serve as a starting point for the familiar tendency to monopolistic closure'.[70] Sociologists and anthropologists have analysed numerous examples of how groups form, develop shared identities and distinguish themselves from outsiders. However, in relation to understanding inequalities of income and wealth, the key issue to consider is how particular groups are able to claim exclusive access and erect barriers that restrict entry to the most valuable resources, particularly private property.[71]

In his *Discourse on the Origin of Inequality*, Rousseau suggested that the enclosure of land and the creation of private property were the origin of economic and social divisions: 'The first man who, having enclosed a piece of ground, bethought himself of saying "This is mine", and found people simple enough to believe him, was the real founder of civil society'.[72] Although Rousseau was not referring to an actual historical incident, real cases of **land enclosure** illustrate the phenomenon of closure. The enclosure of what was previously common land, owned by no one and used communally, to make this the private property of a class of landowners was a major event in English history, with long-term economic and political consequences. Before enclosure, agriculture in England was based on tenant farmers cultivating strips of land within large open fields, and sharing access to common grazing pastures. The first Enclosure Act in England was passed in 1604, and from then until 1914, a further 5,200 such Acts were passed, which applied to over one fifth of the total area of England.[73] This process created the familiar English landscape of fields and hedgerows and improved overall agricultural productivity. However, it also involved a huge transfer of what had been shared resources into private hands. As the evidence presented in this and other chapters has shown, an increase in overall productivity does not necessarily improve living standards for everyone. It took 500 years from 1300 before living standards in Britain doubled; in contrast, after 1929, living standards doubled within 28 years.[74] These figures require careful interpretation, but it is evident that there is no simple relationship between productive efficiency, economic growth and general improvements in living standards.

More contemporary examples of erecting barriers to restrict entry to outsiders are **gated communities**.[75] These prevent outsiders entering exclusive private spaces, such as residential areas created by or for more wealthy groups.[76] What has been described as 'the withdrawal of the moneyed classes from public spaces and civic institutions – a retreat into gated and guarded compounds'[77] – is not a new phenomenon: different forms of residential restriction can be traced back several centuries in England.[78] The replacement of many shared public spaces by privately owned and restricted areas, such as shopping centres and malls, is an associated development that has caused concern.[79] Exclusion need not be imposed by physical barriers – there are residential and commercial 'gilded ghettos' in many cities that are effectively off-limits to all but a small section of the super-rich who can afford to live there, or afford the goods and services they offer.[80]

A gated community is an example of those with wealth 'privating' themselves, that is, withdrawing from mainstream society. Scott argues that the words 'deprivation' and 'privilege' share a common Latin root: *privatus*, which means something that belongs to individuals rather than the public or the state.[81] He suggests that this shared etymology shows the connection between privilege and deprivation.[82] Both privilege and deprivation contrast with the status of shared

citizenship. Those with privileges have special advantages and enjoy private benefits that are not available to the general public. For example, those possessing private resources may be able to ensure privileged treatment in exercising their civil rights by being able to use or manipulate the legal system to their advantage.[83] They may also be able to exercise greater political influence through donations to political organisations or well-funded lobbying, or simply being able to afford the time to engage in political activities.[84] Some privileged groups have no need for some welfare services and therefore little interest in protecting social citizenship rights, if not outright hostility to them. In contrast, the most deprived in society may find themselves excluded from the shared status of equal citizenship if their low income limits their effective civil or political rights.

Citizenship

Citizenship means the rights and duties attached to being a full member of society and is a central concept in Social Policy analysis. Most discussions of citizenship take as their starting point T.H. Marshall's 1948 essay 'Citizenship and Social Class'. Marshall divided citizenship into three analytically distinct sets of rights:

1. **Civil rights**: these are rights necessary for individual freedom, such as the right to own property and the right to justice and fair legal treatment. In England, these rights are often traced back to Magna Carta (in 1215). Marshall argued that in Britain, the principal civil rights had been developed by the 18th century (at least for male adults).
2. **Political rights**: these are the rights necessary to participate in the exercise of political power, such as the right to vote and organise political movements. Marshall argued that in Britain, these rights developed during the 19th century, and involved granting rights that only a privileged few possessed (eg the aristocracy and landowners) to wider sections of society, that is, working-class men and then eventually women.
3. **Social rights**: Marshall defined these as 'the right to share to the full in the social heritage and to live the life of a civilised being according to the standards prevailing in the society'.[85] He suggested that these rights were provided by welfare state institutions, such as the National Health Service, state education and social services. Marshall therefore argued that the social welfare reforms that he observed being introduced in Britain when he was writing in 1948 should be regarded as the latest stage in a historical trend dating back some 250 years rather than a radical departure.

Marshall's account of the components and evolution of citizenship clarifies important aspects of the nature and development of rights, but it has been challenged by many subsequent analysts. It has been suggested that for some groups in some cases, citizenship 'rights' may exist only in theory and are not genuinely enforced. Marshall's historical account has also been described as Anglocentric, that is, specific to England or Britain.[86] Marshall has been accused of implying that there was somehow an inevitable progress in the development of rights, and that he underplays the conflict involved in extending rights, and ignores the fact that rights can be reduced or removed altogether.[87] Critics have also argued that his account does not describe how the rights of women and other groups that have experienced discrimination or exclusion were achieved belatedly and only after considerable struggle, if at all.[88]

Scott suggests that privilege and deprivation are not simply related, but interdependent – that privilege *causes* deprivation. To 'private' something involves depriving others of it by excluding them from access, so that one of the means of preserving wealth simultaneously creates forms of exclusion. To understand this connection between privilege and deprivation, it helps to consider private property ownership as a form of social closure.

Property entitlements and deprivation

Poverty may be caused by an overall lack of resources. Such **availability poverty** is one of the main reasons why poverty has existed for much of human history. The most influential account of this explanation was offered by **Thomas Malthus** (1766–1834) in his 'Essay on the Principles of Population', published in 1798.[89] Bertrand Russell once remarked that 'If a man's greatness is to be measured by his effect upon human life … few men have become greater than Malthus'.[90] Malthus believed that poverty was unavoidable and provided a straightforward explanation for this:

> the power of population is indefinitely greater than the power in the earth to produce subsistence for man. Population, when unchecked, increases in geometrical ratio. Subsistence [ie food supply] increases only in an arithmetical ratio. A slight acquaintance with numbers will show the immensity of the first power as compared with the second.[91]

Malthus argued that as population increased exponentially, the demand for food and other essentials would outstrip supply, resulting in poverty and famine. He believed that it was sentimental and, in fact, socially damaging to provide any welfare support to the 'surplus' population as 'It has appeared, from the inevitable laws of our nature [that] some human beings must suffer from want. These are the unhappy persons who, in the great lottery of life, have drawn a blank'.[92] The only sustainable response to the unavoidable limits of production was for the lower-income households to limit the size of their families.[93]

Malthus's pessimistic outlook was challenged by neoclassical economic theorists in the late 19th century, particularly by Alfred Marshall, who argued in *Principles of Economics*, published in 1890, that poverty would be reduced by increased productivity and economic growth. He pointed to the productivity stimulated by industrialisation in Britain in the 19th century as evidence of this. Even such a hostile critic as Marx was impressed by the immense productivity of industrial capitalism, noting that 'It has been the first to show what man's activity can bring about. It has accomplished wonders far surpassing Egyptian pyramids, Roman aqueducts, and Gothic cathedrals'.[94] However, in contrast to Marx's belief that capitalism would inevitability collapse due to crises and class conflict, Marshall argued that the stimulus of competition would oblige businesses to improve their efficiency and therefore their productivity. The resulting capacity to produce more with less would reduce the prices of goods and services and also enable employers to pay higher wages, improving living standards over time. Marshall believed that the dire predictions of Malthus and Marx could be avoided, provided that improvements in technology, the organisation of production and employees' skills were applied to expand economic output.[95]

However, Marshall's optimism has not always been justified by experience. General living standards may improve as economies transform from subsistence agriculture to industrial production (as occurred in South Korea since the 1960s and China since the 1980s), but after this transition, further improvements in living standards depend on how the benefits of economic growth are distributed.[96] A second type of poverty is therefore not due to any overall lack of resources, but due to how these are shared. Such **distributional poverty** is often the kind that exists in the developed world, where some groups possess abundant resources while others remain deprived.

Poverty can exist – and some people may actually starve – even when there are enough resources to meet everyone's needs. This is made clear by the analysis of famine developed by Amartya Sen, whose views on poverty are discussed in Chapter Four. Sen makes an apparently simple but crucial distinction: 'Starvation is the characteristic of people not *having* enough food to eat. It is not the characteristic of their *being* not enough food to eat'.[97] Mass starvation – and less drastic forms of deprivation – can occur in societies with adequate resources. In fact, there have been occasions where large numbers of people have starved while food was exported elsewhere. One of the most notorious episodes of such 'food countermovement' was the Irish famine of the 1840s.[98] Sen argues that in such circumstances, famine is caused not by an overall lack of food, but by the fact that some groups do not have any *right* to the food that is available. In such cases, starvation or deprivation is due to an **entitlement failure**. Entitlements are rights. Dahrendorf describes them as 'entry tickets' – the rules that legitimise access to provisions, such as food or other resources. Entitlements 'describe a relationship of persons to commodities by which their access to and control over them is "legitimised". Entitlements give people a rightful claim to things'.[99] Those without legitimate entitlement cannot access a resource without breaking the law, and this means that in particular and extreme situations, some people starve not because there is no food to eat, but because the property rights of others prevent them accessing it:

> many, though not all, recent famines seem to have taken place in rather orderly societies without anything 'illegal' about the process leading to starvation. In fact, in guarding ownership rights against the demands of the hungry, the legal forces uphold entitlements, e.g. in the Bengal

famine of 1943 the people who died in front of well-stocked food shops protected by the state were denied food because of lack of legal entitlement and not because of their entitlements being violated.[100]

From this perspective, famine and poverty should not be regarded as merely economic issues of how much is produced. It is not enough to simply ask 'How much is there?', as Malthus implied, but also 'Who gets it, and why?' Answering such questions involves 'going from economic phenomena into social, political and legal issues'.[101]

Thinking about famine, poverty and deprivation as failures of entitlement directs attention to property rights and other form of social closure and how they relate to privilege and exclusion. Parkin identified two main forms of exclusionary social closure in capitalist societies: first, control of the institutions of property; and, second, accreditation, or control over professional qualifications and credentials. Both are social practices and institutions that restrict legitimate access to important resources and social positions to a few:

> property ownership is a form of closure designed to prevent general access to the means of production and its fruits; credentialism is a form of closure designed to control and monitor entry to key positions in the division of labour.[102]

Parkin argues that socio-economic classes are an outcome of the divisions that these different forms of closure create between groups. In contrast to the Marxist view that capitalist societies are divided into two main classes – those who own property and those who do not – Parkin suggests that society is divided by different forms of social closure.[103]

Property and possessions

It is important not to confuse *property* with personal *possessions*. Property refers to resources with a productive potential, that is, assets that can be applied to generate additional value (ie wealth and income), such as land, materials, equipment, plant and machinery, or financial resources that can be invested. In contrast, possessions are consumption goods that are more likely to absorb rather than generate income. Some possessions may be exchanged or sold for more than they cost their owners but this merely redistributes existing assets and does not add to the total sum of resources in an economy.

Property ownership confers power and has social and political consequences beyond those of mere possessions: property 'confers the right to deny men access to the means of life and labour'.[104] Conflating property with possessions leads people to believe that everyone owns some kind of 'property' and therefore all have a stake in the economic and legal system that protects property ownership. Parkin summarises the effects of this confusion:

> If property is simply a specific form of possessions, or a certain bundle of rights, then everyone in society is a proprietor to some degree. On this reckoning there can be no clear social division between owners and non-owners, only a gradual, descending scale from those with very much to those with very little ... [it seems that] The possession of a toothbrush or an oil field confers similar rights and obligations upon their owners, so that property laws cannot be interpreted as class laws.[105]

In theory, in what is perceived to be a socially mobile and meritocratic society, anyone can acquire property and qualifications, and this apparent openness strengthens the legitimacy of these as sources of entitlement. However, in reality, access to educational opportunities and the potential rewards that they confer are far from equally distributed.

Education advantages and the preservation of privilege

In England, only about one fifth of secondary school pupils from the poorest 20% of families achieve the highest grades in their General Certificate of Secondary Education (GCSE) assessments. In contrast, three quarters of those from the richest quintile of households achieve these grades.[106] These results do not reflect innate intellectual differences between socio-economic groups. One of the most detailed studies of education and social mobility in post-Second World War Britain found little correlation between measures of intelligence and academic qualifications, and concluded that that intelligence per se was not an important factor accounting for relative access to higher occupations.[107] Subsequent British studies estimate that about 50% of educational inequality is due to differences in income.[108] US studies have confirmed these results, finding that inherited intelligence quotient (IQ) accounts for only a small percentage of the variation in the occupational positions achieved by children from different backgrounds.[109]

Education is regarded as 'the engine of social mobility' in many societies.[110] However, educational pathways to the most senior and powerful positions in Britain are grossly unequal. For example, in the UK, only 7% of pupils are educated in private schools but this fraction is overwhelmingly represented in the most influential occupations, accounting for 70% of High Court judges, 54% of chief executives of FTSE 100 companies, 54% of top journalists, 45% of top civil servants and 32% of UK Members of Parliament.[111] Of the 30 British schools that were most successful in getting their pupils into Oxford and Cambridge universities, 27 were private (or 'independent', as many prefer to be known). The most successful of all was Westminster, which charges annual boarding fees of almost £34,000.[112] If particular groups or classes can dominate the principal routes to progression and access to elite occupations through privileged education, then equality of opportunity is limited and social mobility is impeded.

The increase in inequality and decline in social mobility in both the US and UK is largely due to **opportunity-hoarding** strategies by higher-income groups.[113]

Social closure and segregation exist at each stage of education. For example, at pre-school age, the Family and Childcare Trust found that some private nurseries in Britain refused to admit children from lower-income households due to concerns from more affluent parents about the damaging effects of 'social mixing'.[114] This closure is repeated and reinforced in primary and secondary education, where parents in the highest income decile are prepared to pay the fees required to send their children to private schools and ensure that their children are educated in an environment geared to high academic attainment and where they mix only with their 'equals' or 'betters' and are safeguarded from 'unsavoury' elements and 'unhelpful' peers.[115] In opting out of public education, these parents are purchasing advantages for their children and 'privating' them from shared citizenship. The social barriers erected by such educational segregation are as effective as if these privileged children lived within exclusive gated communities. Higher-income parents who cannot afford to pay for private education may still be able to secure advantages within the state system as they possess the financial and other resources to make the most of the opportunities available.[116] In parts of England, more affluent parents relocate to the residential catchment areas of state schools with the highest performance scores.[117] Policies that enable parents to choose which state schools their children attend, or that select pupils based on assessments known to have a strong association with income, also reinforce educational and social divisions.[118] Therefore, what might appear to be equal treatment and opportunity in education can actually reinforce inequalities: 'in a stratified society, apparently equitable arrangements for choosing schools can effectively enable those with the material and cultural resources to make the best choices to deny choices to others'.[119]

Social divisions in primary and secondary education are widened beyond higher education. Some of the additional income and wealth accumulated by the highest-paid groups in recent years has been invested in the education and training of their children to secure access to the most competitive and prestigious occupations, including financing postgraduate education and providing support to take unpaid internships.[120]

As shared experiences are eroded and educational divisions widen, important **social networks** become more exclusive and impenetrable to outsiders. One of the most influential ideas in Social Network theory is Granovetter's identification of 'the strength of weak ties', which suggests that information often flows through loose networks between people who have mutual acquaintances but do not necessarily have strong direct relationships.[121] Important information (eg about educational or employment opportunities) may therefore be inaccessible if influential networks become more closed or if different networks and social groups drift apart.[122] Opportunities to mix and interact allow people to become familiar and comfortable with each other and develop trusting relationships or **social capital**. This enables them to exchange 'soft knowledge', such as informal information, know-how, tips about opportunities and advice on how different social systems function and how to use them for maximum effect.[123] If social networks narrow and exchanges become restricted between people 'like themselves', then those regarded as different will be excluded and miss out on opportunities that are supposedly public but, in practice, are closed to those 'in the know'.

Closure and capital

The idea of social capital highlights how social relationships can be assets and resources that can, in some situations, be as valuable as property. Social capital means 'the networks together with shared norms, values and understandings that facilitate co-operation within or among groups'.[124] Many different terms have been used to describe these relationships, such as community spirit, social bonds, community networks, extended friendships, social resources and good neighbourliness, among others.[125] These are different ways to describe the 'social glue' that binds people together and provides the underpinning of trust that allows them to rely on one another for mutual support. Robert Putnam, one of the theorists most closely associated with the concept of social capital, describes these relationships as characterised by 'thick trust'.[126] He distinguishes this bonding social capital with another type of beneficial relationship that he calls bridging social capital. This is not a social glue, but a lubricant. Bridging social capital refers to 'thin' relationships of 'generalised trust' between members of different networks, and there is an obvious resemblance to Granovetter's idea of the importance of weak inter-group ties. As Putnam explains, while bonding social capital is necessary for 'getting by', bridging capital is essential for 'getting ahead'.

Both bonding and bridging social capital are relationships that enable individuals to achieve more with and through others than they could accomplish alone. For this reason, social capital should be regarded as an asset comparable to other productive resources, such as physical capital (eg land, labour, machinery, etc), financial capital or human capital (ie knowledge and skills). Like these other assets, social capital can contribute to productivity by enabling collective action and cooperation, sharing and spreading information, and reducing transaction costs. Recognising these relationships as types of capital highlights the different ways in which they can be invested or exchanged. How different types of capital can be accumulated, 'cashed in' and traded for one another was a central interest in the sociological analysis of **Pierre Bourdieu** (1930–2002). Bourdieu argued that individuals and groups compete to improve or maintain their relative positions by using the different capital resources they possess.[127] A particularly important form is **cultural capital** – the ability to appreciate particular forms of culture (particularly what is defined as 'high culture', such as classical music and art) and recognise what counts as 'good taste'. This knowledge can be used as a resource to mark distinctions between those who are regarded as having more refined and superior judgement and others who are regarded as relatively culturally deprived and socially inferior.[128] One illustration of this is how the images of particular brands are controlled to protect their status as elite products. Manufacturers and retailers of 'high-end' products are careful to market and price their products to maintain brand value by excluding undesirable consumers. For example, the chief executive of the Italian fashion and leather goods company Gucci once explained that although one of their handbags could have been sold at a healthy mark-up for €794, their target customers insisted that the company double the retail price. These customers objected that if a product can be afforded by less wealthy people, it becomes cheapened in the eyes of elite buyers who would not wish to be associated with it.[129] This is a particular form of **conspicuous consumption**, where economic resources are used to highlight cultural distinctions and protect advantages through social closure.[130]

Bourdieu argued that class divisions are reproduced as much through cultural distinctions as by economic resources. Class differences are apparent in people's everyday social activities, lifestyle and culture – what they buy, their tastes and their preferences. Some cultural assets can be used to access educational opportunities, such as entry into prestigious universities.[131] Not only may such knowledge and cultural capital open particular doors, but possessing the 'right' culture may be a necessary in order to capitalise on such opportunities. This relates to Bourdieu's concept of **habitus**.[132] This idea is illustrated by the exchange said to have taken place when the author F. Scott Fitzgerald remarked that 'The rich are different from you and me', to which his fellow writer Ernest Hemingway responded 'Yes, they have more money'.[133] Fitzgerald was referring to the distinctive outlook and lifestyle that inherited or sustained high income and wealth enable, and how this leads those who possess them to develop distinctive experiences and expectations, and become what Weber called a **status group**.[134] Habitus means the 'internalised dispositions' that are acquired within the subculture of a status group – their characteristic habits and beliefs.[135] Bourdieu argued that 'when habitus encounters a social world of which it is the product, it is like a "fish in water": it does not feel the weight of the water and it takes the world about itself for granted'.[136] Those who possess the relevant cultural capital feel more comfortable in higher education institutions or high-status occupations than outsiders, who may be intimidated by the unfamiliar conventions and implicit codes of these alien social settings. The writer and critic Lorna Sage described her experience as a child from a working-class family attending a grammar school as feeling 'like an evacuee or a displaced person'.[137] Bourdieu's own research has shown that students from higher-income households have a smoother transition from their home into academic environments, and adapt more easily to these cultures than those from a different habitus.[138] Other researchers have found that the transition between a 'low-status' social background and high-status university can produce feelings of 'disquiet, ambivalence, insecurity and uncertainty' in students.[139] Bourdieu observed that 'Moving up means raising oneself, climbing and acquiring the marks, the stigmata, of this effort'.[140] The term 'moving up' itself implies leaving behind a 'lower' origin and abandoning, betraying and denigrating a familiar culture (or what others might dismiss as a *lack* of 'culture'). Academic success requires conforming to and internalising the beliefs and norms of a new habitus, and this involves a sacrifice not required by those who do not have to make any cultural adjustment.[141] This is an important factor in the negative 'self-selection' of talented comprehensive school pupils in Britain who feel that the top universities are 'not for the likes of them'.[142] For example, less than half (49%) of 14 year olds from the poorest families in Britain reported that they felt that they were likely to apply and be admitted to university, compared to over three quarters (77%) of children from the richest households.[143] Reflecting this, about half of the children whose parents are professionals aspire to pursue a professional career themselves, compared with only one in six children from families with an average income.[144] A particularly unfortunate feature of these cultural barriers and psychological inhibitions is that when they *do* enter university, students from comprehensive schools often outperform privately educated and grammar school pupils with the same school qualifications.[145] This is further evidence that persistent and widening educational and income inequalities do not reflect ability or intelligence.

The significance of the cultural factors that shape educational and employment opportunities shows that social closure is not necessarily always a deliberate effort by exclusive groups to prevent entry to outsiders.[146] Closure and exclusion can be the unintended outcomes of everyday practices and what particular groups think of as ordinary conventions and pursuing legitimate interests. Most parents want what is best for their children, and higher-income parents cannot be blamed for using their cultural and economic advantages to maximise their children's well-being and opportunities.[147] Even those who believe, in principle, that it is unfair for parents to use exclusive networks, insider knowledge or economic resources to secure advantages for their children might violate this belief when it comes to doing what is best for their own children.[148] As closure may be an unintended consequence of legitimate actions and an outcome of widely supported principles – such as parents' right to send their children to the school of their choice – it is often not recognised as a defence of privilege. There is considerable reluctance among those who benefit from advantages to recognise the fact. Most people who enjoy success like to think that they have earned this through personal merit, and are more likely to see any relative disadvantages that they may have experienced than to recognise the closure that they or their group have imposed on others.[149]

The 'invisible knapsack' of advantage

McIntosh illustrates how discrimination may exist without the deliberate intention and beyond the awareness of those who benefit from it by outlining what she describes as the 'daily effects of white privilege' in the US in the 1980s and 1990s.[150] She shows how racism confers 'unearned advantage and conferred dominance' through 50 propositions that white Americans could take for granted but African-Americans (and other minority racial groups) could not, for example:

• 'I can be pretty sure that my neighbors will be neutral or pleasant to me.'

- 'When I am told about our national heritage or about "civilization" I am shown that people of my color made it what it is.'
- 'I am never asked to speak for all the people of my racial group.'
- 'I can chose blemish cover or bandages in "flesh" color and have them more or less match my skin.'

These experiences demonstrate important aspects of the habitus of white Americans – what they can assume to be 'normal'. McIntosh argues that these norms disadvantage non-white Americans, who become Others outside of 'mainstream' society. McIntosh reveals 'privilege as an invisible package of unearned assets ... an invisible weightless knapsack of special provisions, maps, passports, codebooks, visas, clothes, tools, and blank checks'. Her examples illustrate some of the ways in which 'race is felt and understood at the daily level via everyday encounters'.[151]

McIntosh's broader purpose is to highlight some of the subtle ways in which men may benefit from sexist assumptions and practices, perhaps inadvertently and without being intentionally sexist themselves. She suggests that white people 'are carefully taught not to recognize white privilege, as males are taught not to recognize male privilege'.

As discussed in both Chapters Two and Six, attachment to ideas and beliefs is stronger if they are regarded as disinterested rather than self-serving. The belief that society is open and that equality of opportunity is genuine may blind people to the privileges and unearned advantages that help them to acquire higher incomes and prestigious positions.[152] Believing that high income or occupational success are earned largely through individual merit encourages the view that the lower incomes or deprivation of others is attributable to their deficiencies rather than unequal opportunities. For example, those employed at higher levels in the UK labour market may not appreciate that there is greater competition for jobs at the entry level than there is among professionals, and therefore be mistaken about how easy it is for unemployed people to get a job, particularly applicants in more depressed labour markets or who cannot meet all of the requirements of 'flexible' employment, for example, due to care responsibilities.[153] Widening inequality can reduce interaction and undermine shared experiences between groups, which can lead to a lack of sympathy between and even to hostility towards those judged to be responsible for their own deprivation.[154] The result of allowing unearned advantage to persist unchecked is increased social and political segregation:

> Too great a gap between rich and poor undermines the solidarity that democratic citizenship requires. As inequality deepens, rich and poor live increasingly separate lives. The affluent send their children to successful schools, leaving other schools to the children of families who have no alternative. Private health clubs replace municipal recreation centres and swimming pools. A second or third car removes the need

to rely on public transport. And so on. The affluent secede from public places and services, leaving them to those who can't afford anything else.[155]

If these trends go unchecked, the likely outcomes are widening divisions and increased social tension. In the end, acting as if 'there is no such thing as society' can become a self-fulfilling prophecy.[156]

Conclusions

The question considered in this chapter is how social inequality is maintained. The answer depends on what type of inequality is considered. The principle of ontological equality (that all human beings share a basic equal status) is now almost universally accepted, but there is no agreement over whether opportunities, conditions or outcomes are or ought to be equal. This reflects the dual empirical and normative character of Social Policy: the subject is concerned not only with describing what social conditions are like, but also with proposing how they *ought* to be. This moral dimension raises the question of whether inequality is actually bad at all. It could be argued that inequality encourages people to aspire to success and strive for improvement. As a result, inequality may not only spur people to realise their own potential, but also benefit society generally by stimulating effort and innovation. It is also possible that reducing some inequalities does more harm than good, not only by stifling individual initiative, but by violating important rights and freedoms.

Most advocates of greater equality respond to these objections by arguing that they object to inequalities of income and wealth beyond a certain level, although it is difficult to identify what the threshold might be. Few advocate entirely equal outcomes, so most political and policy debates centre on the extent of equality of opportunity and of conditions, and the relationship between them. Understanding how far and the means by which unequal starting positions result in unequal chances requires careful empirical investigation. The chapter has shown various ways in which the concept of social closure and related ideas can be applied to understand this relationship. However, even if Social Policy analysis successfully demonstrates how inequalities are reproduced, this would still leave open the normative question of why it matters. Supporters of equality of opportunity would offer three answers. The economic case is that large inequalities of income and wealth do not 'trickle down' and benefit the rest of society (see Chapter Six). The super-rich can afford to hire experts to advise them on how best to preserve their assets (eg through elaborate tax avoidance measures), and they do not invest or spend enough themselves to provide mass employment for lower-income groups. The political objection to large income and wealth inequalities is that it can enable some to buy undue power and influence, and this undermines the democratic principle that every citizen should have an equal voice in shaping policy. Finally, the moral objection to privilege is that it is unfair to bestow unearned advantages on those born into good fortune and to discriminate against those who are not lucky enough to inherit such advantages.

It is neither inevitable nor necessary for some of the natural inequalities that exist between people to lead to wide and potentially divisive social inequalities. Allowing this to happen is a matter of policy. Societies can decide how wide they are prepared to allow inequalities of wealth and income to become and choose to limit these.

Social Policy is interested not only in studying the responses to social problems, but also in how these arise in the first place. To understand the causes of social problems requires looking beyond those who experience them, and considering the combination of conditions and choices that create their circumstances. Historically, Social Policy has devoted considerable attention to studying 'the poor' and the conditions of poverty but rather less to understanding how some of the actions of more privileged groups contribute to poverty. There are therefore further interesting possibilities for Social Policy analysis in exploring the implications of Tawney's observation that 'what thoughtful rich people call the problem of poverty, thoughtful poor people call with equal justice a problem of riches'.[157]

Notes

[1] 'Remarks by the President on Economic Mobility', 4 December 2013. Available at: http://www. whitehouse.gov/the-press-office/2013/12/04/remarks-president-economic-mobility (accessed 31 January 2015).

[2] See: http://www.britishpoliticalspeech.org/speech-archive.htm?speech=137 (accessed 31 January 2015).

[3] Blair, T (2001) 'The Government's Agenda for the Future', speech, Enfield, 8 February.

[4] HM Government (2010) *Coalition Programme for Government*. London: HM Government, p 7.

[5] Rousseau, J.-J. (1973) 'A Discourse on the Origin of Inequality', in Rousseau, J.-J., *The Social Contract and Discourses* (trans Cole, G.F.H.). London: Everyman, p 49.

[6] Turner, B. (1986) *Equality*. London: Tavistock, p 35.

[7] Spicker, P. (1988) *Principles of Social Welfare: An Introduction to Thinking About the Welfare State*. London: Routledge, p 71. Available at: https://1cb22603d718a691ce7e453da684fa0463eccf3b. googledrive.com/host/0B67_qju2yrKvTkVleG04X1Y2dzA/Principles%20of%20Social%20 Welfare%20-%20Paul%20Spicker.pdf

[8] Taylor-Gooby, P. (2008) 'Equality, Rights and Social Justice', in Alcock, P., May, M. and Rowlingson, K. (eds) *The Student's Companion to Social Policy* (3rd edn). Oxford: Blackwell.

[9] Although now used favourably to describe a society where opportunities reflect ability and effort, the word 'meritocracy' was initially used satirically to promote a more egalitarian education system, see Young, M. (1958) *The Rise of the Meritocracy, 1870–2033: An Essay on Education and Society*. London: Thames and Hudson.

[10] All-Party Parliamentary Group on Social Mobility (2012) 'Seven Key Truths about Social Mobility', p 5. Available at: http://www.appg-socialmobility.org/ (accessed 17 August 2014).

[11] Willetts, D. (2011) *The Pinch: How the Baby Boomers Stole Their Children's Future and Why They Should Give It Back*. London: Atlantic.

[12] Mason, P. (2012) *Why It's All Kicking Off Everywhere: The New Global Revolutions*. London: Verso.

[13] Dorling, D. (2012) 'Fairness and the Changing Fortunes of People in Britain 1970–2012', Royal Statistical Society Beveridge Memorial Lecture, 27 June.

[14] OECD (Organisation for Economic Co-operation and Development) (2011) 'Divided We Stand: Why Inequality Keeps Rising: Country Note – United Kingdom'. Available at: http://www.bristol.ac.uk/poverty/ESRCJSPS/downloads/research/comparitive/1%20Comparison-General/Report/OECD%20(2011)%20Divided%20We%20Stand%20Why%20Inequality%20Keeps%20Rising.pdf (accessed 17 August 2014).

[15] Gaffney, D. and Baumberg, B. (2014) *Dismantling the Barriers to Social Mobility*. London: Trades Union Congress, p 11.

[16] OECD (2014) 'Focus on Top Incomes and Taxation in OECD Countries: Was the Crisis a Game Changer?'. Available at: http://www.oecd.org/els/soc/OECD2014-FocusOnTopIncomes.pdf (accessed 1 February 2015). See also Starr, P. (2014) 'A Different Road to a Fair Society', *New York Review of Books*, 22 May.

[17] Bauman, Z. (2013) 'Does the Richness of the Few Benefit Us All?', *Social Europe*, 28 January. Available at: http://www.socialeurope.eu/2013/01/does-the-richness-of-the-few-benefit-us-all/ (accessed 1 February 2015).

[18] Saez, E. (2013) 'Striking it Richer: The Evolution of Top Incomes in the United States (Updated with 2012 Preliminary Estimates)', 3 September. Available at: http://eml.berkeley.edu/~saez/saez-UStopincomes-2012.pdf (accessed 1 February 2015).

[19] Fox, J. (2014) 'We Can't Afford to Leave Inequality to the Economists', *Harvard Business Review Blog Network*, 24 January. Available at: http://blogs.hbr.org/2014/01/we-cant-afford-to-leave-inequality-to-the-economists/ (accessed 1 February 2015).

[20] Hardoon, D. (2015) *Having It All and Wanting More*. Oxford: Oxfam. Available at: http://policy-practice.oxfam.org.uk/publications/wealth-having-it-all-and-wanting-more-338125

[21] Fuentes-Nieva, R. and Galasso, M. (2014) 'Working for the Few: Political Capture and Economic Inequality', Oxfam Briefing Paper, 178. Available at: http://www.oxfam.org/sites/www.oxfam.org/files/bp-working-for-few-political-capture-economic-inequality-200114-summ-en.pdf (accessed 1 February 2015).

[22] Hutton, W. (2014) 'Extravagant CEO Pay Doesn't Reflect Performance – It's All About Status', *The Observer*, 19 April.

[23] Bauman (2013). Domhoff, G.W. (2013) 'Wealth, Income, and Power'. Available at: http://www2.ucsc.edu/whorulesamerica/power/wealth.html (accessed 1 February 2015). Mishel, L. and Davis, A. (2014) 'CEO Pay Continues to Rise as Typical Workers are Paid Less', Economic Policy Institute, Wages Incomes and Wealth Report, 12 June. Available at: http://www.epi.org/publication/ceo-pay-continues-to-rise/#_note1 (accessed 1 February 2015).

[24] Hargreaves, D. (2013) 'The Rich Only Get Richer', in Guy, C., Henderson, K., Garnham, A. and Hargreaves, D. (eds) *Busting the Poverty Myths*. London: New Statesman/Webb Memorial Trust, p 12.

[25] Arnsperger, C. and Varoufakis, Y. (2006) 'What is Neoclassical Economics?', *Post-Autistic Economics Review*, 38(1).

[26] Timmins, N. (2011) 'OECD Calls Time on Trickle-down Theory', *Financial Times*, 5 December.

[27] Stiglitz, J. (2012) *The Price of Inequality*. London: Penguin.

[28] Gordon, D. (2014) 'Poverty in the UK', presentation at 'Poverty and Social Exclusion in Scotland and the UK', Edinburgh, New Register House, 20 August. See also: http://www.poverty.ac.uk/pse-research/going-backwards-1983-2012 (accessed 1 February 2015). It might be objected that a relative poverty line increases with rising living standards, but the definition used in the Poverty and Social Exclusion survey is based on the British public's definition of what counts as a necessity and how many people are unable to afford these, and the most recent Poverty and Social Exclusion survey, published in 2013, showed that the public's list of necessities does not always increase.

[29] Friedman, B.J. (2013) '"Brave New Capitalists' Paradise":The Jobs?', *New York Review of Books*, 7 November. 'Real' wages in this context means after adjusting for inflation so that the actual purchasing power can be compared over time.

[30] Blanchflower, D. and Machin, S. (2014) 'Falling Real Wages', *CentrePiece*, 19(1), p 20. Available at: http://cep.lse.ac.uk/pubs/download/cp422.pdf

[31] MacDonald, R. and Shildrick, T. (2013) 'In Work and in Poverty', in Guy, C., Henderson, K., Garnham, A. and Hargreaves, D. (eds) *Busting the Poverty Myths*. London: New Statesman/Webb Memorial Trust, p 21.

[32] Mishel, L. (2012) 'The Wedges between Productivity and Median Compensation Growth', Economic Policy Institute, Issue Brief #330.

[33] Gould, S.J. (2007) 'The Median Isn't the Message', in McGarr, P. and Rose, S. (eds) *The Richness of Life*. London: Vintage.

[34] There is a natural limit to the influence of incomes at the bottom of the scale as (leaving aside debt) no one can earn less than zero.

[35] Basu, K. (2008) 'India's Dilemmas: The Political Economy of Policymaking in a Globalised World', *The Economic and Political Weekly*, 2–8 February.

[36] Toynbee, P. (2003) *Hard Work: Life in Low-Pay Britain*. London: Bloomsbury.

[37] Shildrick, T., MacDonald, R., Webster, C. and Garthwaite, K. (2012) *Poverty and Insecurity: Life in Low-Pay, No-Pay Britain*. Bristol: The Policy Press.

[38] Social Mobility and Child Poverty Commission (2014) *Response to the Consultation on the Child Poverty Strategy 2014 to 2017*. London: Social Mobility and Child Poverty Commission, para 9.

[39] Dolphin, T. and Lawton, K. (2013) *A Job for Everyone: What Should Full Employment Mean in 21st Century Britain?* London: Institute for Public Policy Research, p 15.

[40] Sissons, P. (2011) *The Hourglass and the Escalator: Labour Market Change and Mobility*. London: Work Foundation. As the All-Party Parliamentary Group on Mobility ([2012], p 23) state: 'a number of careers have become "graduate-ised"'.

[41] OECD (2011) 'Divided We Stand: An Overview of Growing Income Inequalities in OECD Countries: Main Findings', p 36. Available at: http://www.oecd.org/els/soc/49499779.pdf (accessed 17 August 2014).

[42] Standing, G. (2011) *The Precariat: The New Dangerous Class*. London: Bloomsbury.

[43] Pyper, D. and McGuinness, F. (2013) *Zero-Hours Contracts*. Standard Note: SN/BT/6553. London: House of Commons Library.

[44] OECD (2014), p 5.

[45] Hutton, 2014. See also Picketty, T. (2014) *Capital in the Twenty-First Century* (trans Goldhammer, A.). Harvard, MA: Harvard University Press.

[46] Runciman, W.G. (1972) *Relative Deprivation and Social Justice*. Harmondsworth: Penguin.

[47] Thompson, E.P. (1971) 'The Moral Economy of the English Crowd in the Eighteenth Century', *Past & Present*, 50.

[48] Rosanvallon, P. (2013) *The Society of Equals*. Harvard, MA: Harvard University Press.

[49] World Health Organisation (no date) 'Trade, Foreign Policy, Diplomacy and Health: Washington Consensus'. Available at: http://www.who.int/trade/glossary/story094/en/ (accessed 1 February 2015).

[50] Seabrook, J. (2008) *Why Do People Think Inequality Is Worse Than Poverty?* York: Joseph Rowntree Foundation, p 2.

[51] Chang, H.-J. (2007) *Bad Samaritans: Rich Nations, Poor Policies and the Threat to the Developing World*. London: Random House, p 27. See also Bauman (2013).

[52] Rose, D. (2005) 'Socio-Economic Classifications: Classes and Scales, Measurement and Theories', paper presented at the First Conference of the European Survey Research Association, Barcelona, 18–22 July.

[53] Gaffney and Baumberg (2014), p 9.

[54] Office for National Statistics (no date) 'SOC2010 Volume 3: The National Statistics Socio-Economic Classification (NS-SEC Rebased on the SOC2010)'. Available at: http://www.ons.gov.uk/ons/guide-method/classifications/current-standard-classifications/soc2010/soc2010-volume-3-ns-sec--rebased-on-soc2010--user-manual/index.html#2 (accessed 1 February 2015).

[55] Giddens, A. (2007) 'You Need Greater Equality to Achieve More Social Mobility', *The Guardian*, 24 May.

[56] HM Government (2013) 'Improving Social Mobility to Create a Fairer Society'. Available at: https://www.gov.uk/government/policies/improving-social-mobility-to-create-a-fairer-society (accessed 1 February 2015).

[57] Milburn, A. (2009) 'Foreword from the Chair', in Panel on Fair Access to the Professions, *Unleashing Aspiration: The Final Report of the Panel on Fair Access to the Professions*. London: Cabinet Office.

[58] Goldthorpe, J.H., in collaboration with Llewellyn, C. and Payne, C. (1987) *Social Mobility and Class Structure in Modern Britain* (2nd edn). Oxford: Clarendon Press.

[59] OECD (2014), p 2.

[6] Breen, R. (2004) *Social Mobility in Europe*. Oxford: Nuffield College. Available at: http://www.uvm.edu/~pdodds/files/papers/others/2004/breen2004a.pdf (accessed 19 August 2014).

[61] Blanden, J., Gregg, P. and Machin, S. (2007) *Recent Changes in Intergenerational Mobility in Britain*. London: Sutton Trust.

[62] Trends in social mobility have also been influenced by the decline in 'cross-class' and corresponding increase in 'assortative' marriages, that is, there is an increasing tendency for people to marry those from the same social class as themselves. This greatly increases household income and widens inequality: 'On average about 40–50% of the covariance between parents' and own permanent family income can be attributed to the person to whom one is married. This effect is driven by strong spouse correlations in human capital' (Ermisch, J., Francesoni, M. and Siedler, T. [2005] *Intergenerational Economic Mobility and Assortative Mating*. Discussion Paper No 1847. Bonn: Institute for the Study of Labor [IZA]). Wolf argues that male and female couples from the same socio-economic background in the US now have more in common with each *other* than either do with members of their own sex from other classes (Wolf, A. [2013] *The XX Factor: How the Rise of Working Women has Created a Far Less Equal World*. London: Crown).

[63] ESRC (Economic and Social Research Council) (2010) 'Briefing: Rebalancing Britain's Public Finances'. Available at: http://www.esrc.ac.uk/news-events-and-publications/evidence-briefings/rebalancing-britain-s-public-finances/ (accessed 1 February 2015).

[64] Fox (2014).

[65] ESRC (no date), p 3.

[66] National Equality Panel (2010) *An Anatomy of Economic Inequality in the UK: Report of the National Equality Panel*. London: Government Equalities Office/Centre for Analysis of Social Exclusion, ch 11.

[67] Murphy, R. (1988) *Social Closure – The Theory of Monopolization and Exclusion*. Oxford: Clarendon Press.

[68] Weber, M. (1978) *Economy and Society: An Outline of Interpretive Sociology* (ed Roth, G. and Wittich, C.). Berkeley, CA: University of California Press, p 343. Original *Wirtschaft und Gesellschaft* (1922).

[69] Parkin, F. (1979) *Marxism and Class Theory: A Bourgeois Critique*. London: Tavistock, p 44.

[70] Weber (1978), p 388.

[71] According to Durkheim's definition: 'the right of property is the right of a given individual to exclude other individuals and collective entities from the usage of a given thing' (Durkheim, E. [1957] *Professional Ethics and Civic Morals*. London: Routledge, p 141).

[72] Rousseau (1973), p 84. He goes on to say: 'From how many crimes, wars, and murders, from how many horrors and misfortunes might not any one have saved mankind, by pulling up the stakes, or filling up the ditch, and crying to his fellows: "Beware of listening to this imposter; you are undone if you once forget that the fruits of the earth belong to us all, and the earth itself to nobody!"'

[73] UK Parliament (no date) 'Enclosing the Land'. Available at: http://www.parliament.uk/about/living-heritage/transformingsociety/towncountry/landscape/overview/enclosingland/ (accessed 1 February 2015).

[74] Department for Business, Innovation and Skills (2014) *Innovation, Research and Growth: Innovation Report 2014*. London: Department for Business, Innovation and Skills, p 6.

[75] Barry, B. (1998) *Social Exclusion, Social Isolation and the Distribution of Income*. London: Centre for Analysis of Social Exclusion.

[76] There are interesting examples of constructing barriers between different income groups that are almost as effective as actual gated communities. A famous (or notorious) example in Britain was Cutteslowe in Oxford, where a wall was built to divide an estate of social housing from a private residential area. This was analysed by sociologists and the subject of an influential book – Collison, P. (1963) *The Cutteslowe Walls. A Study in Social Class*. London: Faber and Faber. An interesting feature of this case was that there had been relatively minor class differences between residents on either side of the wall until it was erected, but the wall itself created a reputation for the residents on either side that widened differences between them. See Scott, P. (2004) *Visible and Invisible Walls: Suburbanisation and the Social Filtering of Working-Class Communities in Interwar Britain*. Reading: Henley Business School. Nelson, M. (2011) 'Gated Communities: Class Walls', *History Today*, 61(11).

[77] Winlow, S. and Hall, S. (2013) *Rethinking Social Exclusion: The End of the Social?* London: Sage, p 3.

[78] Blandy, S. (2006) 'Gated Communities in England: Historical Perspectives and Current Developments', *GeoJournal*, 66(1). In addition to physical barriers, during industrialisation, several British cities developed a distinctive geographic segregation between a poorer east end and a

more affluent west end, corresponding to how the prevailing south-west wind spread pollution. See Morris, R.J. (1999) 'Urban Space and the Industrial City in Britain', *Refresh*, 28(Spring).

[79] Minton, A. (2006) *What Kind of World Are We Building? The Privatisation of Public Space*. London: Royal Institution of Chartered Surveyors. Worpole, K. and Katharine K. (2007) *The Social Value of Public Spaces*. York: Joseph Rowntree Foundation.

[80] Davis, M. and Monk, D. (eds) (2011) *Evil Paradises: Dreamworlds of Neoliberalism*. London: The New Press.

[81] Scott, J. (1994) *Poverty and Wealth: Citizenship, Deprivation and Privilege*. London: Longman.

[82] A similar etymological connection exists between the adjective 'exclusive', the noun 'exclusivity' and the verb to 'exclude', which all derive from the Latin *excludere*, meaning to keep out.

[83] Cole, D. (1999) *No Equal Justice: Race and Class in the American Criminal Justice System*. New York, NY: Norton.

[84] Jacobs, L.R. and Skocpol, T. (eds) (2007) *Inequality and American Democracy: What We Know and What We Need to Learn*. New York, NY: Russell Sage Foundation. Sandel, M. (2012) *What Money Can't Buy: The Moral Limits of Markets*. London: Allen Lane.

[85] Marshall, T.H. and Bottomore, T. (1996) *Citizenship and Social Class*. London: Pluto Classics, p 8.

[86] Mann, M. (1987) 'Ruling Class Strategies and Citizenship', *Sociology*, 21(3).

[87] Turner, B.S. (1990) 'Outline of a Theory of Citizenship', *Sociology*, 24(2).

[88] Lister, R. (1998) *Citizenship: Feminist Perspectives*. London: Macmillan.

[89] Malthus, T. (1798) 'Essay on the Principles of Population'. Available at: http://www.gutenberg.org/files/4239/4239-h/4239-h.htm (accessed 1 February 2015).

[90] Russell, B. (1965) *Legitimacy Versus Industrialism: 1814–1848*. London: Unwin, p 87.

[91] Malthus (1798).

[92] Malthusian ideas of the value of self-interest and the futility of being sentimental about the plight of the poor were the model for Scrooge in Dickens's 1843 *A Christmas Carol*. See Boyer (2012) 'Malthus and Scrooge: How Charles Dickens Put Holly Branch Through the Heart of the Worst Economics Ever', *Forbes Blog*, 24 December. Available at: http://www.forbes.com/sites/jerrybowyer/2012/12/24/malthus-and-scrooge-how-charles-dickens-put-holly-branch-through-the-heart-of-the-worst-economics-ever/ (accessed 1 February 2015).

[93] Chambers, J.D. (1968) *The Workshop of the World: British Economic History, 1820–1880* (2nd edn). Oxford: Oxford University Press, p 133.

[94] Marx, K. and Engels, F. (1968 [1848]) 'Manifesto of the Communist Party', in Marx, K. and Engels, F., *Selected Works in One Volume*. London: Lawrence & Wishart, p 38.

[95] Nasar, S. (2012) *Grand Pursuit: The Story of the People who Made Modern Economics*. London: Forth Estate, pp 64ff.

[96] Contrasting views on the significance of economic growth compared to how this is distributed are reflected in a debate over the impact of economic growth in India. Two of the main participants in this debate are Amartya Sen and the Professor of Economics at Columbia University, Jagdish Bhagwati. See Mehta, P.S and Chatterjee, B. (eds) (2011) *Growth and Poverty: The Great Debate*. Jaipur: CUTS International. Available at: http://cuts-international.org/pdf/Full_Version-Growth_and_Poverty-The_Great_Debate.pdf. The level of economic growth in India over the past 10 years has been second only to China, at roughly 8% per year. However, despite this, Sen argues that there has been little overall improvement in economic and social well-being in India during this time. For example, 50% of Indian households still practised

'open defecation' in 2011 compared with 1% in China. In neighbouring Bangladesh, the figure was 8.4% despite having a lower rate of economic growth than India, see Von Tunzelmann, A. (2013) 'Review of "An Uncertain Glory: India and its Contradictions"', *The Telegraph*, 1 August. Available at: http://www.telegraph.co.uk/culture/books/10211435/An-Uncertain-Glory-India-and-itsContradictions-by-Jean-Dreze-and-Amartya-Sen-review.html. Sen argues that expanded social programmes providing health care, education and social protection are required, as well as greater investment in roads, transport and utilities, in order to spread the benefits of economic growth beyond an elite, see Sen, A. and Drèze, J. (2013) *An Uncertain Glory: India and its Contradiction*. London: Allen Lane. In contrast, Bhagwati advocates economic liberalisation to enable more private sector growth, and regards public spending as a waste of resources, see Bhagwati, J. and Panagariya, A. (2013) *Why Growth Matters*. New York, NY: PublicAffairs.

[97] Sen, A. (1981) *Poverty and Famines: An Essay on Entitlement and Deprivation*. Oxford: Clarendon Press, p 1, emphases in original.

[98] Sen, A. (1981) 'Ingredients in Famine Analysis: Availability and Entitlements', *Quarterly Journal of Economics*, 96(3), p 461.

[99] Dahrendorf, R. (1988) *The Modern Social Conflict: An Essay on the Politics of Liberty*. London: Weidenfield & Nicolson, p 9.

[100] Sen (1981) 'Ingredients of Famine Analysis', p 438.

[101] Sen (1981) *Poverty and Famines*, p 154.

[102] Parkin (1979), pp 47–8.

[103] Parkin (1979, p 89) also suggests that 'exclusion strategies … are frequently employed by one segment of the subordinate class against another', so that significant divisions can exist *within* what Marxists would regard as the 'proletariat', that is, a single propertyless class. This suggests that there is no reason to expect solidarity to exist within a united 'working class', and studies of British labour history have proven this: 'Concern over differentials and relativities occupy as central a place in the history of trade unionism as the class struggle' (Roberts, K., Cook, F.G., Clark, S.C. and Semeneoff, E. [1977] *The Fragmentary Class Structure*. London: Hutchinson, pp 97–8). Women, in particular, have often been excluded from trade unions and other organisations in order to improve working terms and conditions, as men, particularly those in the most skilled trades, were concerned to prevent what they regarded as 'cheap' labour undercutting their wages, see Rose, S.O. (1988) 'Gender Antagonism and Class Conflict: Exclusionary Strategies of Male Trade Unionists in Nineteenth-Century Britain', *Social History*, 13(2). Parkin observes that the US labour movement has had a history of excluding those from certain ethnic groups from joining trade unions, particularly African-Americans.

[104] Macpherson, C.B. (1973) 'A Political Theory of Property', in Macpherson, C.B., *Democratic Theory: Essays in Retrieval*. Oxford: Oxford University Press.

[105] Parkin (1979), p 48.

[106] Hirsch, D. (2007) *Experiences of Poverty and Educational Disadvantage*. York: Joseph Rowntree Foundation. The figures compare the proportion of students who receive grades A★–C in five subjects in GCSE assessments. The GCSE is the principal academic qualification for pupils in secondary education in England, Wales and Northern Ireland (but not Scotland) and is usually taken between the ages of 14 and 16.

[107] Halsey, A.H., Heath, A.F. and Ridge, J.M. (1980) *Origins and Destinations: Family, Class and Education in Modern Britain*. Oxford: Clarendon Press, p 163.

[108] Gregg, P. (2008) 'Childhood Poverty and Life Chances', in Strelitz, J. and Lister, R. (eds) *Why Money Matters: Family Income, Poverty and Children's Lives*. London: Save the Children, p 78.

[109] Bowles, S. and Gintis, H. (2002) 'The Inheritance of Inequality', *Journal of Economic Perspectives*, 16(3).

[110] Gaffney and Baumberg (2014), p 14.

[111] All-Party Parliamentary Group (2012), p 7. Milburn (2009), p 12.

[112] Sutton Trust (2008) *University Admissions by Individual Schools*. London: Sutton Trust. See also: https://www.westminster.org.uk/admissions/fees.html

[113] Tilly, C. (1999) *Durable Inequality*. Berkeley, CA: University of California Press. See also Panel on Fair Access to the Professions (2009) *Unleashing Aspiration: The Final Report of the Panel on Fair Access to the Professions*. London: Cabinet Office, p 15.

[114] Doward, J. and Thomas, M. (2014) 'Underprivileged Two-Year-Olds Being Declined by "Middle-Class" Nurseries', *The Observer*, 24 August. The chief executive of the Family and Childcare Trust commented that 'some [childcare] providers felt that some of the working parents in their nurseries and pre-schools would object to large numbers of vulnerable children being admitted to their setting'. As a result, children from disadvantaged households and communities are denied the opportunity to mix with children from different social backgrounds, which they are known to benefit from. Consequently, the impact of public investment in childcare for more deprived children is reduced, see Rutter, J. and Evans, B. (2012) *2012 London Childcare Survey*. London: Daycare Trust, p 45.

[115] Dorling, D. (2012) *Injustice: Why Social Inequality Persists*. Bristol: The Policy Press, p 132.

[116] Francis, B. and Hutchings, M. (2013) *Parent Power*. London: Sutton Trust.

[117] Nationwide (no date) 'Special Report – High Performing Primary Schools Add Value to Property Prices'. Available at: http://www.nationwide.co.uk/~/media/MainSite/documents/about/house-price-index/primary-school-special.pdf (accessed 1 February 2015).

[118] Ball, S.J. (1993) 'Education Markets, Choice and Social Class: The Market as a Class Strategy in the UK and USA', *British Journal of the Sociology of Education*, 14(1). See also Ball, S.J. (2006) *Education Policy and Social Class: The Selected Works of Stephen J. Ball*. Abingdon: Routledge.

[119] Power, S., Edwards, T., Whitty, G. and Wigfall, V. (2003) *Education and the Middle Class*. Buckingham: Open University Press, p 153.

[120] Clark, T. (2010) 'Is Social Mobility Dead?', *The Guardian*, 10 March. Marcenaro-Gutierrez, O., Micklewright, J. and Vignoles, A. (2014) *Social Mobility and the Importance of Networks: Evidence for Britain*. London: UCL Institute of Education, Centre for Longitudinal Studies. Sutton Trust (2014) 'Internship or Indenture?', Research Briefing, 2 November. Available at: http://www.suttontrust.com/wp-content/uploads/2014/11/Unpaid-Internships.pdf

[121] Granovetter, M. (1973) 'The Strength of Weak Ties', *American Journal of Sociology*, 78(6).

[122] Afridi, A. (2011) *Social Networks: Their Role in Addressing Poverty*. York: Joseph Rowntree Foundation.

[123.] Matthews, P. and Hastings, A. (2013) 'Middle-Class Political Activism and Middle-Class Advantage in Relation to Public Services: A Realist Synthesis of the Evidence Base', *Social Policy & Administration*, 47(1), p 78.

[124] OECD (2011) *How's Life? Measuring Well-Being*. Paris: OECD Publishing, p 171.

[125] Office of National Statistics (2001) *Social Capital – A Review of the Literature*. London: ONS Social Analysis and Reporting Division, Socio-Economic Inequalities Branch, p 6.

[126] Putnam, R. (2000) *Bowling Alone: The Collapse and Revival of American Community*. London: Simon and Schuster.

[127] Bourdieu, P. (1986) 'The Forms of Capital', in Robinson, J.G. (ed) *Handbook of Theory and Research for the Sociology of Education*. New York, NY: Greenwood Press.

[128] Bourdieu, P. (1984) *Distinction: A Social Critique of the Judgement of Taste* (trans Nice, R.). Harvard, MA: Harvard University Press. Hobsbawm argued that signifiers of cultural capital became particularly important in Britain in the middle and later 19th century, when the expansion of mass education threatened the superiority of more advantaged and privileged social classes. It is around this time that particular markers of distinction were developed, such as using old school ties to distinguish one's background and the publication of *Who's Who*. See Hobsbawm, E. (1983) 'Mass-Producing Traditions: Europe 1870–1914', in Hobsbawm, E. and Ranger, T. (eds) *The Invention of Tradition*. Cambridge: Cambridge University Press.

[129] See BBC Radio 4 (2014) 'Price Conscious', *In Business*, 15 May. Available at: http://downloads. bbc.co.uk/podcasts/radio/worldbiz/worldbiz_20140508-2100a.mp3 (accessed 1 February 2014). The Burberry clothing company encountered a similar issue when its previously exclusive and elite brand identity was regarded as tarnished after it became popular with football supporters and those described as lower-class 'Chavs', see 'A Checkered Story: Burberry and Globalisation', *The Economist*, 20 January.

[130] Souiden, N., M'Saad, B. and Pons, F. (2011) 'A Cross-Cultural Analysis of Consumers' Conspicuous Consumption of Branded Fashion Accessories', *Journal of International Consumer Marketing*, 23(5). The concept of 'conspicuous consumption' was created by Thorstein Veblen in 1899 in *The Theory of the Leisure Class*.

[131] Power et al (2003), p 82.

[132] Bourdieu, P. (1993) *Sociology in Question* (trans Nice, R.). London: Sage, p 86.

[133.] Whether this exchange ever really occurred in person or in writing between Fitzgerald and Hemingway is disputed.

[134] Weber, M. (1948) 'Class, Status and Party', in Weber, M., *From Max Weber: Essays In Sociology* (trans and ed Gerth, H.H. and Mills, C.W.). London: Routledge & Kegan Paul, p 187.

[135] Brubaker, R. (1985) 'Rethinking Classical Theory: The Sociological Vision of Pierre Bourdieu', *Theory and Society*, 14(6), p 758.

[136] Bourdieu, P. and Wacquant, L. (1992) *An Invitation to Reflexive Sociology*. Chicago, IL: University of Chicago Press, p 127.

[137] Sage, L.S. (2014) *Bad Blood*. London: Fourth Estate, p 148. See also Jackson, B. and Marsden, D. (1969) *Education and the Working Class*. Harmondsworth: Penguin.

[138] Bourdieu, P. and Passeron, J.-C. (1977) *Reproduction in Education, Society and Culture*. London: Sage.

[139] Reay, D., Crozier, G. and Clayton, J. (2009) '"Strangers in Paradise"? Working-Class Students in Elite Universities', *Sociology*, 43(6), p 1105.

[140] Bourdieu, P. (1985) 'Social Space and the Genesis of Groups', *Theory and Society*, 14(5), p 725. This experience was dramatised in Dennis Potter's (1965) autobiographical television play *Stand Up, Nigel Barton*.

[141] Willis, P. (1977) *Learning to Labour: How Working Class Kids Get Working Class Jobs*. Farnborough: Saxon House.

[142] Power et al (2003).

[143] All-Party Parliamentary Group (2012), p 30.

[144] Milburn (2009), p 7.

[145] All-Party Parliamentary Group (2012), p 27.

[146] Jordan, B. (2006) *A Theory of Poverty and Social Exclusion*. Cambridge: Policy Press.

[147] This is not unique to the UK or the US, see Zhao, Y. (2014) *Who's Afraid of the Big Bad Dragon? Why China Has the Best (and Worst) Education System in the World*. San Francisco, CA: Jossey Bass.

[148] See Calder, J. (2008) 'Labour's Private School Heroes', *New Statesman*, 13 October.

[149] '[T]he privileged in any society have always been desperately reluctant to acknowledge that their privilege arises as a direct outcome of the disadvantage of others. This simple fact is denied with all the vehemence and intellectual dishonesty we are accustomed to hearing from those whose practice is at odds with their purported principles.' Platt, S. (1996) 'Parents Who Pull the Plug', *The Guardian*, 2 July.

[150] McIntosh, P. (1990) 'White Privilege: Unpacking the Invisible Knapsack', *Independent School Magazine*, 49(2), pp 31–6.

[151] Adebayo, D. (2001) 'Young, Gifted, Black', *The Observer*, 25 November.

[152] Seabrook (2008), p 2.

[153] Taulbut, M. and Robinson, M. (2014) 'The Chance to Work in Britain: Matching Unemployed People to Vacancies in Good Times and Bad', *Regional Studies*, 48.

[154] Sampson, A. (2005) *Who Runs This Place? The Anatomy of Britain in the 21st Century*. London: John Murray.

[155] Sandel, M. (2010) 'Towards a Just Society', *The Guardian*, 20 February.

[156] Prime Minister Margret Thatcher made this comment in an interview published in October 1987, and it immediately became a renowned – or infamous – statement. Her supporters argue that the full context clarifies the proposition. Readers can decide upon this for themselves, see: http://www.margaretthatcher.org/speeches/displaydocument.asp?docid=106689

[157] Tawney, R. (1913) 'Poverty as an Industrial Problem', in Tawney, R., *Memoranda on the Problems of Poverty*. London: William Morris Press, p 10.

SIX

Why are people so mistaken about welfare? Myth

> **Myth: key points**
> - Many opinions on welfare issues are profoundly mistaken and resistant to evidence.
> - Myths are deep and unquestioned beliefs that form part of the framework upon which people draw to make sense of information.
> - Media coverage may help perpetuate but does not create welfare myths.
> - People are predisposed to believe what is convenient and comforting, and many views on welfare issues reflect social positions and interests.

Introduction

Most people have little awareness of the details of social policies. The general public have only the vaguest idea of the scale of some important issues or how the institutions established to deal with them actually work.[1] It is unrealistic to expect everyone to have an informed understanding of complex social problems and policies. However, a striking feature of many opinions on social policy issues is that they are not held tentatively. In fact, many people have very firm views on questions of welfare based on what are sometimes rather shaky foundations.[2] This can be demonstrated by the following examples of opinions about social welfare that are widely held in the UK (and in several other countries[3]):

- There is no real poverty in contemporary Britain.
- The welfare state redistributes heavily from the richer to the poorer.
- The best way to reduce poverty is to let wealth 'trickle down' to lower-income groups.
- Social welfare gives too much to the undeserving, is a disincentive to employment and many claimants defraud the system.
- A high level of welfare spending is unaffordable and makes a country economically uncompetitive.

Some of these opinions are discussed in other chapters, where they have been shown to be misconceptions. For example, the first is considered in Chapter Four, where the meaning of 'poverty' is analysed. The second view is discussed both in Chapter One, where the economic dimension of Social Policy is outlined, and in Chapter Three in relation to the 'social division of welfare'. The third proposition is examined in Chapter Five, which considers the persistence of inequality. It is worth considering some of the compelling evidence against the final two opinions.

Welfare fraud and dependency

Surveys of social attitudes have shown that the British public have 'wildly exaggerated' estimates of the scale of welfare support provided to unemployed and single-parent claimants.[4] For example, a majority of respondents in the British Social Attitudes survey believe that unemployment benefits are the largest or second-largest item in the social security budget, and, on average, people think that 41% of the entire welfare budget is spent on benefits to unemployed people.[5] In fact, unemployed benefits make up only 2.5% of the UK benefits bill. Tax credits and other support to those in employment account for 21%, while pensions and other benefits to older people make up 42%. Almost one third of people in Britain believe that more is spent on Jobseeker's Allowance than on old-age pensions. This is not merely a slight overestimate – it is the opposite of the case by a factor of 15: £4.9 billion is spent each year on Jobseeker's Allowance compared with £74.2 billion on pensions.[6] Only 0.1% of claimants who have been receiving benefits in the UK for a decade are unemployed; 2.2% are carers, 6.5% are lone parents and 90.5% are receiving incapacity benefits.[7]

Public understanding of benefit fraud is equally misinformed. As one of the UK's leading experts on the issue noted: 'debates about fraud have on the whole not been too hindered by any rigorous, systematic analysis of the problem'.[8] About 80% of people in Britain believe that 'large numbers falsely claim benefits', and estimate that about one third of all benefit spending is lost on fraudulent claims.[9] In fact, according to the UK government's estimate, only about 0.7% of the total benefit bill is claimed fraudulently, compared to the 2% that is lost due to administrative mistakes.[10] As mentioned in Chapter Two, the proportions and sums of money lost in the UK through abuse of the social security system are far lower than those lost through legal tax avoidance and illegal tax evasion. Tax fraud was estimated to be 12% of the UK **tax gap** in 2012/13, amounting to £4.1 billion.[11] In addition to this, £5.4 billion of tax was not collected due to criminal attacks, £4.4 billion was not collected because of non-payment and £5.9 billion was lost through the hidden economy. The telephone hotline established to enable the British public to report cases of suspected benefit fraud receives over 250,000 calls a year, but only one fifth of these are regarded by officials as sufficiently serious to investigate, and fewer than one in 10 investigations uncover evidence of fraud. In Britain, 74 out of 75 people who thought that a neighbour was committing benefit fraud were mistaken.[12] In fact, if everyone in the UK who was eligible for benefits claimed their full entitlements, an additional £18 billion would be spent on social security. However, underpayment does not trouble the British public as much as the suspicion that claimants are receiving more than they ought.

Concerns that social welfare benefits weaken independence and undermine self-reliance have shaped social policies since at least the English Poor Law of the 16th century. An Act of Parliament was passed in 1530 to arrest 'vacaboundes and ydell persones',[13] and a later law of 1547 declared that 'if anyone refuses to work, he shall be condemned as a slave to the person who has denounced him as an idler'.[14] Punishments inflicted on 'wandering vagabonds' who were judged to be able but unwilling to work in England during this period included whipping, being placed in the stocks, branding, forced labour, imprisonment and even execution for repeat offenders.[15] The children of vagrants would be removed from them and compelled to be apprentices until their 20s to ensure that they did not reproduce their parents' crimes of poverty and idleness.[16]

Anxieties about the moral weakness and economic burden of the undeserving poor were equally common in Britain the 19th century. These concerns were central to the **1834 Poor Law**, described by Bertrand Russell as an Act of 'intolerable cruelty and hardship'.[17] The reason for this is that an important aim of the 1834 Poor Law was to remove 'outdoor relief' (ie income supplements and assistance to reduce poverty) as this was criticised for encouraging deliberate pauperism and enabling people to refuse to work. The 1834 Act replaced outdoor relief with support that required claimants to enter a **workhouse**, where they would be made to earn support through hard labour. Conditions in the workhouses were made **less eligible** than those outside, that is, no one receiving support would be better off than those earning even the lowest income through employment. The principle that workhouse conditions should be unpleasant and uncomfortable to discourage 'malingering' and 'scrounging' was summarised by the 1832 Royal Commission that led to the Act:

> Into such a [work]house none will enter voluntarily; work, confinement and discipline, will deter the indolent and vicious; and nothing but an extreme necessity will induce any to accept the comfort which must be obtained by the surrender of free agency.[18]

The workhouse operated like a prison to deter claims for welfare support, and the Conservative opposition leader Benjamin Disraeli (subsequently prime minister) said that the 1834 Poor Law 'announces to the world that in England poverty is a crime'.[19]

Despite such criticism, and its unpopularity among lower-income groups who feared ever having to claim support, the harshness of the 1834 Poor Law corresponded with mainstream Victorian attitudes. Writing in the 1840 and 1850s, the journalist and social investigator Henry Mayhew recorded public concerns about young vagrants, who were described as 'distinguished by their aversion to continuous labour of any kind ... they are, indeed, essentially the idle and the vagabond'; he also anticipated contemporary concerns about young single parents queue-jumping social housing, as he recorded the views of those convinced that young people were encouraged into 'absconding from their homes, immediately on the least disagreement or restraint' by the availability of cheap lodging houses.[20]

The belief that poverty is caused by moral weakness or self-destructive behaviour did not disappear in the 19th century: in an opinion survey in 2012, the most commonly chosen explanation for child poverty in Britain (selected by 73% of respondents) was that their parents suffered from alcoholism, drug abuse or addiction.[21] In fact, fewer than 4% of benefit claimants with or without children have a reported addiction, and over 60% of children in poverty in the UK live in a household where someone has a job.[22] Fears that welfare support or high benefit levels encourage people to remain unemployed are also exaggerated: unemployed claimants in Denmark can receive up to 90% of their previous wages in benefits but the overall level of unemployment is lower than the UK and the duration of unemployment is shorter.[23] What matters is how welfare support is provided, and there is no evidence that harsh treatment is effective in lowering unemployment.[24] There is even evidence that reducing the conditions attached to welfare benefits can encourage recipients to improve their situation. Experiments in **Unconditional Cash Transfers**, where people experiencing poverty receive money without having to do anything to qualify for this, have found that these do not encourage laziness, frivolous spending or passive dependency: 'Recipients of unconditional cash do not blow it on booze and brothels, as some feared. Households can absorb a surprising amount of cash and put it to good use'.[25] However, it is difficult to imagine many political leaders in the UK or several other countries proposing such a controversial approach to welfare provision.[26]

Is a large welfare state unaffordable?

The German Chancellor Angela Merkel has observed that the population of the European Union makes up only 7% of the global population but accounts for 50% of international welfare spending, while contributing only 25% of the world's economic output: 'The implication is clear enough. If Europe is to compete with the rising economic powers of the east and south, it will have to shrink the state'.[27] As Chapter Three explains, figures on 'welfare' expenditure require careful consideration of what is being counted and what the numbers actually mean. For example, as noted earlier, retirement pensions are the largest single item of UK social security expenditure, and as there are now over three times as many pensioners in the UK than there were in 1948 (when the forerunner of the current form of the basic state pension was introduced) and they are also living longer, it is inevitable that there will be a larger social security budget.[28] It is also a basic principle of scientific analysis that correlation does not mean causation.[29] There is a relationship between population, social policy and economic productivity, but this might be more complicated – in fact, the opposite – of that implied by Chancellor Merkel. Some forms of welfare spending can be regarded as a **social investment** that contributes to economic productivity. For example, expenditure on education improves workforce skills, and social security (known as social protection in some European countries) reduces the financial impact of unemployment, which allows workers to take risks by moving to new jobs and enabling a more dynamic and flexible labour market.[30] Similarly, subsidising childcare helps parents to work, earn wages and pay taxes. Pensions allow older people to spend and consume the goods and services produced by the working population, which stimulates economic growth. The significant point is that a more positive interpretation of the figures that Angela Merkel refers to is possible, and there are alternatives to the ideological implications she draws. As explained in Chapter One, the economic and social effects of different forms of welfare provision should not be automatically assumed, but are matters of empirical Social Policy analysis.

There is no consistent pattern in the relationship between the scale of welfare expenditure and economic growth: some countries that spend more on welfare have increased their gross domestic product (GDP) in recent years, while some lower-spending countries have had a smaller growth rate or have seen their economy shrink. The relationship between social expenditure and economic growth depends on the nature of spending and the structure and resilience of the economy.[31]

Are social policy misconceptions 'myths'?

A notable feature of many welfare debates is how persistent mistaken beliefs are despite years of carefully gathered and widely publicised Social Policy research. For every careful fact-checking website on social welfare and related issues that exists, there are dozens of opinionated falsehoods expressed on blogs, circulated on social media and reported by supposedly respectable mainstream news media.[32] Public opinion analysts distinguish between being *uninformed* through a lack of information about policy and being *misinformed* and confidently holding false beliefs.[33] For example, in 2013, only 47% of Americans were convinced of the evidence in support of Darwin's theory of evolution while 36% believed in Creationism.[34] This scale of reluctance to accept scientific evidence goes beyond a lack of information – such beliefs seem impervious to evidence. These are not opinions reached after calm consideration of the facts. Indeed, some 'facts' that contradict particular beliefs are ignored, or dismissed as irrelevant or wrong.[35] Some views on social policy issues have similar qualities, which suggests that something deeper underlies beliefs about welfare. Social Policy analysts must consider why many people maintain mistaken beliefs with such resilience and passion, and what the source of these ideas might be.[36]

Some commentators suggest that views on welfare and related political issues should be regarded not as considered opinions, but as **social myths** that express deep-rooted beliefs:

> social myths provide much of the rationale for social policy decisions. Such myths form a body of collective beliefs which everyone knows to

be 'right' and to be 'true'. It is easy for a policy maker to accept such myths. They reinforce what he already knows. They are reassuring rather than threatening.[37]

A myth is 'a conviction false yet tenacious'.[38] Myths have several other features that are discussed later, but it is important to recognise that they are not shaken by contrary evidence: 'It is beyond the power of philosophy to destroy the political myths. A myth is in a sense invulnerable. It is impervious to rational arguments; it cannot be refuted by syllogisms'.[39] If this is the case, it has interesting implications for Social Policy as an empirical discipline. One of the functions of social science is to analyse and test beliefs. However, if opinions are immune to carefully collected evidence, there is a danger of relativism and that policies will be determined by 'common sense' prejudices or whichever group has the loudest voice.[40]

However, the situation is not really so relativist and nihilistic: 'There are very few indisputable, unassailable "facts".... [But it] is much easier to be confident about what is wrong. The best we can look for is to get a little nearer the truth – to replace myths with half-truths'.[41] It is not the case that *anything* goes in Social Policy debates and not all opinions are equally valid. There are some statements about social conditions and welfare policies that can be established by careful analysis and robust research irrespective of personal opinion. However, the puzzle remains as to why some well-documented facts are rejected and some beliefs are much more resistant to evidence than others.

The word 'myth' can refer to an explicit story but also a more implicit 'set of systemized beliefs'.[42] In this latter sense, myths are 'internalised preconceptions' and part of the framework through which people interpret information.[43] Myths, in this sense, are part of what the cognitive linguist George Lakoff calls **frames** – the mental structures through which people see and make sense of events.[44] Lakoff suggests that these frames:

> allow human beings to understand reality – and sometimes to create what we take to be reality ... they structure our ideas and concepts, they shape the way we reason.... For the most part, our use of frames is unconscious and automatic.[45]

Myths can be thought of as lenses that filter information and are the basis for organising and explaining experience at a subconscious level: 'It is a property of such myths that they are not judged or questioned by fact, rather facts and theories about the world are assessed by their accordance with our myths'.[46] In many cases and for many social policy issues, the facts do *not* speak for themselves. Instead, what they are taken to say is edited by existing assumptions.

All social groups and communities that persist for some time develop belief systems that help sustain their collective identity. Myths can unify populations, and their role in constructing national identities and binding nations together has been studied at length.[47] The radical social theorist Georges Sorel argued that faith in some social myths could inspire revolutionary action even if there was no realistic foundation for such beliefs.[48] Myths are not deliberate lies, but something that people think ought to be true and do not question; they are comforting internalised fictions. The resonance and resilience of myths is that they are a source of and support for necessary illusions.[49]

Analysing myths

Myths have fascinated scholars for centuries, particularly the legends and religions of ancient Greece and Rome. In the 19th century, such myths were often regarded as primitive belief systems, which were inferior to modern science. However, in the 20th century, a more nuanced view of myths developed and there was greater interest in interpreting the latent meaning of myths and what they revealed about the beliefs of different cultures. Rather than being dismissed as ignorant and outmoded accounts of reality, myths were studied as indications of underlying psychological and moral truths. This reorientation of the relationships between science and myth has implications for the approach that Social Policy has to take towards persistent false beliefs. The conventional approach has been to confront such views with evidence as though they are uninformed. For example, researchers investigating the frequently repeated claim that there are many UK households where three generations have never been employed found not one single such case after exhaustive research. This claim has been comprehensively disproved, and the researchers argue that 'there is a moral duty to expose myths about poverty and people living in poverty'[50] and to rebut what have been described as **zombie theories** – ideas that are 'resistant to evidence and social scientific efforts to kill them off'.[51] Challenging and refuting false claims are important, but the apparent indestructibility of these kinds of myth shows that they are not killed off by scientific proof alone. Some blatantly false convictions can be more compelling than facts, and no amount of carefully collected evidence is enough to rebut some anecdotes and fabrications based on implicit myths.[52]

In addition to denying inconvenient evidence, myths can be flexible and adjusted to accommodate contrary information without compromising core beliefs. Inconvenient evidence may be dismissed or selectively interpreted by what the critic John Berger calls **mystification**: 'the process of explaining away what might otherwise be evident'.[53] For example, studies of attitudes towards welfare in the UK show that some people will go to great lengths to deny the existence of poverty or accept any explanation for it other than individual failure. They will 'reach for outlandish explanations to account for the dissonance from their view', such as suggesting that people experiencing poverty 'don't wear coats because it's fashionable not to', or that 'People in Cornwall don't need so much money – they can go out and cut trees down for fuel'.[54]

It is therefore not enough simply to disprove welfare myths. Views that are held so steadfastly and in the face of all contrary evidence should not be rebutted, but analysed. To dismiss myths as mistaken misunderstands their nature – they are not simply 'wrong', but should be regarded as fictions and stories. A myth is not factually true, but it does express a truth. A myth is defined not by what it says, but what it *does*. Myths serve a need for those who hold them, in particular, they reinforce particular beliefs. Examining common myths uncovers basic impulses and the foundations of belief systems. Myths should be analysed for what they reveal about the functions they perform for a particular culture. The theologian Rudolf Bultman distinguished between 'demythologising' and 'demythicising'.[55] For example, proving that Noah's flood did not actually happen is to **demythicise** it; to interpret the story of the flood as an expression of how a particular society dealt with the mysteries of human life is to **demythologise** it. Social Policy analysis can show particular views to be false (ie demythicise them) but demythologising them involves examining what such views reveal about beliefs, values and social relationships. However, while some beliefs about welfare may be based on myths, they are not mythical in the same way as magic or religion. Statements and opinions about welfare and social policies involve empirical claims about the world that can and should be tested against verifiable facts. However, in addition to this, it is important to understand where false ideas about welfare come from and why they persist.

The mass media and myths

The media play an important role in disseminating and perpetuating welfare myths.[56] For example, public overestimates of the level of abuse of social security in the UK might be influenced by the fact that 30% of all newspaper articles about welfare over a 16-year period referred to fraud.[57] Misrepresentation of welfare issues is not a uniquely British phenomenon – African-Americans make up 27% of those in poverty in the US but feature in 49% of media portrayals of poverty; in contrast, 45% of those experiencing poverty in the US are white but this group appear in only 33% of depictions. Media coverage of poverty in the US is also disproportionately linked to a range of other distinct social problem, such as drugs, crime and gangs, which may distort public perceptions of who experiences poverty and its principal causes.[58]

However, while the mass media may misrepresent some aspects of poverty and the scale and nature of other social problems (notably, crime), this does not mean that the media are the source of public misconceptions or myths. For one thing, changes in public attitudes towards poverty and welfare issues in the UK do not match trends in media coverage.[59] More importantly, people do not passively acquire their views on such issues from whatever the media present to them. As the pioneer of cultural studies Stuart Hall argued, people are not *cultural dopes*, but 'active and often critical participants in the production and negotiation of meaning'.[60] People select which media they consume and choose how to interpret the coverage of events and issues, believing those stories they favour and rejecting or reinterpreting those they find unconvincing.[61] As Galbraith observed, 'people like to hear articulated that which they approve' and will tend to dismiss accounts that contradict firmly held beliefs.[62] The mass media may influence public views of social issues but it does not write on a blank slate and cannot create opinions from thin air. It is more likely that the media reinforces or amplifies existing beliefs by re-presenting what self-selecting audiences expect and by not confronting them with challenging alternative accounts.[63] The commercial mass media responds to competitive pressures, including the demands and preferences of their audiences. As one experienced media insider observed, a skilful 'editor knows his audience', and produces for them a 'closed, complete world view [that] will reassure and underpin the reader's sense of how things are'.[64]

This tendency to encounter messages that reaffirm existing views may be reinforced by social media and the interactions of online communities. This has been described as the **echo chamber** effect,[65] where a preference to engage with those who share opinions reduces encounters with contrary and challenging viewpoints so that, over time, dissenting voices become regarded as marginal and extreme.[66] There is no evidence yet that 'Balkanisation' into exclusive online communities has replaced dialogue within shared spaces, but the commercial interest in enabling and exploiting more personalised online activity could make this a more significant issue in the future.[67] For example, Google is promoting tailored search results to improve the targeting of advertising. Users may benefit by receiving information on relevant products but it could also mean that users with different search histories will retrieve contrasting information about the 'same' issue, and this could undermine the possibility of reaching a shared understanding about the facts of any case.[68] Relying on specialised and preferred rather than shared sources of information reinforces what psychologists call **confirmation bias**: the tendency to recall information that reinforces rather than challenges existing beliefs.[69] This is why scientific methods (including peer review of published findings) and procedures to systematically review all of the available evidence are required in Social Policy analysis (see Chapter One).[70]

Psychologists have also found that media reports can consolidate particular ideas and associations in people's minds, even if these are mistaken or misleading. Everyone relies upon subconscious rules of thumb (ie heuristics [see Chapter Two]) to make sense of information, and things that have been repeated are often more accessible to our memories and become accepted as facts, even if they are untrue or were initially dismissed as implausible.[71] This is particularly the case for people who have not examined the issue seriously and rely on second-hand information and their own unquestioned common sense. The effect can be powerful, and once an idea becomes lodged in the mind, it can be difficult to remove, as political spin doctors, psychologists and journalists well know:

> your world view is altered by the news you get. One story saying that killer French bees are coming to get you might make you laugh. A dozen, over a few days, might make you scared. If you hear that people have indeed died, and this is repeated, and similar stories recur the next spring, and the next, then you may come to believe in killer French

bees. Multiply that a thousand-fold to account for all the running stories in different papers and one understands that power of news. It takes a heroic, or insane, mind to stand outside it.[72]

In such circumstances, only direct personal experience or a robust counter-belief system will challenge a frequently repeated account. However, for many people, much of the time, it is possible to avoid encountering information that disturbs a comfortable prejudice without being deliberately partisan or consciously biased. This is particularly the case if there is any subconscious motivation to hold particular beliefs.

Myths and status legends

People are not neutral in their views on welfare and poverty because (as discussed in Chapter One) these involve not just facts of what *is* the case, but moral convictions about how things *ought* to be. Sociologists have long argued that moral judgements and value systems are not carefully selected from a menu of options, but relate to social conditions. Max Weber suggested that there is an **elective affinity** between what people believe – both factually and morally – and their position in society.[73] This leads everyone to be predisposed to hold views that reflect our experiences and social locations. It is difficult to sustain deeply held views that jar radically with our everyday experiences, although not impossible, as psychological theories of **cognitive dissonance** and the sociological concept of 'dual consciousness' illustrate.[74] Ideas and social experiences interact and mould one another. It is not the case, as some crude versions of Marxism suggest, that material or social conditions *determine* people's values and beliefs, but certain outlooks are compatible with corresponding social experiences and settings.[75] In particular, individuals and groups will tend to acquire 'convenient doctrines' and become attached to views that are psychologically comforting or legitimise any advantages or favourable social status they possess.[76]

Weber described such beneficial beliefs as **status legends**, and they are an important element of the identity of many groups. For example, journalists may regard their profession as holding the powerful to account, exposing scandals and fearlessly seeking the truth. Scientists and academics portray their duty as selflessly pursuing objective knowledge and contributing to the understanding of the world, while some non-scientists and laypeople take pride in their robust common sense and dismiss the pretensions of so-called experts. Weber noted in particular that a wealthy or fortunate person:

> is seldom satisfied with the fact of being fortunate.... Beyond this, he needs to know that he has a *right* to his good fortune. He wants to be convinced that he 'deserves' it, and, above all, that he deserves it in comparison with others. He wishes to be allowed the belief that the

less fortunate also merely experience their due. Good fortune thus wants to be 'legitimate' fortune.[77]

Most people like to feel that they deserve any success they enjoy; that this is a justified reflection of their ability, effort or aspirations. It follows that if success is earned and deserved, then so is any 'failure', such as poverty or the need to receive welfare support. This outlook is reflected and reinforced by the media coverage of welfare and poverty that more wealthy and conventionally successful people prefer to consume and are likely to believe. As a political journalist for a British broadsheet newspaper explained, the reason why there is so little sensitive coverage or sympathetic portrayal of poverty in the mainstream media is because 'people are looking for reassuring images, that things are okay, things are fair, and that people at the bottom are there because it's their fault, and therefore we've all earned and merit our position'.[78] Of course, those who have enjoyed success and wealth often *do* work hard and may have particular abilities or earned valued qualifications. However, this is only a partial account of how most success and wealth is acquired. It ignores the fact that rich and successful people are not the only ones who work hard, and that there are many factors other than merit contributing to the advantages enjoyed by particular groups and individuals (as discussed in Chapter Five).

Relatively few successful and wealthy people are happy to think of themselves as a predatory *Wolf of Wall Street* character, but prefer to believe that they are contributing positive social benefits beyond pursuing their own interests. It has been noted that:

> Man does not live by bread alone. He wants to have a good conscience as he pursues his life-interests. And in pursuing them he develops his capacities to the highest extent only if he believes that in doing so he serves a higher than a purely egoistic purpose.[79]

This is one reason why the rich and wealthy are predisposed to believe in the myth that their riches will 'trickle down' to benefit others and that their success creates a 'rising tide' that improves general living standards, despite the evidence against this.

Aspects of individual psychology and social identity therefore combine to strengthen attachment to particular opinions. An individual's sense of self is invested in certain outlooks that become the framework through which information is filtered and interpreted. The business and organisation theorist Chris Argyris argues that these outlooks become protected by **defensive reasoning**, through which people 'keep private the premises, inferences, and conclusions that shape their behavior and avoid testing them in a truly independent, objective fashion'.[80] This process can lead to orientations and opinions becoming implicit, unquestioned and impenetrable to new information or challenging views. The resilience of beliefs and internalised ideas is strengthened further if they become regarded as disinterested and detached from any selfish interests. The more successful an idea or doctrine is in obscuring its association with the interests of any particular section of society, the more compelling it appears.[81] This leads groups to portray their own beliefs and legitimating ideologies as universal principles. This process is most successful when there appears to be no connection at all between a particular outlook or opinion and any self-interest.[82]

Social Policy analysts should therefore remain alert to the potential association between opinions, social positions and interests, and 'for every idea that we observe we should seek out the status group whose material and ideal way of life it tends to enhance'.[83] This does not mean using **ad hominem** arguments (ie attacking the player rather than the ball) and rejecting certain views simply because they may coincide with or even further the interests of particular groups. Social Policy arguments and positions must be assessed in their own right, and their empirical, distributional and ethical aspects must be analysed critically. However, to understand why some viewpoints may resist the weight of evidence and compelling critique means considering that they may have a deeper appeal beyond their surface appearance. Social Policy analysts must also acknowledge that we ourselves may be just as prone to favouring convenient doctrines and defensive reasoning as anyone else: perhaps claiming to be dedicated to challenging misconceived policies and debunking popular myths is another status legend? To reduce the risk of seeing only what we prefer to believe, Social Policy analysts must confront arguments and evidence that challenge our own positions. The best defence against becoming entrapped by complacency is to be constantly subject to self-criticism and open to public questioning. This is not a comfortable position, but as George Orwell noted: 'To see what is in front of one's nose needs a constant struggle'.[84]

Individualist explanations and blaming the victim

One feature of Social Policy analysis that helps guard against the temptation of simplistic common-sense accounts of social problems is an awareness of the role of structural factors in shaping social conditions. It is more straightforward and often seems obvious to attribute social problems to whatever might be regarded as different about or 'wrong' with those who experience them. It seems reasonable to suggest that the unemployed lack the skills required to secure a job and that people with disabilities have limitations or difficulties that impede them (see Chapter Two). The causal processes in such cases appear straightforward and are intuitively attractive. It is more difficult to identify and trace the complex interactions between social conditions and individual choices that combine to actually create social problems.[85] In fact, from an individualist perspective, it could be argued that some issues are not really *social* problems at all, in the sense that they have no social cause and nor is there any collective obligation to solve them.

However, there are two limitations in explaining social problems by focusing on individuals. The first is that judgements of the attributes or behaviour of those experiencing social problems are often made by those who know little about these groups. There may be little interaction, understanding or sympathy between groups with different opportunities and fortunes, particularly if they are socially segregated by where and how they live, work and socialise (see Chapter Five).[86] The judgements of those who have never experienced social problems or are otherwise unfamiliar with them are often misinformed and based on second-hand accounts – potentially distorted by selective media reporting – or reflect stereotypes and prejudices. A second limitation with individualist accounts of social problems is that they are partial and anti-sociological. Those who experience social problems such as poverty or unemployment do make choices, perhaps even bad ones in some cases, but it is necessary to understand the conditions in which these choices are made because 'Men make their own history, but they do not make it just as they please; they do not make it under circumstances chosen by themselves, but under circumstances directly encountered, given and transmitted from the past'.[87]

Accounts that emphasise individual agency rather than structural causes of social problems are particularly favoured in English-speaking countries with a liberal political tradition.[88] This perspective ties in with the collective self-images and myths of such societies, for example, in the US, the ideals of rugged individualism, a pioneer spirit and the American Dream of success through hard work. There is strong attachment to the idea of Britain as an open society of opportunity and choice.[89] This tendency to favour individual explanations of social problems is the corollary of the status legend that success reflects personal effort and merit rather than other factors, such as unearned advantages.

Focusing on the individuals who experience problems rather than the circumstances that led to their situation can result in **blaming the victim**. Ryan, who popularised this term, outlined four stages that lead to this outcome.[90] The first concerns how an issue is identified and defined. Issues can be constructed so that rather than being interpreted as a result of social structures, responsibility is shifted onto those who are disadvantaged by these structures (see Chapter Two). For example, unemployment is regarded as a supply-side issue concerning the qualities of those who are looking for jobs (eg their lack of skills or low qualifications) rather than an issue of demand, attributable to macroeconomic factors, such as labour-market conditions, or the result of social barriers, such as discrimination. The second stage is to identify something that supposedly marks out whoever experiences the problem as different. A common recent example in the UK is to suggest that poverty and inequality reflect fatalism and a 'poverty of aspirations' within some disadvantaged communities. For example, a minister for employment and welfare reform in the 2005–10 Labour government argued that 'We have not yet managed to crack the cycle of intergenerational poverty. Inequalities in aspiration of parents drive inequalities in attainment for their children at schools. The aspirations of poorer children differ from those who are better off'.[91] In fact, there is no evidence that the aspirations of either children or parents from deprived communities are low, although they may have realistic expectations of the opportunities available to them compared with those from more privileged backgrounds.[92]

The third stage in blaming the victim is to attribute the cause of the problem to whatever is supposedly different about the group who suffers from it. This means that the group themselves can be blamed for their situation and no one else is responsible or under any moral duty to act. More sympathetic victim-blamers might accept that some people simply cannot help themselves and deserve pity rather than criticism, but this still marks them out as Others rather than equals (see 'Othering the poor' in Chapter Two). The final stage of victim blaming is to focus any policy response on removing what is supposedly different about the group in question, that is, to eradicate their pathology and normalise them.

There are two main problems with individualistic accounts of complex social problems. The first is the lack of evidence to support them, and the second is that the policies that follow from them are unsuccessful.[93] For example, there are now generations of evidence demonstrating that there is no such thing as an 'underclass' in the UK.[94] This is about as secure a finding as exists in social science but the fact that varieties of this idea persist in the face of almost 40 years of accumulated research indicates that evidence is not the decisive factor.

In addition to being more straightforward and intuitive, individualistic interpretations of social problems correspond with the principle that people should be regarded as moral agents capable of making choices and responsible for their own lives. This sentiment is so strong in the UK that those who propose alternative, structural explanations for social problems are often criticised for defending immorality. For example, it has been found that unemployed people 'who used structural accounts of unemployment in the company of employed people were sometimes branded as undeserving because their assertion that work was not available was often interpreted as a ruse to conceal their real unwillingness to work'.[95] This resistance to structural accounts of social problems means that responding to distortions, blindspots and myths with rebuttals and refuting evidence is often ineffectual. Not only does this not work, but such denials may actually strengthen people's attachment to false ideas as they reinterpret counter-arguments and misremember confounding evidence to reaffirm their existing opinions.[96]

Many psychologists and cognitive linguists suggest that it is necessary to appreciate that values and emotions are powerful forces in political thinking and that these are unmoved by calculated rationality and even direct appeals to self-interest. For example, Lakoff advocates abandoning arguments that rely on evidence in favour of appealing to moral causes. He suggests that there is no 'middle way' between social conservatives and liberals and that an appeal to an opponent's reason will fail. It is more effective to directly challenge their position by asserting the emotional power of your own moral frame.[97] An alternative approach is advocated by Haidt, who suggests that it is necessary to broaden the basis of an argument so that it appeals to some aspects of an opponent's moral orientation.[98] Irrespective of whichever approach is correct – or even if neither are – it does seem that evidence and logical argument have limited direct impact upon popular views on social problems and welfare policies. This does not mean that Social Policy analysis need not bother carefully documenting social conditions or analysing the complex processes that produce them: facts about social conditions and the impact of policies must be gathered systematically, even if findings are unpalatable for others or even for Social Policy analysts themselves. However, it is important to be aware that other factors may shape popular beliefs and actual policies, and to recognise the limited impact of challenging myths by evidence.

Conclusions

This chapter asked why people are so mistaken about welfare. Reflecting on ideas and opinions on social welfare issues suggests that some beliefs should be regarded as not merely mistaken, but more fundamentally misconceived. More than any other issue considered in this book, attitudes towards welfare reflect the dual nature of Social Policy, that is, its concern not only with empirical matters of fact, but also – and often more importantly – with normative issues and moral judgement. To answer the question considered in this chapter involves understanding that moral beliefs about social policy issues may be resistant and even immune to facts. We all look at the world through frames that shape what we see.[99] The idea that 'the facts speak for themselves' is about as reliable as believing that 'the camera never lies'.[100] However, although everyone interprets the world by perceiving it through a framework of beliefs, these frameworks are not permanent and unchanging. Perceptions *do* change, as shown in attitudes towards sexuality and disability in recent years. Social science (including Social Policy) contributed to some of these changes, and there are valuable lessons to be learned about the nature of such impact from studying the history of social investigation and analysis.

The contribution that Social Policy makes to improving public understanding of social issues and welfare policy involves more than confronting myths with evidence, important as that is. Social Policy can also reframe how issues are understood. Complicating seemingly simple accounts is a virtue of Social Policy analysis, not a vice. Realising that there might be more to an issue than first appears, and pausing to reflect upon familiar but unquestioned certainties, are important steps in developing critical independent thinking. Social Policy analysis should not shy away from directly challenging false claims and beliefs, but its long-term impact may be in undermining such views by providing alternative, more complex, accounts of social issues and 'shaking false self-evidence' to reveal that some of the opinions we hold are not entirely our own, and that perhaps we ought to consider why we are so attached to them.[101]

Notes

[1]   Delli Carpini, M.X. and Keeter, S. (1997) *What Americans Know About Politics and Why It Matters*. New Haven, CT: Yale University Press.

[2] See 'Benefits in Britain: Separating the Facts from the Fiction', *The Observer*, 6 April 2013. Available at: http://www.theguardian.com/politics/2013/apr/06/welfare-britain-facts-myths?CMP=twt_gu

[3] For example, New Zealand Council of Christian Social Services (2009) 'Facts About Poverty in 2009'. Available at: http://www.nzccss.org.nz/site/page.php?page_id=276 (accessed 31 December 2014).

[4] Taylor-Gooby, P., Hastie, C. and Bromley, C. (2003) 'Querulous Citizens: Welfare Knowledge and the Limits to Welfare Reform', *Social Policy and Administration*, 37(1).

[5] Guy, C., Henderson, K., Garnham, A. and Hargreaves, D. (2013) *Busting the Poverty Myths*. London: New Statesman/Webb Memorial Trust, p 6.

[6] Duffy, B., Hall, S., O'Leary, D. and Pope, S. (2013) *Generation Strains*. London: Demos, p 33.

[7] Joint Public Issues Team (2013) 'The Lies We Tell Ourselves: Ending Comfortable Myths About Poverty', p 15. Available at: http://www.jointpublicissues.org.uk/wp-content/uploads/2013/02/Truth-And-Lies-Report-smaller.pdf

[8] Sainsbury, R. (1996) 'Rooting Out Fraud: Innocent Until Proven Fraudulent', *Poverty*, 93(Spring), p 17.

[9] Joint Public Issues Team (2013), p 5. See also Duffy et al (2013), p 33.

[10] Chin, T. (2010) 'The Benefits of Work', in Alexander, N. (ed) *The Community Allowance: A Step up for People and Places*. London: Create Consortium, p 6.

[11] The 'tax gap' is the difference between the amount of tax that HM Revenue & Customs (HMRC) estimates that it should be able to collect compared to what it actually collects. See HMRC (2014) *Measuring Tax Gaps 2014 Edition – Tax Gap Estimates for 2012–13*. London: HM Revenue & Customs.

[12] Joint Public Issues Team (2013), p 22.

[13] Quoted in Williams, R. (1983) *Keywords: A Vocabulary of Culture and Society* (rev edn). London: Fontana, p 326.

[14] Quoted in Russell, B. (1966) *Roads to Freedom: Socialism, Anarchism and Syndicalism* (3rd edn). London: George Allen & Unwin, p 32.

[15] De Schweinitz, K. (1943) *England's Road to Social Security*. New York, NY: Perpetua, pp 20–1.

[16] Pound, J. (1971) *Poverty and Vagrancy in Tudor England*. London: Longman.

[17] Russell, B. (1965) *Legitimacy Versus Industrialism: 1814–1848*. London: Unwin, p 129.

[18] Quoted in De Schweinitz (1943), p 123.

[19] Quoted in De Schweinitz (1943), p 124.

[20] Mayhew, H. (1985 [1851–52]) *London Labour and the London Poor* (ed Neuburg, V.). London: Penguin, pp 370–1.

[21] Church Urban Fund/Church Action on Poverty (2012) *Bias to the Poor? Christian Attitudes to Poverty in this Country*. London: Church Urban Fund, p 3. Respondents were allowed to select more than one explanation.

[22] Joint Public Issues Team (2013), p 4.

[23] Heins, E. (2009) 'Flexicurity: What Can Scotland Learn from Denmark?', paper presented at 'Punching Above Our Weight: Smaller Nations and Regions in the Fight Against Poverty in Europe', Poverty Alliance seminar, Edinburgh, 24 September. Available at: http://povertyalliance.org/userfiles/files/events/EAPN%20Presentations/Flexicurity_Can_Scot_Learn_from_Denmark_Heins_230909.pdf (accessed 31 December 2014).

[24] Layard, R. (1999) *Tackling Unemployment*. London: Palgrave Macmillan.

[25] Kenya, K. (2013) 'Pennies from Heaven', *The Economist*, 26 October. See also Baird, S., Ferreira, F.H.G., Özler, B. and Woolcock, M. (2013) 'Relative Effectiveness of Conditional and Unconditional Cash Transfers for Schooling Outcomes in Developing Countries: A Systematic Review', Campbell Collaboration Library. Available at: http://www.campbellcollaboration.org/lib/project/218/

[26] However, the Child Trust Fund or 'Baby Bonds', introduced in 2005 (before being closed to new cases in 2010), could be regarded as a form of unconditional transfer, albeit not targeted at those in poverty. Available at: https://www.gov.uk/child-trust-funds/overview

[27] Stephens, P. (2014) 'Review of *The Fourth Revolution: The Global Race to Reinvent the State.* by Micklethwait and Wooldridge', *Financial Times*, 30 May.

[28] Spicker, P. (2002) *Poverty and the Welfare State: Dispelling the Myths*. London: Catalyst, p 30.

[29] Sutherland, W.J., Spiegelhalter, D. and Burgman, M. (2013) 'Twenty Tips for Interpreting Scientific Claims', *Nature*, 503, 20 November.

[30] In contrast, austerity measures reduce workers' and employers' investment in education and training, which may reduce productivity, see Taylor-Gooby, P. (2014) 'The Welfare State in Crisis: Reasons to Be Cheerful', *Policy World*, Spring, p 6.

[31] Arjona, R., Ladaique, M. and Pearson M. (2002) 'Social Protection and Growth', *OECD Economic Studies*, No 35.

[32] See, for example: https://fullfact.org/; BBC 'More or Less'. Available at: http://www.bbc.co.uk/programmes/b006qshd; Channel 4 News 'Fact Check'. Available at: http://blogs.channel4.com/factcheck/

[33] Kuklinski, J.H., Quirk, P.J., Jerit, J., Schwieder, D. and Rich, R.F. (2000) 'Misinformation and the Currency of Democratic Citizenship', *Journal of Politics*, 62(3).

[34] 'Americans' Belief in God, Miracles and Heaven Declines', 16 December 2013. Available at: http://www.harrisinteractive.com/NewsRoom/HarrisPolls/tabid/447/ctl/ReadCustom%20Default/mid/1508/ArticleId/1353/Default.aspx (accessed 31 December 2014).

[35] Religious beliefs are not scientific propositions, but of an entirely different nature and so cannot be refuted by evidence. Stephen J. Gould describes science and religion as 'non-overlapping magisteria', see Gould, S.J. (2007) *The Richness of Life*. London: Vintage. However, Creationism is not an article of faith for mainstream Christianity, but purports to be a scientific theory, so it must be assessed in relation to evidence.

[36] Nyhan, B. and Reifler, J. (2010) 'When Corrections Fail: The Persistence of Political Misperceptions', *Political Behavior*, 32(2).

[37] Shanas, E. (1970) 'Social Research and Policy in the Field of Old Age', in Shibutani, T. (ed) *Human Nature and Collective Behaviour: Papers in Honor of Herbert Blumer*. New Brunswick, NJ: Prentice Hall, p 357.

[38] Segal, R.A. (2004) *Myth: A Very Short Introduction*. Oxford: Oxford University Press, p 6.

[39] Cassirer, E. (1946) *The Myth of the State*. New Haven, CT: Yale University Press, p 296.

[40] Lane, R.E. and Sears, D.O. (1964) *Public Opinion*. Englewood Cliffs, NJ: Prentice Hall, p 75.

[41] Spicker, P. (2002) *Poverty and the Welfare State: Dispelling the Myths*. London: Catalyst, p 7.

[42] Sousa, L. and Eusebio, C. (2007) 'When Multi-Problem Poor Individuals' Myths Meet Social Services' Myths', *Journal of Social Work*, 7(2).

[43] Barsky, R.F. (1997) *Noam Chomsky: A Life of Dissent*. Cambridge, MA: MIT Press, pp 195–6.

44   Lakoff, G. (2006) *Thinking Points: Communicating our American Values and Vision*. Berkeley, CA: Rockridge Institute.

45   Williams, Z. (2014) 'George Lakoff: "Conservatives Don't Follow the Polls, They Want to Change Them … Liberals Do Everything Wrong"', *The Guardian*, 1 February.

46   Brockington, D. (2003) 'Myths of Skeptical Environmentalism', *Environmental Science & Policy*, 6(6), p 545.

47   Berger, S. (2009) 'On the Role of Myths and History in the Construction of National Identity in Modern Europe', *European History Quarterly*, 39(3).

48   Sorel, G. (1984 [1908]) *Reflections on Violence* (ed Jennings, G.). Cambridge: Cambridge University Press.

49   'A myth, for someone who believes in it, is not myth but truth.' Mendelson, E. (2013) 'The Strange Power of Norman Mailer', *New York Review of Books*, 21 November, p 21. An alternative use of this term appears in Chomsky, N. (1989) *Necessary Illusions: Thought Control in Democratic Societies*. London: Pluto Press.

50   McDonald, R. and Shildrick, T. (2013) 'In Work and in Poverty', in Guy, C., Henderson, K., Garnham, A. and Hargreaves, D. (eds) *Busting the Poverty Myths*. London: New Statesman/Webb Memorial Trust, p 7.

51   McDonald, R., Shildrick, T. and Furlong, A. (2014) 'In Search of "Intergenerational Cultures of Worklessness": Hunting the Yeti and Shooting Zombies', *Critical Social Policy*, 34(2). The terms 'zombie arguments' and 'theories' also appears in Spicker, P. (2007) *The Idea of Poverty*. Bristol: The Policy Press. See also Spicker's Blog on 21 April 2014. Available at: https://paulspicker. wordpress.com/tag/equalities/

52   While chairman of the UK Supplementary Benefits Commission in the 1970s and 1980s, Professor David Donnison received hundreds of letters claiming that some benefit claimants had received extravagant amounts of state support, all of which were investigated and found to be mere 'folklore' or an 'unlayable ghost' of the public imagination – 'But to demonstrate that did nothing to halt the circulation of a myth which has now taken its place alongside those about Russians marching through England with snow on their boots to join the western front in 1915', Donnison, D. (1982) *The Politics of Poverty*. Oxford: Martin Robertson, p 43.

53   Berger, J. (1972) *Ways of Seeing*. London: BBC/Penguin, p 15.

54   Castell, S. and Thompson, J. (2007) *Understanding Attitudes to Poverty in the UK: Getting the Public's Attention*. York: Joseph Rowntree Foundation, p 17.

55   'The real purpose of myth is not to present an objective picture of the world as it is, but to express man's understanding of himself in the world in which he lives. Myth should be interpreted not cosmologically, but anthropologically, or better still, existentially'. Bultman, R. (1953) 'New Testament and Mythology', in Bultman, R., Lohmeyer, E., Schniewind, J., Thielicke, H. and Farrer, A. (eds) *Kerygma and Myth: A Theological Debate*. New York, NY: Harper & Row, p 10. Available at: http://www.religion.emory.edu/faculty/robbins/Pdfs/BultmannNTMyth.pdf

56   O'Hare, W.P. (2003) *Perceptions and Misperceptions of America's Children: The Role of the Print Media*. Working Paper. Baltimore, MD: KIDS COUNT.

57   Duffy, B., Hall, S., O'Leary, D. and Pope, S. (2013) *Generation Strains: A Demos/IPSOS Mori Report on Changing Attitudes to Welfare*. London: Demos/IPSOS Mori, p 34. See also jointpublicissues. org (no date) 'Truth and Lies about Poverty'. Available at: http://povertyalliance.org/userfiles/ files/EPIC/4th%20Scottish%20Assembly/SATP13_PovertyMyths_ChurchScotland.pdf

[58] Cawson, R.A. and Trice, R. (2000) 'Poverty as We Know It: Media Portrayals of the Poor', *Public Opinion Quarterly*, 65(1), p 54.

[59] Duffy et al (2013), p 38.

[60] Hall, S. (1992) 'Notes on Deconstructing "The Popular"', in Samuel, R. (ed) *People's History and Socialist Theory*. London: Routledge and Kegan Paul, p 447.

[61] Howitt, D. (1982) *The Mass Media and Social Problems*. Oxford: Pergamon.

[62] Galbraith, J.K. (1958) *The Affluent Society*. New York, NY: Houghton Mifflin, p 9.

[63] McKendrick, J.H., Sinclair, S., Irwin, A., O'Donnell, H., Scott, G. and Dobbie, L. (2008) *The Media, Poverty and Public Opinion in the UK*. York: Joseph Rowntree Foundation.

[64] Marr, A. (2005) *My Trade: A Short History of British Journalism*. London: Pan, p 218.

[65] Jamieson, K.H. and Cappella, J.N. (2008) *Echo Chamber: Rush Limbaugh and the Conservative Media Establishment*. Oxford: Oxford University Press.

[66] Martin, A. (2013) 'The Web's "Echo Chamber" Leaves Us None the Wiser', *Wired*, 1 May. Available at: http://www.wired.co.uk/news/archive/2013-05/1/online-stubbornness (accessed 18 January 2015).

[67] Pariser, E. (2012) *The Filter Bubble: What the Internet Is Hiding from You*. London: Penguin.

[68] Hunter, M. (2008) 'Engine Trouble', *Community Care*, 3 April, pp 16–17.

[69] Kahneman, D. (2012) *Thinking, Fast and Slow*. London: Penguin.

[70] See: http://www.campbellcollaboration.org/

[71] Vedantam, S. (2007) 'Persistence of Myths Could Alter Public Policy Approach', *Washington Post*, 4 September.

[72] Marr (2005), p 60.

[73] Weber, M. (1976) *The Protestant Ethic and the Spirit of Capitalism* (trans Parsons, T.). London: George Allen & Unwin.

[74] Parkin, F. (1972) *Class Inequality and Political Order: Social Stratification in Capitalist and Communist Societies*. St Alban's: Paladin.

[75] Scott, A. (1988) 'Imputing Beliefs: A Controversy in the Sociology of Knowledge', *Sociological Review*, 36(1).

[76] Galbraith, J.K. (1994) 'The Good Society Has No Underclass', *The Guardian Weekly*, 6 February. Elsewhere, Galbraith writes: 'We associate truth with convenience, with what most closely accords with self-interest and personal well-being or promises best to avoid awkward effort or unwelcome dislocation of life'. Galbraith, J. (1998) *The Affluent Society* (40th anniversary edn). New York, NY: Houghton Mifflin, p 7.

[77] Weber, M. (1948) 'Social Psychology of the World Religions', in Gerth, H. and Mills, C.W. (eds) *From Max Weber: Essays in Sociology*. London: Routledge and Kegan Paul, p 271, emphasis in original.

[78] Seymour, D. (2009) *Reporting Poverty in the UK: A Practical Guide for Journalists*. York: Joseph Rowntree Foundation, p 27.

[79] Otto Hinze, quoted in Bendix, R. (1977) *Max Weber: An Intellectual Portrait*. Berkeley, CA: University Of California Press, p 47.

[80] Argyris, C. (1991) 'Teaching Smart People How to Learn', *Harvard Business Review*, 69(3), p 103.

[81] Eagleton, T. (1991) *Ideology: An Introduction*. London: Verso, p 56.

[82] Marx described this process in typically acerbic fashion: 'Up to 1846 the Tories passed as the guardians of the traditions of Old England. They were suspected of admiring in the British

Constitution the eighth wonder of the world, to be *laudatores temporis acti*, enthusiasts for the throne, the High Church, the privileges and liberties of the British subject. The fatal year, 1846, with its repeal of the Corn Laws, and the shout of distress which this repeal forced from the Tories, proved that they were enthusiasts for nothing but the rent of land'. Marx, K. (1961 [1852]) *Selected Writings in Sociology and Social Philosophy* (ed Bottomore, T.B. and Rubel, M.). Harmondsworth: Penguin, p 198. '*Laudatores temporis acti*' is a phrase taken from the works of Horace, which means 'admirers of time past'.

[83] Bendix (1977), p 259.

[84] Orwell, G. (1970) 'In Front of Your Nose', in Orwell, S. and Angus, I. (eds) *The Collected Essays, Journalism and Letters of George Orwell, Vol. 4: In Front of Your Nose, 1945–1950*. Harmondsworth: Penguin, p 154.

[85] Parkin ([1972], p 162) quotes a passage from John Steinbeck's *The Grapes of Wrath* that illustrates the lack of transparency in capitalist societies and just how difficult it is to understand the complex structural processes that create outcomes; in this case, why a poor farmer and his family are evicted for defaulting on mortgage payments.

[86] Dorling, D., Rigby, J., Wheeler, B., Ballas, D., Thomas, B., Fahmy, E., Gordon, D. and Lupton, R. (2007) *Poverty and Wealth Across Britain 1968 to 2005*. York: Joseph Rowntree Foundation.

[87] Marx, K. (1968 [1852]) 'The Eighteenth Brumaire of Louis Bonaparte', in Marx, K. and Engels, F., *Selected Works in One Volume*. London: Lawrence & Wishart, p 96.

[88] Seidman, E. and Rappaport, J. (eds) (1986) *Redefining Social Problems*. New York, NY: Plenum Press. For an explanation of the meaning of 'liberal' in this context, see ch 2, n 1.

[89] Cabinet Office (2011) *Opening Doors, Breaking Barriers: A Strategy for Social Mobility*. London: Cabinet Office.

[90] Ryan, W. (1971) *Blaming the Victim*. London: Pantheon.

[91] Murphy, J. (2007) 'Progressive Self-Interest – The Politics of Poverty and Aspiration', in Rossiter, A., Murphy, J., Blanden, J., Harker, L., Gregg, P., Macmillan, L., Sainsbury, R., Phillips, T., Sacks, J. and Batmanghelidjh, C. (eds) *The Politics of Aspiration*. London: Social Market Foundation, p 15.

[92] McKendrick, J.H., Scott, G. and Sinclair, S. (2007) 'Dismissing Disaffection: Young People's Attitudes Towards Education, Employment and Participation in a Deprived Community', *Journal of Youth Studies*, 10(2).

[93] Or, at least, they fail to significantly change social conditions, which might not actually be a failure if the intention of the policy was mainly symbolic (see Chapter Two).

[94] See Rutter, M. and Madge, N. (1976) *Cycles of Disadvantage: A Review of Research*. London: Heinemann. MacNicol, J. (1987) 'In Pursuit of the Underclass', *Journal of Social Policy*, 16(3). Smith, D. (ed) (1992) *Understanding the Underclass*. London: Policy Studies Institute. Morris, L. (1993) 'Is there a British Underclass?', *International Journal of Urban and Regional Research*, 17(3).

[95] Howe (1994), p 326.

[96] Lewandowsky, S., Ecker, U.K.H., Seifert, C.M., Schwarz, N. and Cook, J. (2012) 'Misinformation and Its Correction: Continued Influence and Successful Debiasing', *Psychological Science in the Public Interest*, 13(3).

[97] Lakoff, G. and Welhing, E. (2012) *The Little Blue Book: The Essential Guide to Thinking and Talking Democratic*. New York, NY: Simon and Schuster.

[98] Haidt, J. (2012) *The Righteous Mind: Why Good People are Divided by Politics and Religion*. London: Penguin.

[99] Goffman, E. (1974) *Frame Analysis: An Essay on the Organization of Experience*. New York, NY: Harper & Row.

[100] Epley, N. (2014) *Mindwise: How We Understand What Others Think, Believe, Feel and Want*. London: Allen Lane.

[101] Foucault, M. (1991) 'Questions of Method', in Burchell, G., Gordon, C. and Miller, P. (eds) *The Foucault Effect: Studies in Governmentality*. London: Harvester Wheatsheaf, p 75.

Conclusion: What is the point of Social Policy?

In 2008, the Joseph Rowntree Foundation asked what people in the UK thought were the main 'Social Evils' – the most serious and threatening problems facing society.[1] The issues that troubled people most were the following:

- individualism, consumerism and the decline of community;
- drugs and alcohol abuse;
- a decline of values;
- problems with families and young people;
- inequality and poverty;
- a democratic deficit – unresponsive institutions and political apathy;
- violence and crime;
- gender inequality;
- religious tensions and intolerance;
- social diversity, immigration and intolerance;
- health and care services; and
- environmental issues.

Several other issues could be added to this list of concerns since the research was conducted. For example: living standards have been stagnant or have fallen for several years in many developed countries; many younger people doubt that they will enjoy the opportunities or living standards of previous generations; employment seems less secure and competition for the most attractive jobs is increasingly intense; and fewer people feel that they are able to save and many are struggling with debt, particularly with housing costs. Despite longer-term economic growth and greater overall wealth, there is a widespread sense of instability and social unease in Britain and this is even more apparent in several other countries.[2] The pace and scale of social change feels threatening and beyond control. Many societies appear gripped by what Émile Durkheim called a condition of *anomie*: anxiety and dislocation caused by social upheaval.[3]

Critics might suggest that the discipline of Social Policy has done little to help solve or reduce these social evils. Given the persistence of some of the problems discussed in this book – deprivation, exclusion, unequal opportunities and social tensions – Social Policy might not seem to have an impressive track record in producing solutions. To assess whether this criticism is justified, it is necessary to consider the nature of the impact of Social Policy analysis.

The impact of Social Policy analysis

The social sciences are sometimes criticised for their limited impact on the world compared to the great accomplishments of the natural sciences, such as the exploration of space, the prevention or cure of major diseases, or understanding and manipulating the biochemistry of genetics. These inventions are certainly considerable achievements and have created new opportunities for economic development and possibilities to enhance human well-being. However, invention is not the same as innovation.[4] Invention is the discovery or creation of new knowledge or a new process while innovation is about the impact of this breakthrough and how it is distributed and adopted, and that is a social process. There is nothing inherent in any new technology which ensures that it will contribute to, rather than detract from, well-being.[5] How technologies are used and what impact they have are shaped by beliefs about how resources ought to be distributed and the institutions that implement these principles. These are not scientific issues, but determined by politics, economics and ideology, and these are the subject matter of Social Policy and other social sciences.

Ideas about social issues – such as the appropriate use of technology – can be influenced by social-scientific analysis and debate. For example, the reduction in poverty and the increase in social mobility in the UK in the 30 years after the Second World War, which also occurred across much of the developed world, was as much a result of social policies as of economic growth.[6] As was shown in Chapter Five, economic growth can coexist alongside persistent poverty and stagnating social mobility. The post-war reforms that established (or consolidated and extended) what became known as the welfare state reflected changing outlooks in what governments should and could do, and Social Policy research and analysis contributed to this shift. Rowntree's second study of poverty in York in 1936 (see Chapter Four) was used to calculate the benefit rates proposed in the Beveridge Report of 1942.[7] However, perhaps his original 1901 study had an even more profound influence over the long term – by challenging the view that poverty was a marginal problem and a matter of individual misfortune or personal failing. Social Policy can therefore have a direct effect on technical policy issues, but its more profound impact is often internal and perceptual rather than external and technological. This influence may be gradual and may not be recognised, but changing how issues are conceived is an indispensable stage in any significant policy reform.

However, Social Policy research does not simply land in a clear field, unambiguously point in a single direction and explain precisely what is the case and what ought to be done about it. As was discussed in Chapter One, the issues that Social Policy investigates are not purely matters of fact, but also involve values and beliefs, and these moral orientations colour and cloud views on social issues. Even in natural science, 'Facts do not "speak for themselves"; they are read in the light of theory' and 'New facts, collected in old ways under the guidance of old theories, rarely lead to any substantial revision of thought'.[8] This applies equally to social science. All Social Policy evidence is shaped by ideas about society that influence both the research conducted (Why this topic? Why this way of defining it?) and its reception (What does it tell us? What does it suggest we do?). As was shown in Chapter Six, carefully collected evidence does not always determine policy: if British and American policymakers applied the findings of criminological evidence, neither country would imprison so many people.[9]

Policymakers and practitioners who focus on 'getting things done' may be impatient with analysts and theorists, and 'often view research as the opposite of action rather than the opposite of ignorance'.[10] However, action can be the opposite of thinking, and ill-considered actions may exacerbate social problems. Acting or basing policy on gut instinct, intuition or personal experience can be a cover for prejudice, perhaps unintentional but harmful nevertheless. Social Policy analysis requires reflecting on and testing the representativeness of individual experience or practical expertise. Martin Rein once suggested that 'What is needed in social policy is not so much good tools but good questions'.[11] Practical people might not welcome the questions and doubts raised by Social Policy analysis and may hope for a degree of certainty that valid, reliable and representative social research rarely provides. As one Social Policy analyst explained:

> That's part of the reason why governments like think-tanks. Think-tanks say: 'What you need to do is A, B and C'. If someone comes to me, I will say 'Well, you could do A, B and C, but these are the following problems associated with them' ... but someone who makes policy doesn't want ifs and buts.[12]

Social Policy therefore contributes to addressing social problems by asking questions, clarifying thinking and analysing options. As was shown in Chapter Two, it is possible to 'solve' a social problem by making it disappear through redefining it or delegitimising it rather than genuinely changing conditions. Therefore, debating how problems are defined and interrogating discourses are necessary rather than self-indulgent activities, and just as important as evaluating the impact of policies. Policymakers may not be interested in reconceptualising social issues, but an important role of Social Policy analysis is to oblige them – and every citizen with an interest in social conditions – to stop and think; to consider why an issue is thought of as it is, what causes problems and what outcomes different interventions might produce. The word 'analysis' comes from the ancient Greek for loosening or unravelling, and means unpicking something. Analysis means questioning assumptions about social conditions and beliefs about their causes, deconstructing the rationales for policies, challenging the quality of arguments, examining the soundness of methods, and testing the validity of evidence. The duty of Social Policy analysis is to provoke debate and discussion rather than to provide definitive solutions. Those looking for simple answers and comforting certainty should look elsewhere.

It might seem that the ills and evils that confront every society are insoluble and determined by global forces and factors beyond the control of national governments. However, there is more scope for action than some might believe or be willing to acknowledge. While there are certain common challenges and concerns across the developed world, not all national economic and welfare systems are the same. The widening inequalities discussed in Chapter Five, for example, are neither universal nor inevitable, but a matter of policy. Between 1980 and 2007, the share of income going to the top 1% in the US increased by 135% but by only 76% in Canada over the same period and even less in Japan.[13] These variations reflect the level of **predistribution** in different countries, that is, the extent of income and wealth inequality before taking taxation and welfare policies into account.[14] Those countries that experienced the greatest widening of inequality chose this outcome by deregulating labour markets and reducing the top rates of tax. Significantly, they did not enjoy any corresponding increase in economic growth, let alone well-being, as a result.[15]

Political and economic systems are human creations (albeit complex and sensitive ones), and we cannot simply resign responsibility for how they function or their effects on people. They are the result of choices we have made. In 1972, the international think tank the Club of Rome produced a famous report on The Limits to Growth that argued, among many other things, that the principal problems facing the world could not be solved by purely technological developments, which often create their own negative side effects; rather, 'the need will quickly become evident for social innovation to match technical change, for radical reform of institutions and political processes at all levels'.[16] While some of the alarming predictions in this report have not come true (yet), this argument remains compelling – social change is a matter of politics and morality, not technocratic tinkering. This book has shown that ideas about 'social problems' are not fixed: some are solved, in various ways, and new ones emerge. Social Policy analysis shows that social problems cannot be fatalistically accepted as inevitable. The only limits to *social* growth are set by our imagination and will. Social Policy is about ideas of the good society, about how we should live together to extend and advance well-being. There are few subjects more deserving of our attention.

Notes

[1]   Watt, B. (2008) *What Are Today's Social Evils?* York: Joseph Rowntree Foundation.

[2]   Orton, M. (2015) *Something's Not Right: Insecurity and an Anxious Nation.* London: Compass. See also OECD (Organisation for Economic Co-operation and Development) (no date) 'Better Life Index'. Available at: http://www.oecdbetterlifeindex.org/topics/life-satisfaction/

[3]   Durkheim, E. (1970 [1897]) *Suicide: A Study in Sociology* (trans Spaulding, J.A. and Simpson, G.). London: Routledge.

[4]   Conger, S. (1996) 'Social Inventions', *The Innovation Journal*, 1(2).

[5]   Wolpert, L. (2000) *The Unnatural Nature of Science* (2nd edn). London: Faber and Faber.

6   Milburn, S. (2009) 'Foreword from the Chair', in Panel on Fair Access to the Professions (ed) *Unleashing Aspiration: The Final Report of the Panel on Fair Access to the Professions*. London: Cabinet Office, p 6.

7   Veit-Wilson, J. (1998) *Setting Adequacy Standards: How Governments Define Minimum Incomes*. Bristol: The Policy Press, p 40.

8. Gould, S.J. (2007) *The Richness of Life* (ed McGarr, P. and Rose, S.). London: Vintage, p 291.

9   Wilson, D. and Ashton, J. (2001) *What Everyone in Britain Should Know About Crime and Punishment*. Oxford: Blackstone. See also Hari, J. (2015) *Chasing the Scream: The First and Last Days of the War on Drugs*. London: Bloomsbury.

10 Court, J. (2004) 'The Political Context in Developing Countries', in Overseas Development Institute (ed) *Research and Policy in Development: Does Evidence Matter?* London: Overseas Development Institute, p 16.

11 Rein, M. (1978) *Social Policy*. New York, NY: Random House, p x.

12 Hugh Bochel quoted in Corbyn, Z. (2009) 'I Can't Hear You', *Times Higher Education*, 26 March, p 33.

13 Starr, P (2014) 'A Different Road to a Fair Society', *New York Review*, 22 May.

14 OECD (2008) *Are We Growing Unequal? New Evidence on Changes in Poverty and Incomes Over the Past 20 Years*. Paris: OECD Publishing. Available at: http://www.oecd.org/els/soc/41494435.pdf

15 Ostry, J.D., Berg, A. and Tsangarides, C.G. (2014) 'Redistribution, Inequality, and Growth', IMF Staff Discussion Note, SDN/14/02. Available at: https://www.imf.org/external/pubs/ft/sdn/2014/sdn1402.pdf (accessed 1 February 2015).

16 Meadows, D.H., Meadows, D.L., Render, J. and Behrens, W.W. (1972) *The Limits to Growth: A Report for the Club of Rome's Project on the Predicament of Mankind*. New York, NY: Universe Books, pp 193–4.

References

Adebayo, D. (2001) 'Young, Gifted, Black', *The Observer*, 25 November.

Afridi, A. (2011) *Social Networks: Their Role in Addressing Poverty*. York: Joseph Rowntree Foundation.

Aghai, V. (2014) *America's Shrinking Middle Class*. Bloomington, IN: AuthorHouse.

Alcock, P. (2004) 'The Influence of Dynamic Perspectives on Poverty Analysis and Anti-Poverty Policy in the UK', *Journal of Social Policy*, 33(3).

Alcock, P. (2005) 'From Social Security to Social Inclusion: The Changing Policy Climate', *Benefits: The Journal of Poverty and Social Justice*, 43(2).

Alcock, P., May, M. and Rowlingson, K. (eds) (2008) *The Student's Companion to Social Policy* (3rd edition). Oxford: Blackwell.

Alexander, N. (ed) (2010) *The Community Allowance: A Step Up for People and Places*. London: Create Consortium.

All-Party Parliamentary Group on Social Mobility (2012) 'Seven Key Truths about Social Mobility'. Available at: http://www.appg-socialmobility.org/

Alter, A. (2103) 'Can't Follow this Column? Try Changing the Typeface', *Wired*, October.

Althusser, L. (1969) *For Marx* (trans Brewster, B.). Harmondsworth: Penguin.

Argyris, C. (1991) 'Teaching Smart People How to Learn', *Harvard Business Review*, 69(3).

Arjona, R., Ladaique, M. and Pearson M. (2002) 'Social Protection and Growth', *OECD Economic Studies*, No. 35.

Arnsperger, C. and Varoufakis, Y. (2006) 'What is Neoclassical Economics?', in Atkinson, A.B. and Hills, J. (eds) *Exclusion, Employment and Opportunity*, London: Centre for Analysis of Social Exclusion.

Axford, N. (2010) 'Is Social Exclusion a Useful Concept in Children's Services?', *British Journal of Social Work*, 40(3).

Babich, B.E. (1994) *Nietzsche's Philosophy of Science: Reflecting Science on the Ground of Art*. Albany, NY: State University of New York Press.

Baird, S., Ferreira, F.H.G., Özler, B. and Woolcock, M. (2013) 'Relative Effectiveness of Conditional and Unconditional Cash Transfers for Schooling Outcomes in Developing Countries: A Systematic Review', Campbell Collaboration Library. Available at: http://www.campbellcollaboration.org/lib/project/218/

Ball, S.J. (1993) 'Education Markets, Choice and Social Class: The Market as a Class Strategy in the UK and USA', *British Journal of the Sociology of Education*, 14(1).

Ball, S.J. (2006) *Education Policy and Social Class: The Selected Works of Stephen J. Ball*. Abingdon: Routledge.

Barnes, C. (1991) *Disabled People in Britain and Discrimination: A Case for Anti-Discrimination Legislation*. London: Hurst and Company.

Barnes, C. and Mercer, G. (2005) 'Disability, Work, and Welfare: Challenging the Social Exclusion of Disabled People', *Work Employment & Society*, 19(3).

Barry, B. (1998) *Social Exclusion, Social Isolation and the Distribution of Income*, CASEpaper12. London: LSE/CASE.

Barsky, R.F. (1997) *Noam Chomsky: A Life of Dissent*. Cambridge, MA: MIT Press.

Basu, K. (2008) 'India's Dilemmas: The Political Economy of Policymaking in a Globalised World', *The Economic and Political Weekly*, 2–8 February.

Bauer, M.W., Jordan, A., Green-Pedersen, C. and Héritier, A. (eds) (2012) *Dismantling Public Policy: Preferences, Strategies and Effects*. Oxford: Oxford University Press.

Bauman, Z. (2013) 'Does the Richness of the Few Benefit Us All?', *Social Europe*, 28 January.

BBC Radio 4 (2014) 'Price Conscious', *In Business*, 15 May.

Becker, H.S. (1963) *Outsiders: Studies in the Sociology of Deviance*. Glencoe, IL: Free Press.

Becker, H.S. (1970) 'Whose Side Are We On?', in Douglas, J.D. (ed) *The Relevance of Sociology*. New York, NY: Appleton-Century-Crofts.

Becker, S. (ed) (1991) *Windows of Opportunity: Public Policy and the Poor*. London: Child Poverty Action Group.

Béland, D. and Peterson, K. (eds) *Analysing Social Policy Concepts and Language: Comparative and Transnational Perspectives*. Bristol: The Policy Press.

Bendix, R. (1977) *Max Weber: An Intellectual Portrait*. Berkeley, CA: University of California Press.

Bennet, C. (2009) 'The Beauty Industry Is at It Again … It's Not a Pretty Sight', *The Observer*, 18 January.

Beresford, P. (2002) 'User Involvement in Research and Evaluation: Liberation or Regulation?', *Social Policy and Society*, 1(2).

Beresford, P., Green, D., Lister, R. and Woodward, K. (1999) *Poverty First Hand: Poor People Speak for Themselves*. London: Child Poverty Action Group.

Berger, J. (1972) *Ways of Seeing*. London: BBC/Penguin.

Berger, P.L. and Luckmann, T. (1967) *The Social Construction of Reality: A Treatise in the Sociology of Knowledge*. Harmondsworth: Penguin.

Berger, S. (2009) 'On the Role of Myths and History in the Construction of National Identity in Modern Europe', *European History Quarterly*, 39(3).

Berlin, I. (1969) *Four Essays on Liberty*. Oxford: Oxford University Press.

Bhagwati, J. and Panagariya, A. (2013) *Why Growth Matters*. New York, NY: PublicAffairs.

Blair, T. (1999) Beveridge Lecture, Toynbee Hall London, 18 March.

Blair, T. (2001) 'The Government's Agenda for the Future', speech, Enfield, 8 February.

Blanchflower, D. and Machin, S. (2014) 'Falling Real Wages', *CentrePiece*, 19(1).

Blanden, J., Gregg, P. and Machin, S. (2007) *Recent Changes in Intergenerational Mobility in Britain*. London: Sutton Trust.

Blandy, S. (2006) 'Gated Communities in England: Historical Perspectives and Current Developments', *GeoJournal*, 66(1).

Boghossian, P. (2001) 'What is Social Construction?', *Times Literary Supplement*, 23 February.

Bonoli, G. (1997) 'Classifying Welfare States: A Two-dimension Approach', *Journal of Social Policy*, 26(3).

Boo, K. (2102) *Behind the Beautiful Forevers: Life, Death and Hope in a Mumbai Slum*. London: Portobello Books.

Boote, D.N. and Beile, P. (2005) 'Scholars Before Researchers: On the Centrality of the Dissertation Literature Review in Research Preparation', *Educational Researcher*, 34(6).

Bourdieu, P. (1984) *Distinction: A Social Critique of the Judgement of Taste* (trans Nice, R.). Harvard, MA: Harvard University Press.

Bourdieu, P. (1985) 'Social Space and the Genesis of Groups', *Theory and Society*, 14(5).

Bourdieu, P. (1993) *Sociology in Question* (trans Nice, R.). London: Sage.

Bourdieu, P. and Passeron, J.-C. (1977) *Reproduction in Education, Society and Culture*. London: Sage.

Bourdieu, P. and Wacquant, L. (1992) *An Invitation to Reflexive Sociology*. Chicago, IL: University of Chicago Press.

Bowles, S. and Gintis, H. (2002) 'The Inheritance of Inequality', *Journal of Economic Perspectives*, 16(3).

Boyer, J. (2012) 'Malthus and Scrooge: How Charles Dickens Put Holly Branch Through the Heart of the Worst Economics Ever', *Forbes Blog*, 24 December.

Bradshaw, J., Gordon, D., Levitas, R., Middleton, S., Pantazis, C., Payne, S. and Townsend, P. (1998) *Perceptions of Poverty and Social Exclusion*. Bristol: Townsend Centre for International Poverty Research.

Breen, R. (2004) *Social Mobility in Europe*. Oxford: Nuffield College. Available at: http://www.uvm.edu/~pdodds/files/papers/others/2004/breen2004a.pdf

Brockington, D. (2003) 'Myths of Skeptical Environmentalism', *Environmental Science & Policy*, 6(6).

Brubaker, R. (1985) 'Rethinking Classical Theory: The Sociological Vision of Pierre Bourdieu', *Theory and Society*, 14(6).

Buckner, L. and Yeandle, S. (2011) *Valuing Carers, 2011 – Calculating the Value Carer's Support*. London: Carers UK.

Bultman, R., Lohmeyer, E., Schniewind, J., Thielicke, H. and Farrer, A. (1953) *Kerygma and Myth: A Theological Debate*. New York, NY: Harper & Row.

Burchardt, T. (2004) 'Capabilities and Disability: The Capabilities Framework and the Social Model of Disability', *Disability and Society*, 19(7).

Burchardt, T. and Hills, J. (1999) *Private Welfare and Public Policy*. York: Joseph Rowntree Foundation.

Burchell, G., Gordon, C. and Miller, P. (1991) (eds) *The Foucault Effect: Studies in Governmentality*. London: Harvester Wheatsheaf.

Burden, T. (1998) *Social Policy and Welfare: A Clear Guide*. London: Pluto Press.

Burns, H. (2012) *Kilbrandon's Vision – Healthier Lives, Better Futures. The Tenth Kilbrandon Lecture*. Edinburgh: Scottish Government.

Byrne, D. (1999) *Social Exclusion*. Buckingham: Open University Press.

Cabinet Office (2011) *Opening Doors, Breaking Barriers: A Strategy for Social Mobility*. London: Cabinet Office.

Calder, J. (2008) 'Labour's Private School Heroes', *New Statesman*, 13 October.

Cameron, A. (2005) 'Geographies of Welfare and Exclusion: Initial Report', *Progress in Human Geography*, 29(2).

Carlat, D. (2010) *Unhinged: The Trouble with Psychiatry – A Doctor's Revelations about a Profession in Crisis*. New York, NY: Free Press.

Cassirer, E. (1946) *The Myth of the State*. New Haven, CT: Yale University Press.

Castell, S. and Thompson, J. (2007) *Understanding Attitudes to Poverty in the UK: Getting the Public's Attention*. York: Joseph Rowntree Foundation.

Cawson, R.A. and Trice, R. (2000) 'Poverty as We Know It: Media Portrayals of the Poor', *Public Opinion Quarterly*, 65(1).

Chalabi, M. (2013) 'Crime, Teen Pregnancy and Job-seekers: What Do We Overestimate?', *The Guardian*, 9 July.

Chambers, J.D. (1968) *The Workshop of the World: British Economic History, 1820– 1880* (2nd edn). Oxford: Oxford University Press.

Chang, H.-J. (2007) *Bad Samaritans: Rich Nations, Poor Policies and the Threat to the Developing World*. London: Random House.

Chang, H.-J. (2014) *Economics: The User's Guide*. London: Pelican.

Choitz, V. (1998) *An Inclusive Society: Strategies for Tackling Poverty* (Summary). London: Institute for Public Policy Research.

Chomsky, N. (1989) *Necessary Illusions: Thought Control in Democratic Societies*. London: Pluto Press.

Church Urban Fund/Church Action on Poverty (2012) *Bias to the Poor? Christian Attitudes to Poverty in this Country*. London: Church Urban Fund.

Clark, T. (2010) 'Is Social Mobility Dead?', *The Guardian*, 10 March.

Clark, T. and Health, A. (2014) *Hard Times: The Divisive Toll of the Economic Slump*. Newhaven, CT: Yale University Press.

Clery, E., Lee, L. and Kunz, S. (2013) *Public Attitudes to Poverty and Welfare, 1983–2011: Analysis Using British Social Attitudes Data*. York: Joseph Rowntree Foundation.

Cohen, R., Coxall, J., Craig, G. and Sadiq-Sangster, A. (1992) *Hardship Britain: Being Poor in the 1990s*. London: Child Poverty Action Group.

Cole, D. (1999) *No Equal Justice: Race and Class in the American Criminal Justice System*. New York, NY: Norton.

Collison, P. (1963) *The Cutteslowe Walls: A Study in Social Class*. London: Faber and Faber.

Conger, S. (1996) 'Social Inventions', *The Innovation Journal*, 1(2).

Conrad, P. and Angell, A. (2004) 'Homosexuality and Remedicalization', *Society*, 41(5).

Cookson, R., Sainsbury, R. and Glendinning, C. (eds) (2004) *Jonathan Bradshaw on Social Policy: Selected Writings 1972–2001*. York: York Publishing Services.

Cooper, G. (1998) 'Disabled Demand End to "Apartheid"', *The Independent*, 27 May.

Corbyn, Z. (2009) 'I Can't Hear You', *Times Higher Education*, 26 March.

Corker, M. (2005) *Disabling Language: Analysing the Discourse of Disability*. London: Routledge.

Court, J. (2004) 'The Political Context in Developing Countries', in Overseas Development Institute (ed) *Research and Policy in Development: Does Evidence Matter?* London: Overseas Development Institute.

Dahrendorf, R. (1988) *The Modern Social Conflict: An Essay on the Politics of Liberty*. London: Weidenfield & Nicolson.

Davies, H. and Nutley, S. (2002) *Evidence-Based Policy and Practice: Moving from Rhetoric to Reality*. Discussion Paper. St Andrews: Research Unit For Research Utilisation.

Davis, M. and Monk, D. (eds) (2011) *Evil Paradises: Dreamworlds of Neoliberalism*. London: The New Press.

Dawkins, R. (1986) *The Blind Watchmaker: Why the Evidence of Evolution Reveals a Universe without Design*. London: Penguin.

Dawkins, R. (2007) 'Why Darwin Matters', *The Guardian*, 9 February.

Dean, H. (2006) *Social Policy*. Cambridge: Policy Press.

Dean, H. and Taylor-Gooby, P. (1992) *Dependency Culture: The Explosion of a Myth*. Hemel Hempstead: Harvester Wheatsheaf.

Dean, M. (1997) 'Haunted by the Breadline', *The Guardian*, 1 October.

Delli Carpini, M.X. and Keeter, S. (1997) *What Americans Know About Politics and Why It Matters*. New Haven, CT: Yale University Press.

Department for Business, Innovation and Skills (2014) *Innovation, Research and Growth: Innovation Report 2014*. London: Department for Business, Innovation and Skills.

Department for Communities and Local Government (2012) 'Helping Troubled Families Turn Their Lives Around'. Available at: https://www.gov.uk/government/policies/helping-troubled-families-turn-their-lives-around

De Schweinitz, K. (1943) *England's Road to Social Security*. New York, NY: Perpetua.

Dixon, M. and Margo, J. (2006) *Population Politics*. London: Institute for Public Policy Research.

Dolphin, T. and Lawton, K. (2013) *A Job for Everyone: What Should Full Employment Mean in 21st Century Britain?* London: Institute for Public Policy Research.

Domhoff, G.W. (2013) 'Wealth, Income, and Power'. Available at: http://www2.ucsc.edu/whorulesamerica/power/wealth.html

Donnison, D. (1982) *The Politics Of Poverty*. Oxford: Martin Robertson.

Dorling, D. (2012a) 'Fairness and the Changing Fortunes of People in Britain 1970–2012', Royal Statistical Society Beveridge Memorial Lecture, 27 June.

Dorling, D. (2012b) *Injustice: Why Social Inequality Persists*. Bristol: The Policy Press.

Dorling, D., Rigby, J., Wheeler, B., Ballas, D., Thomas, B., Fahmy, E., Gordon, D. and Lupton, R. (2007) *Poverty and Wealth Across Britain 1968 to 2005*. York: Joseph Rowntree Foundation.

Doward, J. and Thomas, M. (2014) 'Underprivileged Two-Year-Olds Being Declined by "Middle-Class" Nurseries', *The Observer*, 24 August.

Duffy, B., Hall, S., O'Leary, D. and Pope, S. (2013) *Generation Strains: A Demos/ IPSOS Mori Report on Changing Attitudes to Welfare*. London: Demos/IPSOS Mori.

Durkheim, É. (1957) *Professional Ethics and Civic Morals*. London: Routledge.

Durkheim, É. (1970) *Suicide: A Study in Sociology* (trans Spaulding, J.A. and Simpson, G.). London: Routledge.

Durkheim, É. (1984) *The Division of Labour in Society* (trans Halls, W.D.). Basingstoke: Macmillan.

Dworkin, R. (2011) *Justice for Hedgehogs*. Cambridge, MA: Harvard University Press.

DWP (Department for Work and Pensions) (2007) *Opportunities for All: Indicators Update 2007*. London: Department for Work and Pensions, Family, Poverty and Work Division.

DWP (2012) *Measuring Child Poverty: A Consultation on Better Measures of Child Poverty*, (Cm 8483). London: Department for Work and Pensions.

DWP (2014) *Fraud and Error in the Benefit System: Preliminary 2013/14 Estimates (Great Britain)*. London: DWP Information, Governance and Security Directorate.

Eagleton, T. (1991) *Ideology: An Introduction*. London: Verso.

Economics Online (no date) '*Measuring Unemployment*'. Available at: http://www. economicsonline.co.uk/Managing_the_economy/Measuring_unemployment. html

Edelman, M. (1964) *The Symbolic Uses of Politics*. Urbana, IL: University of Illinois Press.

Edelman, M. (1977) *Political Language: Words that Succeed and Policies that Fail*. New York, NY: Academic Press.

Ellison, N. and Pierson, C. (eds) (1998) *Developments in British Social Policy*. Houndmills: Macmillan.

Engels, F. (1844) 'The Condition of the Working-Class in England'. Available at: http://www.gutenberg.org/files/17306/17306-h/17306-h.htm

Epley, N. (2014) *Mindwise: How We Understand What Others Think, Believe, Feel and Want*. London: Allen Lane.

Equality and Human Rights Commission (2011) 'Sex and Power, 2011'. Available at: http://www.equalityhumanrights.com/publication/sex-and-power-2011

Ermisch, J., Franceseoni, M. and Siedler, T. (2005) *Intergenerational Economic Mobility and Assortative Mating*. Discussion Paper No. 1847. Bonn: Institute for the Study of Labor (IZA).

ESRC (Economic and Social Research Council) (2010) 'Briefing: Rebalancing Britain's Public Finances'. Available at: http://www.esrc.ac.uk/news-events-and-publications/evidence-briefings/rebalancing-britain-s-public-finances/

Eterno, J.A. and Silverman, E.B. (2012) *The Crime Numbers Game: Management by Manipulation*. Boca Raton: CRC Press.

European Commission's Expert Group on Gender and Employment (2009) *Gender Segregation in the Labour Market: Root Causes, Implications and Policy Responses in the EU*. Luxembourg: European Commission Directorate-General for Employment, Social Affairs and Equal Opportunities.

Evers, A., Pijl, M. and Ungerson, C. (eds) (1994) *Payments for Care*. Aldershot: Avebury.

Farmelo, G. (ed) (2003) *It Must Be Beautiful: Great Equations of Modern Science*. London: Granta.

Ferrera, M. (1996) 'The "Southern Model" of Welfare in Social Europe', *Journal of European Social Policy*, 6(1).

Foote, G. (1997) *The Labour Party's Political Thought: A History* (3rd edn). Basingstoke: Macmillan.

Fox, J. (2014) 'We Can't Afford to Leave Inequality to the Economists', *Harvard Business Review Blog Network*, 24 January. Available at: http://blogs.hbr.org/2014/01/we-cant-afford-to-leave-inequality-to-the-economists/

Francis, B. and Hutchings, M. (2013) *Parent Power*. London: Sutton Trust.

Friedman, B.J. (2013) '"Brave New Capitalists' Paradise": The jobs?', *New York Review of Books*, 7 November.

Fuentes-Nieva, R. and Galasso, M. (2014) 'Working for the Few: Political Capture and Economic Inequality'. Oxfam Briefing Paper.

Fuertes, V. and McQuaid, R. (2012) 'Recurrent Poverty and the Low-Pay–no-Pay Poverty Cycle', *Scottish Anti-Poverty Review*, 15(Winter).

Fukuda-Parr, S. (2003) 'The Human Development Paradigm: Operationalizing Sen's Ideas on Capabilities', *Feminist Economics*, 9(2/3).

Fukuda-Parr S. and Shiva Kumar, A.K. (eds) (2003) *Readings in Human Development*. New York, NY: Oxford University Press.

Furedi, F. (2008) 'Medicalisation in a Therapy Culture', in Wainwright, D. (ed) *A Sociology of Health*. London: Sage.

Gaffney, D. and Baumberg, B. (2014) *Dismantling the Barriers to Social Mobility*. London: Trades Union Congress.

Galbraith, J.K. (1958) *The Affluent Society*. New York, NY: Houghton Mifflin.

Galbraith, J.K. (1994) 'The Good Society has no Underclass', *The Guardian Weekly*, 6 February.

Galbraith, J.K. (1998) *The Affluent Society* (40th anniversary edn). New York, NY: Houghton Mifflin.

George, V. and Page, R. (eds) (1995) *Modern Thinkers on Welfare*. London: Prentice Hall/Harvester Wheatsheaf.

Gibbs, D. (1995) 'The Law Giveth and the Law Taketh Away', *The Observer*, 7 May.

Giddens, A. (1976) *New Rules of Sociological Method: A Positive Critique of Interpretative Sociologies*. London: Hutchinson.

Giddens, A. (1986) *Sociology: A Brief but Critical Introduction*. London: Palgrave Macmillan.

Giddens, A. (2007) 'You Need Greater Equality to Achieve More Social Mobility', *The Guardian*, 24 May.

Gilens, M. (1999) *Why Americans Hate Welfare: Race, Media, and the Politics of Antipoverty Policy*. Chicago, IL: University of Chicago Press.

Ginn, J. and Arber, S. (1993) 'Pension Penalties: The Gendered Division of Occupational Welfare', *Work, Employment & Society*, 7(1).

Ginsberg, J., Mohebbi, M.H., Patel, R.S., Brammer, L., Smolinski, M.S. and Brilliant, L. (2009) 'Detecting Influenza Epidemics Using Search Engine Query Data', *Nature*, 457, 19 February.

Goffman, E. (1974) *Frame Analysis: An Essay on the Organization of Experience*. New York, NY: Harper & Row.

Goldthorpe, J.H., in collaboration with Llewallyn, C. and Payne, C. (1987) *Social Mobility and Class Structure in Modern Britain* (2nd edn). Oxford: Clarendon Press.

Gordon, D. (2014) 'Poverty in the UK', presentation at 'Poverty and Social Exclusion in Scotland and the UK', New Register House, Edinburgh, 20 August.

Gordon, D. and Townsend, P. (eds) (2000) *Breadline Europe: The Measurement of Poverty*. Bristol: The Policy Press.

Gore, C. and Figueiredo, J.B. (eds) (1997) *Social Exclusion and Anti-Poverty Policy*. Geneva: International Institute of Labour Studies.

Gould, S.J. (2007) *The Richness of Life* (ed McGarr, P. and Rose, S.). London: Vintage.

Goulden, C. (2010) *Cycles of Poverty, Unemployment and Low Pay*. York: Joseph Rowntree Foundation.

Gouldner, A.V. (1970) *The Coming Crisis of Western Sociology*. London: Heinemann.

Gouldner, A.V. (1973) *For Sociology: Renewal and Critique in Sociology Today*. London: Allen Lane.

Gramsci, A. (1971) *Selections from Prison Notebooks* (ed and trans by Hoare, Q. and Smith, G.N.). London: Lawrence & Wishart.

Granovetter, M. (1973) 'The Strength of Weak Ties', *American Journal of Sociology*, 78(6).

Gubrium, E.K., Pellissery, S. and Lødemel, I. (eds) (2013) *The Shame of it: Global Perspectives on Anti-Poverty Policies*. Bristol: The Policy Press.

Guy, C., Henderson, K., Garnham, A. and Hargreaves, D. (2013) *Busting the Poverty Myths*. London: New Statesman/Webb Memorial Trust.

Haidt, J. (2012) *The Righteous Mind: Why Good People are Divided by Politics and Religion*. London: Penguin.

Haines, H.H. (1979) 'Cognitive Claims Making, Enclosure and the Depoliticisation of Social Problems', *Sociological Quarterly*, 20(1).

Halsey, A.H, Heath, A.F. and Ridge, J.M. (1980) *Origins and Destinations: Family, Class and Education in Modern Britain*. Oxford: Clarendon Press.

Hamilton, C. (2004) *Growth Fetish*. London: Pluto.

Hardoon, D. (2015) *Having It All and Wanting More*. Oxford: Oxfam.

Hari, J. (2015) *Chasing the Scream: The First and Last Days of the War on Drugs*. London: Bloomsbury.

Hatfield, I. (2015) *Self-Employment in Europe*. London: Institute for Public Policy Research.

Haynes, L., Service, O., Goldacre, B. and Torgerson, D. (2012) *Test, Learn, Adapt: Developing Public Policy with Randomised Controlled Trials*. London: Cabinet Office Behavioural Insights Team.

Heffer, S. (2008) 'Do Nothing', BBC Radio 4, 9 and 16 January. Available at: http://www.bbc.co.uk/programmes/b008s4ds/broadcasts/2008/01

Heins, E. (2009) 'Flexicurity: What Can Scotland Learn from Denmark?', paper presented at 'Punching Above our Weight: Smaller Nations and Regions in the Fight Against Poverty in Europe', Poverty Alliance seminar, Edinburgh, 24 September.

Hennessey, P. (1996) 'The Glories and Blemishes of the British Governing Class', *Fabian Review*, 108(1).

Hennock, E.P. (2007) *The Origin of the Welfare State in England and Germany, 1850–1914: Social Policies Compared*. Cambridge: Cambridge University Press.

Heslop, P. (2013) 'Disabled People and Their Relationship with Poverty', Poverty and Social Exclusion in the UK, Working Paper – Methods Series No. 23, Bristol.

Hills, J. (1997) 'A CASE for Investigation', *LSE Magazine*, 9(2).

Hills, J. (ed) (1999) *Persistent Poverty and Lifetime Inequality: The Evidence*. CASEreport 5. London: Centre for Analysis of Social Exclusion/HM Treasury.

Hills, J. (2004) *Inequality and the State*. Oxford: Oxford University Press.

Hills, J. (2014) *Good Times, Bad Times: The Welfare Myth of Them and Us*. Bristol: The Policy Press.

Hills, J., Le Grand, J. and Piachaud, D. (eds) (2002) *Understanding Social Exclusion*. Oxford: Oxford University Press.

Himmelweit, S. and Land, H. (2008) *Reducing Gender Differences to Create a Sustainable Care System*. York: Joseph Rowntree Foundation.

Hinds, K. (2000) *Social Exclusion: What Is It, and How Can We Measure It in a Meaningful Way?* 15 November. Edinburgh: Royal Statistical Society/Social Research Association.

Hirsch, D. (2007) *Experiences of Poverty and Educational Disadvantage*. York: Joseph Rowntree Foundation.

Hirsch, D. (2013) *An Estimate of the Costs of Child Poverty in 2013*. Loughborough: Centre for Research in Social Policy.

HM Government (2010) *Coalition Programme for Government*. London: HM Government.

HM Government (2013) 'Improving Social Mobility to Create a Fairer Society'. Available at: https://www.gov.uk/government/policies/improving-social-mobility-to-create-a-fairer-society

HMRC (HM Revenue & Customs) (2014) *Measuring Tax Gaps 2014 Edition – Tax Gap Estimates for 2012–13*. London: HM Revenue & Customs.

HM Treasury (2014) *Public Expenditure Statistical Analyses, 2014*. Cm 8902. London: HM Treasury.

HM Treasury and DWP (Department for Work and Pensions) (2003) *Full Employment in Every Region*. London: Office of the Deputy Prime Minister.

Hobsbawm, E. (1994) *The Age of Extremes: The Short Twentieth Century, 1914–1991*. London: Michael Joseph.

Hobsbawm, E. and Ranger, T. (eds) (1983) *The Invention of Tradition*. Cambridge: Cambridge University Press.

Hofstadter, D. (1982) 'Default Assumptions', *Scientific American*, 247(4).

Hood, C. (2006) 'Gaming in Targetworld: The Targets Approach to Managing British Public Services', *Public Administration Review*, 66(4).

Hooper, C., Thompson, M., Laver-Bradbury, C. and Gale, C. (eds) (2012) *Child and Adolescent Mental Health: Theory and Practice* (2nd edn). London: CRC Press.

Hough, M. and Park, A. (2011) 'How Malleable are Attitudes to Crime and Punishment? Findings from a British Deliberative Poll', in Roberts, J. and Hough, M. (eds) *Changing Attitudes to Punishment: Public Opinion, Crime and Justice* (3rd edn). Abingdon: Routledge.

Howard, C. (1999) *The Hidden Welfare State: Tax Expenditures and Social Policy in the United States*. Princeton, NJ: Princeton University Press.

Howarth, C., Kenway, P., Palmer, G. and Miorelli, R. (1999) *Monitoring Poverty and Social Exclusion, 1999*. York: Joseph Rowntree Foundation/New Policy Institute.

Howitt, D. (1982) *The Mass Media and Social Problems*. Oxford: Pergamon.

Hunter, M. (2008) 'Engine Trouble', *Community Care*, 3 April.

Hutton, W. (2014a) 'This Pensions "Freedom" Will Be a Long-Term Disaster', *The Observer*, 23 March.

Hutton, W. (2014b) 'Capitalism Simply Isn't Working', *The Observer*, 13 April.

Hutton, W. (2014c) 'Extravagant CEO Pay Doesn't Reflect Performance – It's All About Status', *The Observer*, 19 April.

Hyman, R. (1972) *Strikes*. Glasgow: Fontana/Collins.

Ignatieff, M. (2013) *Fire and Ashes: Success and Failure in Politics*. London: Harvard University Press.

Illich, I. (1973) *Tools for Conviviality*. New York, NY: Harper & Row.

Independent Living in Scotland (2010) 'Human Rights and Self-Directed Support'. Glasgow: ILiS Policy Briefing 3.

Ipsos MORI (2013) 'Perceptions Are Not Reality – the Top 10 We Get Wrong'. Available at: https://www.ipsos-mori.com/researchpublications/researcharchive/3188/Perceptions-are-not-reality-the-top-10-we-get-wrong.aspx

Jackson, T. (2013) 'New Economic Model Needed not Relentless Consumer Demand', *The Guardian*, 17 January.

Jacobs, L.R. and Skocpol, T. (eds) (2007) *Inequality and American Democracy: What We Know and What We Need to Learn*. New York, NY: Russell Sage Foundation.

Jamieson, K.H. and Cappella, J.N. (2008) *Echo Chamber: Rush Limbaugh and the Conservative Media Establishment*. Oxford: Oxford University Press.

Jo, Y.N. (2012) 'Psycho-Social Dimensions of Poverty: When Poverty Becomes Shameful', *Critical Social Policy*, 33(3).

Joint Public Issues Team (2013) 'The Lies We Tell Ourselves: Ending Comfortable Myths About Poverty'. Available at: http://www.jointpublicissues.org.uk/wp-content/uploads/2013/02/Truth-And-Lies-Report-smaller.pdf

Jones, K. (1991) *The Making of Social Policy in Britain, 1830–1990*. London: Athlone.

Jordan, B. (2006) *A Theory of Poverty and Social Exclusion*. Cambridge: Policy Press.

Kahneman, D. (2012) *Thinking, Fast and Slow*. London: Penguin.

Kemp, P.A. (2005) 'Escape Routes from Poverty', *Benefits*, 13(3).

Kempson, E. and Collard, S. (2012) *Developing a Vision for Financial Inclusion*. Dorking: Friends Provident Foundation.

Kenya, K. (2013) 'Pennies from Heaven', *The Economist*, 26 October.

Keynes, J.M. (1936) *The General Theory of Employment, Interest and Money*. Cambridge: Cambridge University Press.

Kuklinski, J.H., Quirk, P.J., Jerit, J., Schwieder, D. and Rich, R.F. (2000) 'Misinformation and the Currency of Democratic Citizenship', *Journal of Politics*, 62(3).

Lakoff, G. (2006) *Thinking Points: Communicating Our American Values and Vision*. Berkeley, CA: Rockridge Institute.

Lakoff, G. and Welhing, E. (2012) *The Little Blue Book: The Essential Guide to Thinking and Talking Democratic*. New York, NY: Simon and Schuster.

Lanchester, J. (2014) 'There's Poverty in the UK, But We Are Better off Calling it Inequality', *The Guardian*, 5 September.

Lane, R.E. and Sears, D.O. (1964) *Public Opinion*. Englewood Cliffs, NJ: Prentice Hall.

Lanzieri, G. (2013) *Towards a 'Baby Recession' in Europe? Differential Fertility Trends During the Economic Crisis*. Luxembourg: Eurostat.

Layard, R. (1999) *Tackling Unemployment*. London: Palgrave Macmillan.

Lazer, D., Kennedy, R., King, G. and Vespignani, A. (2014) 'The Parable of Google Flu: Traps in Big Data Analysis', *Science*, 343(14).

Lee, P. and Murie, A. (1999) *Literature Review of Social Exclusion*. Edinburgh: The Scottish Office Central Research Unit.

Lenoir, R. (1974) *Les Exclus: Un Francais sur Dix*. Paris: Editions du Seuil.

Levitas, R. (1996) 'The Concept of Social Exclusion and the New Durkheimian Hegemony', *Critical Social Policy*, 46.

Levitas, R. (1998) *The Inclusive Society? Social Exclusion and New Labour*. London: Macmillan.

Levitas R. (2012) *There May be 'Trouble' Ahead: What We Know About Those 120,000 'Troubled' Families*. Policy Working Paper 3. Bristol: Poverty and Social Exclusion in the UK.

Levitas, R., Pantazis, C., Fahmy, E., Gordon, D., Lloyd, E. and Patsios, D. (2007) *The Multi-Dimensional Analysis of Social Exclusion*. Bristol: Department of Sociology and School for Social Policy, Townsend Centre for the International Study of Poverty and Bristol Institute for Public Affairs.

Levitt, S.D. and Dubner, S.J. (2007) *Freakonomics: A Rogue Economist Explores the Hidden Side of Everything*. London: Penguin.

Levitt, S.D. and Dubner, S.J. (2014) 'Think Like a Freak Extract: Joining the Dots between Hot Dogs, Van Halen and David Cameron', *The Observer*, 11 May.

Lewandowsky, S., Ecker, U.K.H., Seifert, C.M., Schwarz, N. and Cook, J. (2012) 'Misinformation and its Correction: Continued Influence and Successful Debiasing', *Psychological Science in the Public Interest*, 13(3).

Lewin, K. (1951) *Field Theory in Social Science; Selected Theoretical Papers* (ed Cartwright, D.). New York, NY: Harper & Row.

Lewis, J. (1992) 'Gender and the Development of Welfare Regimes', *Journal of European Social Policy*, 2(3).

Lister, R. (1997) *Citizenship: Feminist Perspectives*. Basingstoke: Macmillan.

Lister, R. (2004) *Poverty*. Cambridge: Polity.

Lister, R. (2008) 'Povertyism and Othering: Why They Matter', presentation delivered at TUC Conference, 'Challenging Povertyism', 17 October.

Lodge, D. (1992) *The Art of Fiction*. London: Penguin.

Lombard, N. and McMillan, L. (eds) (2013) *Violence Against Women: Current Theory and Practice for Working with Domestic Abuse, Sexual Violence and Exploitation*. London: Jessica Kingsley.

Luckhaus, L. (2000) 'Equal Treatment, Social Protection and Income Security for Women', *International Labour Review*, 139(2).

Lukács, G. (1971 [1923]) *History and Class Consciousness* (trans Livingstone, R.) Boston, MA: MIT Press.

Lukes, S. (1968) 'Methodological Individualism Reconsidered', *British Journal of Sociology*, 19(2).

MacDonald, R., Shildrick, T. and Furlong, A. (2014) 'In Search of "Intergenerational Cultures of Worklessness": Hunting the Yeti and Shooting Zombies', *Critical Social Policy*, 34(2).

MacInnes, T., Aldridge, H., Bushe, S., Kenway, P. and Tinson, A. (2013) *Monitoring Poverty and Social Exclusion 2013*. York: Joseph Rowntree Foundation.

MacInnes, T., Aldridge, H., Bushe, S., Tinson, A. and Born, T.B. (2014) *Monitoring Poverty and Social Exclusion, 2014*. York: Joseph Rowntree Foundation.

MacNicol, J. (1987) 'In Pursuit of the Underclass', *Journal of Social Policy*, 16(3).

Macpherson, C.B. (1973) *Democratic Theory: Essays in Retrieval*. Oxford: Oxford University Press.

McCormack, K. (2004) 'Resisting the Welfare Mother: The Power of Welfare Discourse and Tactics of Resistance', *Critical Sociology*, 30(2).

McIntosh, P. (1990) 'White Privilege: Unpacking the Invisible Knapsack', *Independent School Magazine*, 49(2).

McKendrick, J.H. (2011) *Writing and Talking About Poverty – Briefing Paper 26*. Edinburgh: Scottish Government.

McKendrick, J.H., Scott, G. and Sinclair, S. (2007) 'Dismissing Disaffection: Young People's Attitudes Towards Education, Employment and Participation in a Deprived Community', *Journal of Youth Studies*, 10(2).

McKendrick, J.H., Sinclair, S., Irwin, A., O'Donnell, H., Scott, G. and Dobbie, L. (2008) *The Media, Poverty and Public Opinion in the UK*. York: Joseph Rowntree Foundation.

McVeigh, T. (2015) 'Net Porn Filters Block Sex Abuse Charity Sites', *The Observer*, 25 January.

Machiavelli, N. (1972) *The Prince, Selections from the Discourses and Other Writings* (ed Plamenatz, J.). London: Fontana/Collins, pp 71–2.

Maddox, B. (2013) 'DNA's Double Helix: 60 Years Since Life's Deep Molecular Secret was Discovered', *The Guardian*, 22 February.

Malthus, T. (1798) 'Essay on the Principles of Population'. Available at: http://www.gutenberg.org/files/4239/4239-h/4239-h.htm

Mandelson, P. (1997) *Labour's Next Steps: Tackling Social Exclusion*. Pamphlet 581. London: Fabian Society.

Mann, K. (1992) *The Making of an English 'Underclass': The Social Divisions of Welfare and Labour*. Milton Keynes: Open University Press.

Mann, M. (1987) 'Ruling Class Strategies and Citizenship', *Sociology*, 21(3).

Mannheim, K. (1936) *Ideology and Utopia: An Introduction to the Sociology of Knowledge* (trans Wirth, L. and Shils, E.). London: Routledge & Kegan Paul.

Manning, N. (ed) (1985) *Social Problems and Welfare Ideology*. Aldershot: Gower.

Manning, N. and Page, R. (eds) (1992) *Social Policy Review 4*. Canterbury: Social Policy Association.

Marçal, K. (2015) *Who Cooked Adam Smith's Dinner?* London: Portobello.

Marcenaro-Gutierrez, O., Micklewright, J. and Vignoles, A. (2014) *Social Mobility and the Importance of Networks: Evidence for Britain*. London: UCL Institute of Education, Centre for Longitudinal Studies

Marr, A. (2005) *My Trade: A Short History of British Journalism*. London: Pan.

Marsh, A. and Mullins, D. (1998) 'The Social Exclusion Perspective and Housing Studies: Origins, Applications and Limitations', *Housing Studies*, 13(6).

Marshall, T.H. and Bottomore, T. (1996) *Citizenship and Social Class*. London: Pluto.

Martin, A. (2013) 'The Web's "Echo Chamber" Leaves Us None the Wiser', *Wired*, 1 May.

Marx, K. (1961) *Selected Writings in Sociology and Social Philosophy* (ed Bottomore, T.B. and Rubel, M.). Harmondsworth: Penguin.

Marx, K. and Engels, F. (1968) *Selected Works in One Volume*. London: Lawrence and Wishart.

Marx, K. and Engels, F. (1974) *The German Ideology: Part One* (2nd edn) (ed Arthur, C.J). London: Lawrence and Wishart.

Mason, P. (2012) *Why It's All Kicking Off Everywhere: The New Global Revolutions.* London: Verso.

Mathias, P. (1969) *The First Industrial Nation: An Economic History of Britain, 1700–1914.* London: Methuen.

Mattelart, A. and Sugelaub, S. (eds) (1979) *Communication and Class Struggle, Vol. 1.* New York, NY: International General.

Matthews, P. and Hastings, A. (2013) 'Middle-Class Political Activism and Middle-Class Advantage in Relation to Public Services: A Realist Synthesis of the Evidence Base', *Social Policy & Administration*, 47(1).

Mayhew, H. (1985) *London Labour and the London Poor* (ed Neuburg, V.). London: Penguin.

Meadows, D.H., Meadows, D.L., Render, J. and Behrens, W.W. (1972) *The Limits to Growth: A Report for the Club of Rome's Project on the Predicament of Mankind.* New York, NY: Universe Books.

Mehta, P.S. and Chatterjee, B. (eds) (2011) *Growth and Poverty: The Great Debate.* Jaipur: CUTS International.

Mendelson, E. (2013) 'The Strange Power of Norman Mailer', *New York Review of Books*, 21 November.

Micklethwait, J. and Wooldridge, A. (2014) *The Fourth Revolution: The Global Race to Reinvent the State.* London: Penguin.

Milburn, S. (2009) 'Foreword from the Chair', in Panel on Fair Access to the Professions (ed) *Unleashing Aspiration: The Final Report of the Panel on Fair Access to the Professions.* London: Cabinet Office.

Milligan, B. (2014) 'The Truth About Welfare Spending: Facts or Propaganda?', BBC News.

Mills, C.W. (1970) *The Sociological Imagination.* Harmondsworth: Penguin.

Minton, A. (2006) *What Kind of World Are We Building? The Privatisation of Public Space.* London: Royal Institution of Chartered Surveyors.

Mishel, L. (2012) 'The Wedges between Productivity and Median Compensation Growth', Issue Brief #330, Economic Policy Institute.

Mishel, L. and Davis, A. (2014) 'CEO Pay Continues to Rise as Typical Workers are Paid Less', Wages Incomes and Wealth Report, Economic Policy Institute, 12 June.

Moore, J. (1989) *The End of the Line for Poverty.* London: Conservative Political Centre.

Morris, L. (1993) 'Is There a British Underclass?', *International Journal of Urban and Regional Research*, 17(3).

Morris, R.J. (1999) 'Urban Space and the Industrial City in Britain', *Refresh*, 28(Spring).

Murphy, R. (1988) *Social Closure – The Theory of Monopolization and Exclusion.* Oxford: Clarendon Press.

Nasar, S. (2012) *Grand Pursuit: The Story of the People Who Made Modern Economics*. London: Forth Estate.

National Centre for Social Research (no date) 'British Social Attitudes, 31'. Available at: http://www.bsa-31.natcen.ac.uk/read-the-report/benefits/public-attitudes-to-the-benefits-system-are-they-changing.aspx

National Equality Panel (2010) *An Anatomy of Economic Inequality in the UK: Report of the National Equality Panel*. London: Government Equalities Office/Centre for Analysis of Social Exclusion.

Nationwide (no date) 'Special Report – High Performing Primary Schools add Value to Property Prices'. Available at: http://www.nationwide.co.uk/~/media/MainSite/documents/about/house-price-index/primary-school-special.pdf

Naughton, J. (2014) 'Google and the Flu: How Big Data Will Help us Make Gigantic Mistakes', *The Observer*, 6 April.

Nelson, M. (2011) 'Gated Communities: Class Walls', *History Today*, 61(11).

New Zealand Council of Christian Social Services (2009) 'Facts About Poverty in 2009'. Available at: http://www.nzccss.org.nz/site/page.php?page_id=276

Nickell, S and Van Ours, J. (2000) 'Mirage or Miracle? Labour Market Performance in Britain and the Netherlands', *CentrePiece*, 5(1).

Niemietz, K. (2011) *A New Understanding of Poverty: Poverty Measurement and Policy Implications*. London: Institute of Economic Affairs.

Noble, M., Wright, G., Dibben, C., Smith, G.A.N., McLennan, D., Anttila, C., Barnes, H., Mokhtar, C., Noble, S., Avenell, D., Gardner, J., Covizzi, I. and Lloyd, M. (2003) *The English Indices of Deprivation, 2004 (Revised)*. London: Office of the Deputy Prime Minister/Neighbourhood Renewal Unit.

Nussbaum, M.C. (2011) *Creating Capabilities: The Human Development Approach*. Cambridge, MA: Harvard University Press.

Nyhan, B. and Reifler, J. (2010) 'When Corrections Fail: The Persistence of Political Misperceptions', *Political Behavior*, 32(2).

OECD (Organisation for Economic Co-operation and Development) (2008) *Are We Growing Unequal? New Evidence on Changes in Poverty and Incomes Over the Past 20 Years*. Paris: OECD Publishing.

OECD (2010) 'A Family Affair: Intergenerational Social Mobility across OECD Countries'. Available at: http://www.oecd.org/tax/public-finance/chapter%205%20gfg%202010.pdf

OECD (2011a) 'Divided We Stand: Why Inequality Keeps Rising: Country Note – United Kingdom'. Available at: http://www.bristol.ac.uk/poverty/ESRCJSPS/downloads/research/comparitive/1%20Comparison-General/Report/OECD%20(2011)%20Divided%20We%20Stand%20Why%20Inequality%20Keeps%20Rising.pdf

OECD (2011b) *How's Life? Measuring Well-Being*. Paris: OECD Publishing.

OECD (2014) 'Focus on Top Incomes and Taxation in OECD Countries: Was the Crisis a Game Changer?' Available at: http://www.oecd.org/els/soc/OECD2014-FocusOnTopIncomes.pdf

Office for Budget Responsibility (2014) 'Welfare Trends Report'. Available at: http://budgetresponsibility.org.uk/welfare-trends-report-october-2014/

Office for Disability Issues/Department for Work and Pensions (2014) 'Disability Facts and Figures'. Available at: https://www.gov.uk/government/publications/disability-facts-and-figures/disability-facts-and-figures

Office for National Statistics (no date) 'SOC2010 Volume 3: The National Statistics Socio-Economic Classification (NS-SEC Rebased on the SOC2010)'. Available at: http://www.ons.gov.uk/ons/guide-method/classifications/current-standard-classifications/soc2010/soc2010-volume-3-ns-sec--rebased-on-soc2010--user-manual/index.html#2

Office for National Statistics (2001) *Social Capital – A Review of the Literature*. London: ONS Social Analysis and Reporting Division, Socio-Economic Inequalities Branch.

Office for National Statistics (2012) *Family Spending, 2012 Edition*. London: Office for National Statistics.

Office of the Third Sector (2008) *Participation in Regular Volunteering*. Briefing Note for Local Strategic Partnerships, No 16. London: Cabinet Office.

O'Hare, W.P. (2003) *Perceptions and Misperceptions of America's Children: The Role of the Print Media*. Working Paper. Baltimore, MA: KIDS COUNT.

Olson, P. and Champlin D. (1998) 'Ending Corporate Welfare as We Know It: An Institutional Analysis of the Dual Structure of Welfare', *Journal of Economic Issues*, 32(3).

Oppenheim, C. and Harker, L. (1996) *Poverty: The Facts* (3rd edn). London: Child Poverty Action Group.

Orr, H.A. (2013) 'Awaiting a New Darwin', *The New York Review of Books*, 7 February.

Orshansky, M. (1969) 'How Poverty Is Measured', *Monthly Labor Review*, 92(2).

Orwell, G. (1970) *The Collected Essays, Journalism and Letters of George Orwell, Vol. 4: In Front of Your Nose, 1945–1950* (ed Orwell, S. and Angus, I.). Harmondsworth: Penguin.

Osborne, H. (2014) 'Cost of Raising a Child Surges Past £225,000', *The Guardian*, 23 January.

Ostry, J.D., Berg, A. and Tsangarides, C.G. (2014) 'Redistribution, Inequality, and Growth', IMF Staff Discussion Note, SDN/14/02.

Oxfam (2010) 'Something for Nothing: Changing Negative Attitudes to People Living in Poverty'. Available at: http://policy-practice.oxfam.org.uk/publications/something-for-nothing-changing-negative-attitudes-to-people-living-in-poverty-114046

Palan, R., Murphy, R. and Chavagneux, C. (2010) *Tax Havens: How Globalization Really Works*. Ithaca, NY: Cornell University Press.

Panel on Fair Access to the Professions (2009) *Unleashing Aspiration: The Final Report of the Panel on Fair Access to the Professions*. London: Cabinet Office.

Pariser, E. (2012) *The Filter Bubble: What the Internet Is Hiding from You*. London: Penguin.

Parkin, F. (1972) *Class Inequality and Political Order: Social Stratification in Capitalist and Communist Societies*. St Alban's: Paladin.

Parkin, F. (1979) *Marxism and Class Theory: A Bourgeois Critique*. London: Tavistock.

Parton, N. (2006) *Safeguarding Childhood: Early Intervention and Surveillance in a Late Modern Society*. Basingstoke: Palgrave Macmillan.

Pascal, G. (1986) *Social Policy: A Feminist Analysis*. London: Routledge.

Paxton, R.O. (2013) 'Vichy Lives! In a Way', *New York Review of Books*, 25 April.

Payments Council (2010) *The Way We Pay, 2010: The UK's Payment Revolution*. London: Payments Council.

Percy-Smith, J. (ed) (2000) *Policy Responses to Social Exclusion: Towards Inclusion*. Maidenhead: Open University Press.

Perfect, D. (2012) *Gender Pay Gaps, 2012*. London: Equality and Human Rights Commission.

Petrosino, A. and Turpin-Petrosino, C. (2003) 'Scared Straight and other Juvenile Awareness Programs for Preventing Juvenile Delinquency: A Systematic Review of the Randomized Experimental Evidence', *Annals of the American Academy of Political and Social Science*, 589(1).

Piachaud, D. (1987) 'Problems in the Definition and Measurement of Poverty', *Journal of Social Policy*, 16(2).

Picketty, T. (2014) *Capital in the Twenty-First Century* (trans Goldhammer, A.). Harvard, MA: Harvard University Press.

Pierson, P. (1996) 'The New Politics of the Welfare State', *World Politics*, 48(2).

Pinker, R. (1971) *Social Theory and Social Policy*. London: Heinemann.

Platt, J. (1992) 'The Contribution of Social Science', in Loney, M. (ed) *The State or the Market: Politics and Welfare in Contemporary Britain*. London: Sage.

Platt, S. (1996) 'Parents Who Pull the Plug', *The Guardian*, 2 July.

Pound, J. (1971) *Poverty and Vagrancy in Tudor England*. London: Longman.

Poverty Truth Commission (no date) *Nothing About Us Without Us is for Us: Findings of The Poverty Truth Commission, March 2009–April 2011*. Glasgow: Poverty Truth Commission. Available at: http://www.faithincommunityscotland.org/wp-content/themes/charitas-wpl/files/doc_14401207062012_30031_Poverty_Truth_Commission_A5_report_-_small.pdf

Powell, M., Boyne, G. and Ashworth, R. (2001) 'Towards a Geography of People Poverty and Place Poverty', *Policy & Politics*, 29(2).

Power, M. (1994) *The Audit Explosion*. London: DEMOS.

Power, S., Edwards, T., Whitty, G. and Wigfall, V. (2003) *Education and the Middle Class*. Buckingham: Open University Press.

Purdum, T.S. (1995) 'Clinton Takes on Violent Television', *New York Times*, 11 July.

Putnam, R. (2000) *Bowling Alone: The Collapse and Revival of American Community*. London: Simon and Schuster.

Pyper, D. and McGuinness, F. (2013) 'Zero-Hours Contracts', House of Commons Library Standard Note: SN/BT/6553, London.

Reay, D., Crozier, G. and Clayton, J. (2009) '"Strangers in Paradise"? Working-Class Students in Elite Universities', *Sociology*, 43(6).

Rees, J., Whitworth, A. and Carter, E. (2013) *Support For All in the UK Work Programme? Differential Payments, Same Old Problem*. Working Paper 115. Birmingham: Third Sector Research Centre.

Reeskens, T. and Van Oorschot, W. (2013) 'Equity, Equality, or Need? A Study of Popular Preferences for Welfare Redistribution Principles Across 24 European Countries', *Journal of European Public Policy*, 20(8).

Rein, M. (1978) *Social Policy*. New York, NY: Random House.

Reyles, D.Z. (2007) *The Ability to Go About without Shame: A Proposal for Internationally Comparable Indicators of Shame and Humiliation*. Working Paper No. 03. Oxford: Oxford Poverty & Human Development Initiative.

Ringen, S. (1988) 'Direct and Indirect Measures of Poverty', *Journal of Social Policy*, 17(3).

Robbins, L. (1935) *An Essay on the Nature and Significance of Economic Science*. London: MacMillan.

Roberts, K., Cook, F.G., Clark, S.C. and Semeneoff, E. (1977) *The Fragmentary Class Structure*. London: Hutchinson.

Robertson, A. (ed) (1997) *Unemployment, Social Security and the Social Division of Welfare: A Festschrift in Honour of Adrian Sinfield*. Social Policy Series No. 13. Edinburgh: New Waverley Papers.

Robinson, J.G. (ed) (1986) *Handbook of Theory and Research for the Sociology of Education*. New York, NY: Greenwood Press.

Robinson, P. (2000) 'Active Labour-Market Policies: A Case of Evidence-based Policy-Making?', *Oxford Review of Economic Policy*, 16(1).

Room, G. (ed) (1995) *Beyond the Threshold: The Measurement and Analysis of Social Exclusion*. Bristol: The Policy Press.

Rosanvallon, P. (2013) *The Society of Equals*. Harvard, MA: Harvard University Press.

Rose, D. (2005) 'Socio-Economic Classifications: Classes and Scales, Measurement and Theories', paper presented at the First Conference of the European Survey Research Association, Barcelona, 18–22 July.

Rose, H. (1981) 'Rereading Titmuss: The Sexual Division of Welfare', *Journal of Social Policy*, 10(4).

Rose, S. (2013) 'Swamp-Man Strikes Again', *The Guardian*, 18 May.

Rose, S.O. (1988) 'Gender Antagonism and Class Conflict: Exclusionary Strategies of Male Trade Unionists in Nineteenth-Century Britain', *Social History*, 13(2).

Rosenfield, J. (2010) '"The Meaning of Poverty" and Contemporary Quantitative Poverty Research', *British Journal of Sociology*, 61.

Rossiter, A., Murphy, J., Blanden, J., Harker, L., Gregg, P., Macmillan, L., Sainsbury, R., Phillips, T., Sacks, J. and Batmanghelidjh, C. (eds) (2007) *The Politics of Aspiration*. London: Social Market Foundation.

Rousseau, J.-J. (1973) *The Social Contract and Discourses* (trans Cole, G.D.H.). London: Everyman.

Rowntree, B.S. (1901) *Poverty: A Study of Town Life*. London: Macmillan.

Rubington, E. and Weinberg, S. (eds) *The Study of Social Problems: Seven Perspectives* (5th edn). Oxford: Open University Press.

Runciman, W.G. (1972) *Relative Deprivation and Social Justice*. Harmondsworth: Penguin.

Russell, B. (1965) *Legitimacy Versus Industrialism: 1814–1848*. London: Unwin.

Russell, B. (1966) *Roads to Freedom: Socialism, Anarchism and Syndicalism* (3rd edn). London: George Allen & Unwin.

Rutter, J. and Evans, B. (2012) *2012 London Childcare Survey*. London: Daycare Trust.

Rutter, M. and Madge, N. (1976) *Cycles of Disadvantage: A Review of Research*. London: Heinemann.

Ryan, W. (1971) *Blaming the Victim*. London: Pantheon.

Saez, E. (2013) 'Striking it Richer: The Evolution of Top Incomes in the United States (Updated with 2012 Preliminary Estimates)', 3 September. Available at: http://eml.berkeley.edu/~saez/saez-UStopincomes-2012.pdf

Sage, L.S. (2014) *Bad Blood*. London: Fourth Estate.

Said, E.W. (1994) *Representations of the Intellectual: The 1993 Reith Lectures*. London: Vintage.

Sainsbury, R. (1996) 'Rooting Out Fraud: Innocent Until Proven Fraudulent', *Poverty*, 93(Spring).

Salais, R. and Villeneuve, R. (eds) (2004) *Europe and the Politics of Capabilities*. Cambridge: Cambridge University Press.

Sampson, A. (2005) *Who Runs This Place? The Anatomy of Britain in the 21st Century*. London: John Murray.

Samuel, R. (ed) (1992) *People's History and Socialist Theory*. London: Routledge and Kegan Paul.

Sandel, M. (2010) 'Towards a Just Society', *The Guardian*, 20 February.

Sandel, M. (2012) *What Money Can't Buy: The Moral Limits of Markets*. London: Allen Lane.

Sartori, G. (1970) 'Concept Misformation in Comparative Politics', *The American Political Science Review*, 64(4).

Scott, A. (1988) 'Imputing Beliefs: A Controversy in the Sociology of Knowledge', *Sociological Review*, 36(1).

Scott, J. (1994) *Poverty and Wealth: Citizenship, Deprivation and Privilege*. London: Longman.

Scott, P. (2004) *Visible and Invisible Walls: Suburbanisation and the Social Filtering of Working-Class Communities in Interwar Britain*. Reading: Henley Business School.

Scott, W.R. and Meyer, J.W. (1994) *Institutional Environments and Organizations*. London: Sage.

Scottish Executive (2004) *Social Justice: A Scotland Where Everyone Matters*. Edinburgh: Scottish Executive.

Seabrook, J. (2008) *Why Do People Think Inequality Is Worse Than Poverty?* York: Joseph Rowntree Foundation.

Sefton, T. (2002) *Recent Changes in the Distribution of the Social Wage*. York: Joseph Rowntree Foundation.

Segal, R.A. (2004) *Myth: A Very Short Introduction*. Oxford: Oxford University Press.

Seidman, E. and Rappaport, J. (eds) (1986) *Redefining Social Problems*. New York, NY: Plenum Press.

Sen, A. (1981a) *Poverty and Famines: An Essay on Entitlement and Deprivation*. Oxford: Clarendon Press.

Sen, A. (1981b) 'Ingredients in Famine Analysis: Availability and Entitlements', *Quarterly Journal of Economics*, 96(3).

Sen, A. (1983) 'Poor, Relatively Speaking', *Oxford Economic Papers*, 25(2).

Sen, A. (1992) *Inequality Re-Examined*. Oxford: Clarendon Press.

Sen, A. (1997) *Resources, Values and Development*. Cambridge, MA: Harvard University Press.

Sen, A. (1999a) *Development as Freedom*. Oxford: Oxford University Press.

Sen, A. (1999b) *Commodities and Capabilities*. Oxford: Oxford University Press.

Sen, A. (2000) *Social Exclusion: Concept, Application, and Scrutiny*. Social Development Papers No 1. Manila: Office of Environment and Social Development, Asian Development Bank.

Sen, A. (2005) 'Human Rights and Capabilities', *Journal of Human Development*, 6(2).

Sen, A. (2010) *The Idea of Justice*. London: Penguin.

Sen, A. and Drèze, J. (2013) *An Uncertain Glory: India and its Contradiction*. London: Allen Lane.

Seymour, D. (2009) *Reporting Poverty in the UK: A Practical Guide for Journalists*. York: Joseph Rowntree Foundation.

Sherman, A., Greenstein, R. and Ruffing, K. (2012) 'Contrary to 'Entitlement Society' Rhetoric, Over Nine-Tenths of Entitlement Benefits Go to Elderly, Disabled, or Working Households', Center on Budget and Policy Priorities.

Shibutani, T. (ed) (1970) *Human Nature and Collective Behaviour: Papers in Honor of Herbert Blumer*. New Brunswick, NJ: Prentice Hall.

Shildrick, T., MacDonald, R., Furlong, A., Roden, J. and Crow, R. (2012a) *Are 'Cultures of Worklessness' Passed Down the Generations?* York: Joseph Rowntree Foundation.

Shildrick, T., MacDonald, R., Webster, C. and Garthwaite, K. (2012b) *Poverty and Insecurity: Life in Low-Pay, No-Pay Britain*. Bristol: The Policy Press.

Silver, Ü.H. (1994) 'Social Exclusion and Social Solidarity: Three Paradigms', *International Labour Review*, 133(5/6).

Sinclair, S. (2001) *Financial Inclusion: An Introductory Survey*. Edinburgh: Centre for Research into Socially Inclusive Services.

Sinfield, A. (1978) 'Analyses in the Social Division of Welfare', *Journal of Social Policy*, 7(2).

Sinfield, A. (1985) 'Being Out of Work', in Littler, C. (ed) *The Experience of Work*. Aldershot: Gower.

Sinfield, A. (1989) *Social Security and its Social Division: A Challenge for Sociological Analysis*. Social Policy Series No 2. Edinburgh: New Waverley Papers.

Sinfield, A. (ed) (1993) *Poverty, Inequality and Justice*. Social Policy Series No 6. Edinburgh: New Waverley Papers.

Sinfield, A. (2000) 'Tax Benefits in Non-State Pensions', *European Journal of Social Security*, 2(2).

Sinfield, A. (2014) 'How Can We Reduce Poverty Without Improving its Prevention?', *Poverty*, 147.

Sissons, P. (2011) *The Hourglass and the Escalator: Labour Market Change and Mobility*. London: Work Foundation.

Skelton, D. (2013) 'Reviving the Tory Tradition of Social Reform', in Derbyshire, J. (ed) *Poverty in the UK: Can It Be Eradicated?* London: Prospect Publishing.

Smith, A. (1776) *An Inquiry in the Nature and Causes of the Wealth of Nation*. London: Methuen (1904 edition).

Smith, D. (ed) (1992) *Understanding the Underclass*. London: Policy Studies Institute.

Social Exclusion Task Force (no date) *Families at Risk: Background on Families with Multiple Disadvantages*. London: Cabinet Office.

Social Mobility and Child Poverty Commission (2014) *Response to the Consultation on the Child Poverty Strategy 2014 to 2017*. London: Social Mobility and Child Poverty Commission.

Social Policy Association (2009) 'Guidelines on Research Ethics'. Available at: http://www.social-policy.org.uk/downloads/SPA_code_ethics_jan09.pdf

Sorel, G. (1984) *Reflections on Violence* (ed Jennings, G.). Cambridge: Cambridge University Press.

Souiden, N., M'Saad, B. and Pons, F. (2011) 'A Cross-Cultural Analysis of Consumers' Conspicuous Consumption of Branded Fashion Accessories', *Journal of International Consumer Marketing*, 23(5).

Sousa, L. and Eusebio, C. (2007) 'When Multi-Problem Poor Individuals' Myths Meet Social Services Myths', *Journal of Social Work*, 7(2).

Spector, M. and Kitsuse, J.I. (1987) *Constructing Social Problems*. New York, NY: Aldine de Gruyter.

Spicker, P. (1988) *Principles of Social Welfare: An Introduction to Thinking About the Welfare State*. London: Routledge.

Spicker, P. (2002) *Poverty and the Welfare State: Dispelling the Myths*. London: Catalyst.

Spicker, P. (2004) 'Developing Indicators: Issues in the Use of Quantitative Data About Poverty', *Policy and Politics*, 32(4).

Spicker, P. (2007) *The Idea of Poverty*. Bristol: The Policy Press.

Srinivasan, S. (2007) 'No Democracy Without Justice: Political Freedom in Amartya Sen's Capability Approach', *Journal of Human Development*, 8(3).

StamfordPlus.com (2009) 'Dodd Introduces Bill to Modernize Poverty Measurement', 10 August, Available at: http://www.stamfordplus.com/stm/information/nws1/publish/News_1/Dodd-introduces-bill-to-modernize-poverty-measurement_printer.shtml

Standing, G. (2011) *The Precariat: The New Dangerous Class*. London: Bloomsbury.

Starr, P. (2014) 'A Different Road to a Fair Society', *New York Review*, 22 May.

Stephens, P. (2014) 'Review of *The Fourth Revolution: The Global Race to Reinvent the State* by Micklethwait and Wooldridge', *Financial Times*, 30 May.

Stewart, T. (2010) 'Addressing Financial Exclusion Among Families Living in Poverty', *Journal of Poverty and Social Justice*, 18(2).

Stiglitz, J. (2012) *The Price of Inequality*. London: Penguin.

Stoller, T. (2013) 'Antipoverty Debate Needs to be Conducted with the Right Language', Joseph Rowntree Foundation Blog, 3 May. Available at: http://www.jrf.org.uk/blog/2013/05/antipoverty-debate-right-language

Strathearn, P. (2001) *Mendeleyev's Dream: The Quest for the Elements*. London: Thomas Dunne Books.

Strelitz, J. and Lister, R. (eds) (2008) *Why Money Matters: Family Income, Poverty and Children's Lives*. London: Save the Children.

Surry, S.S. (1973) *Pathways to Tax Reform: The Concept of Tax Expenditures*. Cambridge, MA: Harvard University Press.

Suskind, R. (2004) 'Faith, Certainty and the Presidency of George W. Bush', *The New York Times Magazine*, 17 October.

Sutherland, W.J., Spiegelhalter, D. and Burgman, M. (2013) 'Twenty Tips for Interpreting Scientific Claims', *Nature*, 503(20 November).

Sutton Trust (2008) *University Admissions by Individual Schools*. London: Sutton Trust.

Sutton Trust (2014) 'Internship or Indenture?', Research Briefing, 2 November.

Taulbut, M. and Robinson, M. (2014) 'The Chance to Work in Britain: Matching Unemployed People to Vacancies in Good Times and Bad', *Regional Studies*, 48.

Tawney, R. (1913) *Memoranda on the Problems of Poverty*. London: William Morris Press.

Taylor-Gooby, P. (2014) 'The Welfare State in Crisis: Reasons to Be Cheerful', *Policy World* (Spring).

Taylor-Gooby, P., Hastie, C. and Bromley, C. (2003) 'Querulous Citizens: Welfare Knowledge and the Limits to Welfare Reform', *Social Policy and Administration*, 37(1).

Teasdale, S. (2011) 'What's in a Name? the Construction of Social Enterprise', *Public Policy and Administration*, 27(2).

Thomas, W.I. and Thomas, D.S. (1928) *The Child in America: Behavior Problems and Programs*. New York, NY: Knopf.

Thompson, E.P. (1971) 'The Moral Economy of the English Crowd in the Eighteenth Century', *Past & Present*, 50.

Tierney, J. and O'Neill, M. (2010) *Criminology Theory and Context* (3rd edn). Abingdon: Routledge.

Tilly, C. (1999) *Durable Inequality*. Berkeley, CA: University of California Press.

Timmins, N. (2011) 'OECD Calls Time on Trickle-Down Theory', *Financial Times*, 5 December.

Titmuss, R.M. (1958) *Essays on 'The Welfare State'*. London: George Allen & Unwin.

Titmuss, R.M. (1962) *Income Distribution and Social Change: A Study in Criticism*. London: George Allen & Unwin.

Titmuss, R.M. (1963) 'The Welfare State: Images and Realities', *Social Service Review*, xxxvi(1).

Titmuss, R.M. (1970) *The Gift Relationship: From Human Blood to Social Policy*. London: Penguin.

Titmuss, R.M. (1974) *Social Policy: An Introduction*. London: George Allen & Unwin.

Tomlinson, M. and Walker, R. (2010) *Recurrent Poverty: The Impact of Family and Labour Market Changes*. York: Joseph Rowntree Foundation.

Townsend, P. (1976) *Sociology and Social Policy*. Harmondsworth: Penguin.

Townsend, P. (1979) *Poverty in the United Kingdom*. London: Penguin.

Townsend, P. (2010) 'The Meaning of Poverty', *British Journal of Sociology*, 61.

Toynbee, P. (2003) *Hard Work: Life in Low-Pay Britain*. London: Bloomsbury.

TUC (Trades Union Congress) (2009) 'Decent Pensions for All: Why Public Sector Pensions Are Affordable and the Real Challenge Is the Collapse of Private Sector Pensions'. Available at: http://publicservicepensioners.org.uk/pdfs/TUC%20Decent%20Pensions%20for%20All.pdf

Tucker, I. (2012) 'Science Writing: How Do You Make Complex Issues Accessible and Readable?', *The Observer*, 2 December.

Tudor Hart, J. (1971) 'The Inverse Care Law', *The Lancet*, 297.

Turner, B. (1986) *Equality*. London: Tavistock.

Turner, B.S. (1990) 'Outline of a Theory of Citizenship', *Sociology*, 24(2).

UK Coalition Against Poverty (2008) *Communicating Poverty*. Liverpool: UK Coalition Against Poverty.

UK Parliament (no date) 'Enclosing the Land'. Available at: http://www.parliament.uk/about/living-heritage/transformingsociety/towncountry/landscape/overview/enclosingland/

United Nations (no date) 'Enable: Development and Human Rights for All'. Available at: http://www.un.org/disabilities/default.asp?id=279

United Nations (1995) 'World Summit for Social Development'. Available at: http://www.un.org/esa/socdev/wssd/text-version/agreements/poach2.htm

United Nations World Water Assessment Programme (2012) 'Facts and Figures: Managing Water Under Uncertainty and Risk', United Nations WWD Report 4.

Unterhalter, E. (2003) 'Crossing Disciplinary Boundaries: The Potential of Sen's Capability Approach for Sociologists of Education', *British Journal of Sociology of Education*, 24(5),

Vandenbroucke, F. (2014) 'We Must Act Now to Defuse Europe's Timebomb', *Europe's World*, 15 June. Available at: http://europesworld.org/2014/06/15/we-must-act-now-to-defuse-europes-child-poverty-timebomb/#.U63FEU1OV94

Veit-Wilson, J. (1998) *Setting Adequacy Standards: How Governments Define Minimum Incomes*. Bristol: The Policy Press.

Veit-Wilson J. (2013) 'Measuring Child Poverty: A Response to the Consultation', 12 February. Available at: https://northeastchildpoverty. wordpress.com/2013/02/12/measuring-child-poverty-a-response-to-the-consultation/

Vedantam, S. (2007) 'Persistence of Myths Could Alter Public Policy Approach', *Washington Post*, 4 September.

Von Tunzelmann, A. (2013) 'Review of "An Uncertain Glory: India and its Contradictions"', *The Telegraph*, 1 August.

Walker, A. (1984) *Social Planning: A Strategy for Socialist Welfare*. Oxford: Basil Blackwell.

Walker, A. and Walker, C. (eds) (1997) *Britain Divided: The Growth of Social Exclusion in the 1980s and 1990s*. London: Child Poverty Action Group.

Walker, R. (2009) 'Eyelash of the Beholder', *New York Times*, 31 July.

Walker, R. and Chase, E. (2014) 'Adding to the Shame of Poverty: The Public, Politicians and the Media', *Poverty*, 148(Summer).

Watt, B. (2008) *What Are Today's Social Evils?* York: Joseph Rowntree Foundation.

Weber, M. (1948) *From Max Weber: Essays in Sociology* (trans and ed Gerth, H.H. and Mills, C.W.). London: Routledge & Kegan Paul.

Weber, M. (1976) *The Protestant Ethic and the Spirit of Capitalism* (trans Parsons, T.). London: George Allen & Unwin.

Weber, M. (1978) *Economy and Society: An Outline of Interpretive Sociology* (ed Roth, G. and Wittich, C.). Berkeley, CA: University of California Press.

Weinberg, S. (2013) 'Physics: What We Do and Don't Know', *New York Review of Books*, 7 November.

Welshman, J. (2013) *Underclass: A History of the Excluded since 1880* (2nd edn). London: Bloomsbury.

Witcher, S. (2013) *Inclusive Equality: A Vision for Social Justice*. Bristol: The Policy Press.

Willetts, D. (2011) *The Pinch: How the Baby Boomers Stole Their Children's Future and Why They Should Give It Back*. London: Atlantic.

Williams, R. (1983) *Keywords: A Vocabulary of Culture and Society* (rev edn). London: Fontana.

Williams, Z. (2014) 'George Lakoff: "Conservatives Don't Follow the Polls, They Want to Change Them ... Liberals Do Everything Wrong"', *The Guardian*, 1 February.

Willis, P. (1977) *Learning to Labour: How Working Class Kids Get Working Class Jobs*. Farnborough: Saxon House.

Wilson, D. and Ashton, J. (2001) *What Everyone in Britain Should Know About Crime and Punishment*. Oxford: Blackstone.

Wilson, S., Meagher, G. and Hermes, K. (2012) 'The Social Division of Welfare Knowledge: Policy Stratification and Perceptions of Welfare Reform in Australia', *Policy & Politics*, 40(3).

Winlow, S. and Hall, S. (2013) *Rethinking Social Exclusion: The End of the Social?* London: Sage.

Wolf, A. (2013) *The XX Factor: How the Rise of Working Women Has Created a Far Less Equal World*. London: Crown.

Wolf, N. (1991) *The Beauty Myth: How Images of Beauty are Used Against Women*. London: Vintage.

Wolpert, L. (2000) *The Unnatural Nature of Science* (2nd edn). London: Faber and Faber.

Worpole, K. and Katharine, K. (2007) *The Social Value of Public Spaces*. York: Joseph Rowntree Foundation.

WWF (World Wildlife Fund) (2012) 'Living Planet Report 2012: Biodiversity, Biocapacity and Better Choices'. Available at: http://www.footprintnetwork. org/images/uploads/LPR_2012.pdf

York Consulting (2010) *Turning Around the Lives of Families with Multiple Problems: An Evaluation of the Family and Young Carer Pathfinders Programme*. Research Report DFE-RR154. London: Department for Education.

Young, M. (1958) *The Rise of the Meritocracy, 1870–2033: An Essay on Education and Society*. London: Thames and Hudson.

Zhao, Y. (2014) *Who's Afraid of the Big Bad Dragon? Why China has the Best (and Worst) Education System in the World*. San Francisco, CA: Jossey Bass.

Index

Page references for notes are followed by n